DJUNA

DJUNA

The Formidable Miss Barnes

Andrew Field

University of Texas Press, Austin

International Standard Book Number 0-292-71546-3
Library of Congress Catalog Number 85-50940

First University of Texas Press Edition, 1985

The author gratefully acknowledges permission from the following sources to reprint material in this book:

Mrs. T. S. Eliot for a line from an unpublished letter by T. S. Eliot.
Faber & Faber Ltd.; Farrar, Straus & Giroux; New Directions Publishing Corporation; and Djuna Barnes for material from works by Djuna Barnes.
Fleet Press Corporation for lines from *The Divine Comedy of Pavel Tchelitchew* by Parker Tyler, copyright 1969 by Parker Tyler.
Grand Street for lines from "Rite of Spring" by Djuna Barnes, reprinted from *Grand Street,* Spring 1982.
Harcourt Brace Jovanovich, Inc., for material from *The Heart to Artemis* by Bryher, copyright 1962 by Bryher; and from *Shadow of Light* by Maurice Sterne, copyright 1965 by Maurice Sterne.
David Higham Associates Ltd. for material from *Drawn from Life* by Stella Bowen (Collins), copyright 1941 by Stella Bowen.
Horizon Press for material from *My Thirty Years' War* by Margaret Anderson, copyright 1969 by Margaret Anderson.
The New Yorker Magazine, Inc., for "Quarry" by Djuna Barnes, reprinted from *The New Yorker,* December 27, 1969, copyright © 1969 by The New Yorker Magazine, Inc.; and for "The Walking-Mort" by Djuna Barnes, reprinted from *The New Yorker,* May 15, 1971, copyright © 1971 by The New Yorker Magazine, Inc.
Oxford University Press Canada for material from *Memoirs of Montparnasse* by John Glassco, copyright © 1970 Oxford University Press Canada.
Random House, Inc., for lines from *The Autobiography of Alice B. Toklas* by Gertrude Stein, copyright 1933 by Gertrude Stein.
Russell & Volkening, Inc., for material from *The Letters of Ezra Pound, 1907–1941,* edited by D. D. Paige, copyright © 1950 by D. D. Paige, renewed 1978 by D. D. Paige.
Universe Books for material from *Out of This Century* by Peggy Guggenheim, copyright © 1946, 1960, and 1970 by Peggy Guggenheim.
Yale University, Collection of American Literature, Beinecke Rare Book and Manuscript Library for quotation from an unpublished letter by Eugene O'Neill to Djuna Barnes.

Requests for permission to reproduce material from this work should be sent to Permissions, University of Texas Press, Box 7819, Austin, Texas 78713.

A biographical inscription:

TO MEG,
this book, all my books

. . . Tell them almost anything, but give them facts.
—*Facts,* I said slowly—*My God, have we come to that? . . .*
—*Oh, indeed,* he said scornfully. —*Are you going to be purely personal?*
—*I am—everyone is who writes well.*

DJUNA BARNES,
The New York Tribune
February 16, 1919

DJUNA

CHAPTER ONE

This is the story of Djuna Barnes. It is a tale of two cultures, three generations, and a major writer of our time. She was born in 1892 in Cornwall-on-Hudson in New York State, the daughter of an eccentric father who was an unsuccessful American artist. Her mother, Elizabeth Chappell, was English and had studied violin in London prior to her marriage. Miss Barnes was the last survivor of the great generation of early twentieth-century modernists in English literature.

Both Djuna and Barnes have their stories as names. She was named after a character in *The Wandering Jew*. It is said that a little brother mispronounced the name, and it became and remained Djuna. Her father's surname was actually Budington, but he changed it out of dislike for his father. Much else in her life, particularly her early life, is even less certain. Her complicated family history would feed her and gnaw at her all her life. It would supply the basis of her art.

Miss Barnes never attended school, except for a brief period as an art student in New York, nor would the family have wanted tutors even if it could have afforded them. After the separation of her parents, who had left Cornwall-on-Hudson and been living on a small farm on Long Island, she worked as a freelance journalist and artist in Manhattan, Brooklyn and the Bronx. She would get fifteen dollars for a picture or article. That was quite a lot. Among the papers to which she contributed were *The Brooklyn Daily Eagle, The World, The New York Press, The Morning Telegraph* and *The New York Tribune.* Her father was a spoiled bohemian; Cornwall-on-Hudson was a watering place of literary New York (which it has, curiously enough, become once again as this is being written nearly seventy years later), and thus it was both natural and inevitable that after a short time on Long Island the young Miss Barnes went to Greenwich Village, which by 1913 was entering its high period as a centrepoint for a new stage of American culture. She described herself, in a sketch about the salon of Mabel Dodge, as naive and exceedingly timid when she came to the Village. It is left out of thumbnail sketches of her life that she had heavy responsibilities in her years as a journalist, for she was for a time the main source of support for her mother and three young brothers, and she also had to assume the burden of the cost of her grandmother's hospitalization.

Most descriptions of her in this period have her tall and dashing and strange. She was an impressionistic young journalist who specialized in colourful interviews, action pieces such as fire rescue techniques and courtroom scenes, and more often than not she illustrated her own pieces with striking drawings in the manner of Beardsley. Among the well-known people with whom she associated during this period prior to World War I were Edmund Wilson (friend and ardent admirer at first), Edna St. Vincent Millay (neither), Eugene O'Neill (another great admirer), and Peggy Guggenheim, who was to become her astringent friend and parsimonious benefactress for many decades in her later life.

Her first book appeared in November 1915, when she was twenty-three. It was called *The Book of Repulsive Women*, a pamphlet publication of eight poems (termed Rhythms) and five drawings issued as one of *Bruno's Chap Books* by Guido Bruno, a petty and disreputable profiteer in poetry and publishing in whose chapbooks a certain amount of her early work appeared. She was unsure at that stage in her life whether she intended to be a writer or an artist. Apart from his own considerable eccentric interest, Guido Bruno is of note in the life of Djuna Barnes because she modelled the character of Felix Volkbein, who is the first character presented in her most famous novel, *Nightwood* (1936), largely upon him. She was also friendly with Frank Harris, whose literary secretary Bruno became for a time.

The Book of Repulsive Women was scarcely noticed. That was something which frequently happened with Bruno publications, though in this case there may have been a double reason because the poems in it have some images so bold for their time that they could not even be recognized for purposes of suppression, as were much tamer books by authors such as Kreymborg and Dreiser. There will be some debates as to the period of her life when women lovers first became important. However, there can be no doubt that a powerful wave of feminist assertion, which began in America in the mid-nineteenth century (Miss Barnes' grandmother Zadel was active in that movement), reached its apogee in Greenwich Village just prior to World War I, where women of every disposition, including lesbian, flourished. The woman with whom Miss Barnes was closest in these early years was Mary Pyne, an actress and Village beauty who lived with the famous "tramp poet" of the Village, Harry Kemp. She died of influenza after having been tended by Djuna Barnes before going to hospital. Another unusual lady from the Village with whom she was friendly was the Baroness Elsa von Freytag-Loringhoven, who would stride the streets dressed in little more than a Mexican blanket and who once followed William Carlos Williams to New Jersey after he had made the near-fatal error of complimenting her. The Baroness was America's contribution to the Dada movement. She later followed Djuna Barnes to Paris, where she gassed herself. Miss Barnes became her literary executor.

In this pre-expatriation period Djuna Barnes had affairs with many men and lived in common-law marriage—according to family information provided after her death—to one, Courtenay Lemon, for a little more than two years. The main testimony to their time together comes from the journals of Edmund Wilson and the memoirs of the painter Maurice Sterne, another man with whom she had a very brief connection. Lemon was a libertarian and was engaged in writing a history of criticism, which never appeared. Djuna Barnes told Edmund Wilson that for a brief time she had been overwhelmed by the power of his intellect. They separated in 1919. Lemon was one of those from the Village who never went to Paris. He was for many years the chief script reader for the Theatre Guild in New York.

An earlier and interesting love affair, in 1914, about which we know from a 1938 letter, a discarded portion of *Nightwood,* and a jocular greeting note that he sent to her decades later, was with the German Harvard graduate Putzi Hanfstaengl, who twenty years later enjoyed fame of a sort by being the jester in Adolf Hitler's court. Djuna Barnes herself was "political" only for the brief moment when, probably under the influence of Lemon, she did some anti-war drawings for the Pacifist movement prior to America's entry into the First World War. In later years she reacted violently to suggestions that the "decadence" of *Nightwood* had anything at all to do with the spirit of Nazism and remained absolutely apolitical through the decades of depression, communism, fascism, war and McCarthyism.

More typical of the men with whom she associated were the major artist Marsden Hartley, who was sexually ambivalent (a great many of the men with whom she was friendly throughout her life fit this description), and the minor writer Laurence Vail, who was briefly married to Peggy Guggenheim and who epitomized the wildness of the Village at its most sophisticated. Although she did not have much money, Miss Barnes herself cut a very dashing figure when she was young. She was tall, angular, large-breasted, and swished about in a black cape which eventually became something like her insigne.

When she went to Paris in 1919 or 1920 (she was unsure which year it had been), it was as an accomplished journalist with a distinctive style—half a century later she would have been termed a "new journalist"—and a certain amount of artistic recognition given on promissory note. She had appeared in *The Little Review*, although she never was close to the clique of the Misses Anderson and Heap, and *Smart Set,* and one of the things she came to Paris with were letters of introduction to Ezra Pound and James Joyce. Joyce was one of the very few people in her life to whose genius she gave full deference, though she was also, according to Janet Flanner, the only person in Paris to call him Jim to his face. In 1922 she wrote an article about him for *Vanity Fair,* using the phrase "silence, cunning, and exile." That would become the most famous descriptive label about Joyce (taken from *Portrait of the Artist as a Young Man*), but few would notice how the phrase applied to her work as well, or how clearly her work stands in the post-Joycean tradition. James Joyce was her artistic role model, and secret rival, too.

In the beginning Miss Barnes stayed at a little hotel on the rue Jacob which was largely populated by expatriate Americans, particularly those grouped around Harold Loeb's journal *Broom.* One incident in the boisterous months of her residence at the small hotel found its way into Hemingway's *The Sun Also Rises.* Hemingway and Barnes were breezy acquaintances, but she did not move in the expatriation's front circle of fame and money. She was among the poets and actors, mostly homosexual, and the many women artists, of all manner and sort, who furnished the fascinating background texture of the expatriation. She was, of course, acquainted with Sylvia Beach of Shakespeare & Co. and Gertrude Stein, and she appeared in the famous salon of "the Amazon," Natalie Barney.

Barnes was one of those who followed the currency fluctuations to Berlin in the early 1920s. (The availability of soft drugs in Berlin was also important to the expatriate writers.) By then she knew Thelma Wood, a young sculptress from Missouri who would become her lover and the prototype for the figure of Robin Vote in *Nightwood.* She is the T. W. to whom the novel *Ryder* is dedicated. The photographer Berenice Abbott, who was assistant to Man Ray, and the actor Harrison Dowd were both in Berlin. Both of them were to remain friends over many years. Marsden Hartley was in Berlin then, too. She renewed her acquaintanceship with Charlie Chaplin, whom she had met during the time she was connected with the Provincetown Players. The grotesque atmosphere of Berlin during those years must surely have contributed something to the gloomy air of *Nightwood,* which may be vouchsafed by the fact that Robert McAlmon, another friend who lasted, wrote an unsuccessful story called *Miss Knight* which was set in Berlin and based in large part upon the

16

same Paris expatriate character from whom Djuna Barnes drew her greatest creation, Dr. O'Connor in *Nightwood.*

Barnes followed when the American artists left Berlin. For most of the next decade she lived tempestuously with Thelma Wood. They lived together first in a flat on the boulevard St.-Germain, and subsequently in a much grander place which Djuna Barnes purchased with literary monies on rue St.-Romain. The artist Mina Loy, who was her best friend during this period of her life, had a flat in the same building. The first serious Barnes book, called simply *A Book,* appeared in 1923. It was a collection of poems, stories, plays and drawings. The stories in particular are striking for their sparse, stark emotional quality. That book, which was published by Horace Liveright, the publisher of most of the outstanding expatriate avantgarde writers, didn't make money, but she did a lot of anonymous journalism for *McCall's.* Her 1928 novel *Ryder,* a bawdy mock-Elizabethan chronicle of the Barnes family history, did briefly make the best-seller lists, and that, with the *McCall's* money, gave her enough for the flat purchase at the end of 1928. During the Twenties Barnes wrote articles on a fairly regular basis for *Vanity Fair, The New York Tribune, Charm, Theatre Guild Magazine* and *McCall's.*

The famous anonymous book she wrote, a comic hortatory to the expatriate lesbian ladies of Paris, was *Ladies Almanack,* published in 1929. Miss Barnes herself and others sold it on the streets of Paris.

She had plans to import copies of *Ladies Almanack* to America, but they came to nothing. Copies of *Ryder* were questioned at the New York Post Office when Liveright tried to ship them to Paris, because of obscene spots in the long poem in the novel.

Miss Barnes had a serious drinking problem in Paris, and it got worse as her difficulties with Thelma increased. Frequently Djuna would have to go out in search of her lover, who would be totally drunk and lurching from bar to bar. Thelma Wood was an extremely striking woman, and she was also a talented silverpoint artist. The relationship between the two women was both passionate and intensely domestic. Thelma would threaten to leave Djuna on a nightly basis, but the Barnes efforts to end the relationship were in the end decisive. Starting from the Twenties, Miss Barnes suffered a series of what she once referred to as —*my famous breakdowns,* involving severely heavy drinking and hospitalization in Paris, London and New York.

The affair was over by the end of 1931. She began at once to work on the story of that romance, which was first called *Bow Down* and subsequently *Nightwood.* Early in 1933 her friend Charles Henri

Ford went to Tangiers on the urging of his friend Paul Bowles, and Ford in turn wrote to her urging her to join him. He had known her when he came to Greenwich Village from Mississippi, and in early 1931 he moved into her Paris flat to care for her after she had a minor operation in Paris. Ford was to type her manuscript in Morocco. She disliked Tangiers intensely at first, largely due to unfortunate housing circumstances. The rats were at her stockings. Then she discovered that she was pregnant, the result of a brief affair with a French painter. She returned to Paris where she had an abortion and subsequently went with the entourage of Peggy Guggenheim to England where she lived at a rented country manor called Hayford Hall, and it was here that *Nightwood* was largely written.

Many people visited Hayford Hall, but the prime residents were Barnes and Guggenheim, the critic John Holms, who was Peggy Guggenheim's lover, and the writers Emily Coleman and Antonia White, who have both had a deserved reappreciation in recent years. It was a most lively artistic household, and it is curious that "Hangover Hall" has waited so long, apart from the memoirs of Peggy Guggenheim herself, to have its little place in literary history. Barnes was given the most ornate and also gloomiest bedroom because it was the general opinion that it suited her Gothic personality. John Holms, who it is agreed possessed a brilliance which evades conveyance, was the centre of the household, which had many intense conversations and quarrels. There was a certain calm remove in his personality. It is said that he rarely bothered to finish a sentence unless he was very excited about something, and yet he was likely to respond to any topic with the statement that he had been thinking very deeply about that. He died unexpectedly under anaesthetic in a minor operation in January 1934, and the death broke off the Guggenheim summers. Barnes dedicated *Nightwood* to him and Peggy. The poet Edwin Muir was a great friend and admirer of John Holms, and he became an even greater admirer of Djuna Barnes, though oddly enough he never met her during her English years. Muir's opinion helped Eliot get the difficult subject past Faber's editorial board, and subsequently he published an opinion of the novel which praised Miss Barnes in certain respects over Joyce. The real credit for the acceptance of *Nightwood,* however, belonged to Emily Coleman. Eliot called her Little Annie Oakley (because of her manner and because she lived on Oakley Street), and in subsequent years felt that the publication of the novel was the primary achievement of his career at Faber.

Miss Barnes went to London and took an extremely large room over an antique shop on Old Church Street, which her friends dubbed Nightmare Abbey. The flat received its light primarily from an overhead skylight, which leaked badly when it rained. Though King's Road and a garish cinema were close at hand, the old church was then still standing, and she went there often to pray. There was also a pub on the corner, and she went there even more frequently. During these London days Miss Barnes saw a good deal of two friends, Peter Hoare (later he was knighted) and S—, who became her lover and who is still alive. She was attracted to him because he had —*the stamp of death upon him.* She loved him, in fact was almost desperate to have a proper love and even marriage. He drifted into treating her like a sister.

Everything had come apart in Paris. She had no inclination to return to the United States. When she furnished an autobiographical statement for the first edition of Stanley Kunitz's *Twentieth Century Authors,* published in 1942, she indicated that it was her intention to remain in England forever. The war forced her to return to America two years before that stated intention even made it into print.

She had gone to Paris in 1939 with Peggy Guggenheim to sell her flat and wind up her affairs there, but she was, like many others, taken completely unawares by the sudden sound of jackboots. In *Out of This Century* (1946), Peggy Guggenheim describes how she got Djuna a passage on the same boat as the painter Tanguy and saw her off in October —in a complete state of collapse. Peggy asked Tanguy to look after her, which he didn't. Throughout the voyage the passengers kept terrified watch for German submarines at the ship's rail. Barnes' gloom and tension over being back in the United States were considerably increased by a period of extreme poverty in New York. A trip she took to visit Emily Coleman in Arizona didn't help much. She was even less at home in the American West than she had been in Morocco.

Peggy Guggenheim came to New York in July 1941, and through her Barnes was drawn back into art, though it was a selection of several oil paintings and drawings Miss Barnes had done in the Thirties which were exhibited (but not sold) at the Guggenheim gallery in 1943. There were friends in New York. She saw a bit of Ruth Ford, the actress and sister of Charles Henri; Berenice Abbott; Marcel Duchamp. She at first lived with her ageing mother. Neither of them was happy about it. Though her physical needs were not at all great, Miss Barnes had absolutely nothing to live on. By a fluke, she obtained an inexpensive apartment on Patchin Place in the Village (one room with appendages), where she was to live for more than forty years in what she became fond of describing as her "Trappist" period. Peggy Guggenheim, with whom she had quarreled, began to

19

help her financially again. E. E. Cummings had an apartment on Patchin Place, too, and from time to time he would throw open the sash and bawl out: —*Are ya still alive, Djuna?!* Once, when she was sick, he brought her chicken soup.

Nightwood, though it had been rejected by seven major American publishers, did appear in New York in 1937, thanks entirely to Eliot's Introduction and his connections, but it was indifferently reviewed in *The New York Times* by Alfred Kazin, and many other American critics wasted considerable effort quarreling with and qualifying Eliot. Clifton Fadiman had championed the novel in *The New Yorker* (where Djuna's old friend Janet Flanner also had a good word to say about it) and compared Dr. O'Connor in the novel with Joyce's Stephen Dedalus, but he correctly voiced the fear that the novel would be —visited with a *succès de snobisme. Nightwood* made no deep impression on the broad reading public in either England or America, although it became and still is a novel known to all serious writers and poets and eventually achieved the considerable distinction of managing to stay in print for nearly fifty years as a result of a small but steady cult demand of several thousand copies a year.

After Edwin Muir and Emily Coleman, the greatest enthusiast for *Nightwood* was Dylan Thomas, who wrote: —It isn't a lah-de-dah prose poem, because it's about what some very real human people feel, think, and do. It's *Nightwood* by Djuna Barnes, and one of the three great prose books ever written by a woman.

Edwin Muir drew his friend Dag Hammarskjöld into his enthusiasm, and the diplomat-aesthete made time from his U.N. obligations to become the Swedish co-translator of her 1958 play *The Antiphon,* which was produced in Stockholm in 1961. Miss Barnes told Peggy Guggenheim after Hammarskjöld's death in Africa that he had told her that he hoped that he was preparing the way for her to receive the Nobel Prize.

Her contemporaries among American writers and especially the younger generation tended to notice her, draw from her, but at the same time be rather dismissive of her. A prominent case in point is Faulkner, who actually cites Barnes, unfavourably, in *The Town* and in *Intruder in the Dust,* even though his own prose style manifestly owes her more than a little. By the 1960s, perhaps feeling that her last hope really had gone down in flames, Miss Barnes grew resentful and unreasonable. One of the several writers whom she accused of theft was Lawrence Durrell, who had used a fleeting Barnes scene in his fiction, clearly by way of a bow in her direction. In a tribute to her published on her eightieth birthday in 1972, Durrell wrote: —One is glad to be living in the same epoch as Djuna Barnes.

The Antiphon, her second major work, was published largely out of a sense of duty and friendship on the part of Eliot. He didn't much like it. Edwin Muir did, and he helped her to edit the manuscript which had taken her nearly a decade to produce and afterwards publicly praised it as —one of the greatest things that has been written in our time. Eliot, in his awkwardness, compared the play to an atomic explosion, though he credited it with one of the great last acts in the language. The play had the enthusiasm of other important poets such as Richard Eberhart and Howard Nemerov.

Muir arranged a reading of *The Antiphon* at Harvard, and Miss Barnes travelled there to witness it with Eliot. The reading was inept; the occasion a sour one. The play had no other presentation in English. It was really a poem rather than a drama, and its story,—the bone which cannot be sensed beneath the embroidery of its language in Eberhart's elegant formula, was the familiar Barnes tale: her family. But no one knew. The play was a fish that unexpectedly broke the ice of silence, a silence of twenty years from the publication of *Nightwood.*

How adequately does one describe years of silence in biography, the genre least suited to the needs and contours of silence?

The signs of it had long been present. When she surfaced to publish one small poem in *The New Yorker* in 1971, Henry Raymont was allowed to see her for a feature article in *The New York Times.* She spoke of herself when she was a young woman in the Village: —*It was all so very, very desperate. Years ago I used to see people, I had to, I was a newspaperman, among other things. And I used to be rather the life of the party. I was rather gay and silly and bright and all that sort of stuff and wasted a lot of time. I used to be invited by people who said, "Get Djuna for dinner, she's amusing." So I stopped it.*

The silence, then, was not a sudden turn in her life but simply a potentiality that came to the fore when various other things such as sense of self, love, accomplishment and fame had in one way or the other played themselves out. If "Uncle Tom" (for that was what she called Eliot) and Dag Hammarskjöld had lived. If she had had a sympathetic partner in life. The odds were against that in the circles in which she moved throughout her mature life.

Apart from her great friends and a few members of her family, it was chiefly her publishers with whom she fought. James Laughlin of New Directions was the American publisher of *Nightwood,* and he had to endure most of it because his editorial offices were in the Village. After one onslaught he almost lost his temper and started to tell her that, although he had learned at his mother's knee always to be respectful towards women . . . And ever after she would spot him walking in the Village and brandish her cane imperiously under his nose while demanding of him: —*And how are your mother's knees, Mr. Laughlin?* She was, he told me, the only person he was ever frightened of in his life. His face still showed it years later as he recounted his meetings with the formidable Miss Barnes.

Years of silence, broken by some quarrels, a few breakdowns, being put into a sanatorium twice against her will by heavy family pressure, odd, unsatisfactory reestablishment of contact with people of her past. She no longer wandered into churches to pray, but her essential religious orthodoxy grew stronger. She gave up drink, stopped smoking, began to take vitamins. In her little apartment the television set faced the complete *Oxford English Dictionary* across her table-desk. Her story and that now were her world. Little shopping expeditions. Sometimes six months could slide by without a conversation with anyone. There was an errand man who occasionally brought in the groceries from the store, but he spoke almost no English, though he did sometimes bring her flowers. She was able to afford his services because of an unexpected gift of several thousand dollars, which she received from Samuel Beckett. Various neighbours tried to keep an eye out for her. Patchin Place's residents had changed, but there were still editors and people connected with the arts, and everyone knew who she was. On one occasion, in 1963, she came forcefully out of her lair to join a neighbourhood protest movement after an investor purchased Patchin Place with the intention of demolishing and developing the site. It was an indication of how the Barnes cult was growing that an occasional young poet would encamp on her doorstep in the hope of seeing her, though the encounter would never be anything more than a rude injunction from the window above to move on from the doorstep.

Years of spotted silence. The *OED*. Daily struggles with slips of paper, first for *The Antiphon* and later for what was to be her last collection of poems, in piles all over the floor and her large table-desk. The fear oft-expressed in letters, not without some pride, that she was going a bit crazy.

—*How old are you?* Miss Barnes asked me. (I had just turned forty.) —*Oh, that's the age! Now you'll see, you'll see what life has in store for you!!*

Such a span of silence that perhaps not even her old friend Beckett, who once used to boast of his friendship with her by taking friends to see the dangerous comic loo that was immortalized in *Nightwood,* could register it fully.

Eat sparingly. Wallow in a laundry-basket mass of manuscripts.

Resist letters and knocks on the door. Every once in a while, however, yield suddenly to a telephone call that rambles past the hour, and then return to silence and brooding, interspersed with the television news and *Time* magazine.

The Times Literary Supplement came, too, that last looping thread back to the maternal and literary English side when, in 1958, the poet Burns Singer reviewed the Faber edition of *The Antiphon* and wrote:

> —*The Antiphon,* because of its uncompromising bitterness and its equally uncompromising language, is even less likely than *Nightwood* to prove popular, but it is probable that there will always be one or two eccentrics who think that it gives its author the first place among women who have written in the English language.

So what if no one notices? The great and the lesser but real artists have all noticed. If there are only a few bits of praise, those bits are far richer than the others with flashy careers and contracts ever managed to receive.

—*Look at the way those young thugs have taken over the city. It's not safe to walk the streets any more!*

—*You have come too late to write a book about me, Mr. Field.*

By the 1970s the Guggenheim support was supplemented by some contributions from Natalie Barney, who was still living in Paris and had just entered into a new love affair in her eighties. And then, after strained negotiations with four universities—Miss Barnes acted as her own agent and sent Princeton, Yale and Harvard packing after it became clear to her that they felt that they would be doing *her* a favour by *accepting* her papers—the papers were sold to the University of Maryland (a book dealer by this time had entered the picture), fifty boxes and several of her paintings for a generous sum paid out to her on an annual basis which would considerably ease the poverty of her last years.

For a few years before her death a little cluster of sensitive men attended to her needs in various ways. One she had met years before when she had been seeking help in restoring her paintings. She claimed—quite unfairly—that he had ruined her painting but had at least got her to hospital on time and so had to be forgiven. Another was a fervent admirer of Miss Barnes, who, moreover, was able to find just the right tone in talking with her, and so she began to talk more on the telephone. He took her out to buy bedroom slippers at Altman's. Finally a minimally acceptable pair was found. She wanted to pay by cheque but had no identification with her. —*I am Djuna*

23

Barnes. I was a friend of T. S. Eliot and James Joyce. To which the saleslady replied: —*That's very nice, lady, but do you have a driver's license?* Barnes was indignant. She drew herself up so she was tall again. —*Do I* look *like the sort of person who would have a driver's license?!*

Another young man named Hank O'Neal had come highly recommended by her photographer friend Berenice Abbott. He helped take charge of her financial affairs, and by attending to various permissions, translations and royalties, managed to bring them into order, though there was a rift with the young man when he presumed to exercise too much autonomy. In fact, O'Neal performed great services for her in putting her affairs in order. In 1980 there was some talk of a Presidential Medal, but like the other grand prospect, it also came to nothing. She did receive a grant from The National Endowment for the Arts in 1981. An editor, Irene Skolnick, who was a great admirer of her work, took over the task of trying to keep her affairs in order and became her literary agent.

She had survived and was now only one of a handful left from her generation. Death, which had made two tentative visits in terrifying circumstances, could come now simply and peacefully, to a great writer, though not a writer for everyone. People usually make the mistake, Miss Barnes herself has informed us, of ascribing too much to last words. The important thing is that she never relented, never became a sweet little old lady who retired to the country to take up knitting with a cat, a canary and a parrot, as she had once described her distant future with confident self-mockery to Robert McAlmon in the 1920s. She was always a slightly unlikely person, or made herself so even as she composed her mannered stories. It furnished both distinction and protection of a sort. Her father had said that the great man lives alone, and that if people clamber over you you will perish.

ii

One could tell the story of Djuna Barnes in an entirely different manner as a psychological study: *Young Woman Barnes,* that book might have been called.

If we take occasional comments in her letters, references to her youth in her early journalism, and those elements and passages in the novel *Ryder* for which there is reasonably substantial evidence of references to actual events and people from her life, then there are many more than the five "facts" from which Freud constructed his controversial life of Leonardo. There are several score "facts" for the childhood of Miss Barnes.

She was the only girl in a family of five children, the second born, though there were children by other mothers as well. (Years later she had a half-brother and half-sister from her father's second marriage, but she herself was adult by then.) It is unclear whether or not she was at first named Djalma after the Prince in Eugène Sue's novel and then the name was changed to Djuna as a result of a brother's mispronunciation, or whether the mispronunciation and name change occurred almost simultaneously. It all depends upon which brother it was. It is one of the very few stories about her childhood that Miss Barnes has told repeatedly. In some versions (such as the interview given to a *Time* reporter in January 1943) it is a younger brother who is cited. The problem is that if it was indeed a younger brother the name change would have taken place in about 1901 or 1902 since the next child, Zendon, was born January 8, 1900, when Miss Barnes was seven and a half. The story could be correct, since we are told that Wendell, the father figure in *Ryder,* changed his own name freely and whimsically when young, or it could refer (as it does in a 1967 letter) to a mispronunciation by her elder brother Thurn, who, born in June 1890, was exactly two years older than she and at just the right age to get the name wrong. The elder brother theory has it that her father noticed how Thurn called the moon *una* and combined that with the Sue character.

Names are a distinctive oddity on the paternal side of the family. If the evidence of *Ryder* is to be followed—the birthdate of Wendell Ryder —in the winter of the year 1865 coincides with her father's birthdate—Djuna's father adopted so many names by the time he was fifteen that a great number of them slipped his mind in later years. He kept one for as long as three years, but finally ended by keeping for the rest of his life the name he was given by his future wife. Miss Barnes' father was born Henry Budington (no middle name). When his parents were divorced in 1879, his mother, Zadel, reverted to her maiden name, Barnes, and the final Christian name he settled on was Wald. Wald Barnes married Elizabeth Chappell from Rutland, England, whom he met in London, in 1889. Besides Thurn, Djuna and Zendon, they had two other boys, Saxon and Shangar, born in 1902 and 1904. Shangar changed his name to Charles Chappell. Thurn dropped the name and called himself Bud.

The names of the children are in perfect concord with the names of characters in Barnes' fiction, particularly when one draws together all the early ephemeral short stories and the light pieces written for

25

Vogue and *Smart Set* and *Theatre Guild Magazine.* These names have the style of *almost* proper European forms. Pilaat Korb. Lupa. Mitzi Ting. Fifine. Lady Olivia Lookover. That sort of name, wonderful names, names that belong to the world of Firbank and Gogol. This tradition of anarchic appellation has at least a three-generation span. Zadel Barnes was a reasonably frequent contributor to *Leslie's Weekly* and *Harper's New Monthly Magazine* in the 1870s and 1880s. Her major work was a long poem called *Meg—A Pastoral,* which was published in *Harper's.* Her *Harper's* poems and stories also show a fair sampling of the exotic names which were much favoured during the Victorian period of English letters, though her odd names entered by way of tales from other nations, probably an imitation of Longfellow, whom she knew. Her early pieces were published under the name "Z. B. Budington," while later works appeared under Z. B. Gustafson, her second and last, but also not permanent, husband. One of her longest *Harper's* pieces, *Voice of Christmas Past,* is a remarkably full incantation of all the marvellously named characters of Dickens. In her own poems and stories one may encounter names like Bernadotte, Sigfrid, Baron Johann Berg von Linde.

Naming is important. Djuna Barnes does one highly significant thing in naming her fictional characters, and she does it with such consistency that we are entitled to examine her practice as more than a narrative peculiarity and see in it a psychological signature.

Put simply, Barnes does tend to use both real names and characters, but the characters and the names are never matched. The wife of Ryder is not named Elizabeth but Amelia. The explanation is that the real prototype behind Kate Careless, Wendell's lover in the novel, is the operatic contralto Marguerite d'Alvarez, whose full name was Marguerite *Amelia* Alvarez de Rocafuerte. The grandmother of the novel is not named Zadel but Sophia, which it happens is the name of her grandfather's *second* wife, Sophia Steele Billings, whom he married less than two years after the divorce from Zadel.

We are told that Wendell Ryder enters on his succession of names out of objection to having to carry his father's name. Both the father and the grandfather of Miss Barnes were named Henry. But the interesting naming coincidence in regard to Wendell is the family name Ryder, which is very likely drawn from Albert Pinkham Ryder who was one of the two or three most esteemed American painters (three of his paintings are in the Metropolitan Museum in New York City) when Miss Barnes was an art student in New York, and whose personal life was known to her as well since her friend Marsden Hartley actually knew Ryder and considered him the greatest

American painter. One of Hartley's best-known paintings is of Ryder, and one of his poems was entitled *Albert Ryder—Moonlightist.* In his Introduction to a 1921 book by Hartley, Waldo Frank wrote: — Hartley is in some ways a continuance of Ryder. Ryder, like Wald Barnes, was of New England Methodist whaling stock, and, in fact, the Ryder and Budington families had relatives in common. Albert Ryder mixed arts, in his case writing lovely and slightly strange poetry to accompany his paintings:

> In the morning ashen-hued
> came nymphs dancing through the wood.

It is then clear that we have a disadvantageous comparison with her father the failed artist and eccentric set up against a successful artist and much more benign eccentric.

One need not involve oneself in arbitrary readings of emotional repressions and sexual transferences to explain the Barnesian pattern of naming. Let us agree merely that there is considerable evidence of family hostility in naming the grandmother by the step-grandmother who succeeded her, the mother by the mistress, and the father by the artist who was what Wald Barnes failed to be.

Another interesting such linkage may be observed in an article which Miss Barnes wrote about Synge in 1917. It also contains her first clear memory:

> ... the year nineteen hundred was the first year that I remember as being anything more specific than time that passed pleasantly and time that passed in tears. Synge first touched the Irish in me as nineteen hundred touched the attaining of a long desire; mother that day had presented me with a brother. I remember the brother but hazily, the little pair of boots over the arm that held him, I remember plainly. One should be remembered for something, for to be forgotten is to be remembered for all that was unimportant and evil.

That passage is an extraordinary little reverie for a Sunday newspaper article (in the sense that it has no *obvious* tie to what she is writing about) that does connect with her father's assertions that it is well to be famous and that he would live on in the brooding of his children, which indeed was fact. But it does not seem to have much to do with John Millington Synge.

The aside in her Synge article must refer to Synge the man also compared in her mind with her father, for the Irish playwright was a contemporary of Wald Barnes and like him was not only a writer, but also a musician and a painter. Once again, as with Albert Ryder,

27

there is the matter of success or failure, both human and artistic. This light smoke of paternal denigration was, of course, totally imperceptible in 1917, and required the clear anger-transferences of *Ryder* to be decoded. If there be any doubt, the matter is made explicit enough in Chapter Twenty-four of the novel, where Wendell (Wald) says to his mother about Julie (Djuna):

> —*Keep her,* says Wendell, *she is none of mine. Did I not hear her deriding me greatly?*

Synge wrote at some length of people like Wald Barnes who live and perish by the conceit of their whimsies. For his weakness and his heedless fancies about himself, Christy Mahon, the hero of *The Playboy of the Western World,* could well be Wald Barnes, and the young Djuna would not have missed that. The play is a mock-tragic patricide in which the supposedly murdered father keeps storming or crawling back on stage.

In *Ryder,* the fourteen-year-old Julie, her breast bared, flies at the father's mistress with murderous intent, saying over and over to her father:

> —*You, you, you!* . . . for she looked upon [the mistress] not so much as the disease as the manifestation of such emanating directly from her father . . .

A Greenwich Village memoirist observed the mature Miss Barnes hissing at an enemy: —*I hate you, I hate you, I hate you!* and that, the whole novel informs us, is the subtext of the daughter's steel-hammer pronouns. She hated him as he had hated his father.

Synge was very important for Djuna Barnes. There are only two writers to whom Miss Barnes has paid such full obeisance, Synge and James Joyce. The article makes clear that she read everything available on him. There are references to obscure Synge prose pieces as well as the six plays, and she refers to memoirists and the 1913 biography by Bourgeois. The Barnes article shows that Synge is important to her in terms of the time at which she read him as well as for his art and his themes. For her, *Deirdre of the Sorrows* (1910) was: —the first song that had come into my ears to stay. She would then probably have read Synge's play in 1911 or 1912 when she was nineteen or twenty, and the real events which were to go into *Ryder* were only two years behind and still molten in her mind.

The conclusion of the *Morning Telegraph* article (February 18, 1917) is an ecstatic affirmation of the power of Synge for Barnes:

28

—It is enough that, turning back to look on Synge, I have more courage to go forward—that I can read at least eight books without having to say that I was duped into fruitless hours of attention, or into the temporary anguish of undiscovering a discovery. Mary in *The Well of Saints* did not want to see again, preferring darkness to such tragic and illuming light as that let in on her and her Martin when the Saint touched them with the holy healing waters—so sometimes I also do not want to be awakened from the certain joyous blindness that was Synge's.

Miss Barnes was twenty-four when she wrote that.

Probably as a direct result of her intense admiration for Synge and Joyce, Miss Barnes throughout her life would take pains to emphasize that she had Irish blood. That may well be the case through her grandmother Zadel's family, which remains obscure, but that Irish element in Miss Barnes is in the main a matter of willful nurture. You'll remember, Meg, how she suddenly startled you by taking you by the chin and moving her face within inches of yours to examine your features with approbation. —*It's good to have some Irish blood.*

Miss Barnes praised the brutality which went hand in hand with the song in Synge's work. In this she stands entirely above what we have with ever greater carelessness since the eighteenth century come to term neurosis. Her art proves that she knows herself. The guilt described by Freud in *Mourning and Melancholia* does not seem applicable when we look at Barnes. There is instead a potent rage which is finely articulated. It quivers but manages to maintain a very quiet, contained surface. Contrary forces of bestiality and rectitude play menacingly in her mind and on her pages.

The prime symbol of fear and hatred in the child's dream is the bird. A dream of a bird was central to Freud's analysis in his *Leonardo da Vinci*, which, as is well known, came unstuck through a mistranslation in the biography which he was using. But the bird is a well-enough documented phenomenon in childhood hypochondria. Barnes has these "horrid birds" of childhood both in her writing and in her illustrations. They may be transposed to her art from actual dreams—probably are—but there is a difference, for in Barnes the beak is not the devouring vagina of the psychiatric textbook. All of Wendell's women in *Ryder* see an insect-bird which is as gigantic as it is explicit, though not exactly threatening:

—So here rose up a figure in each brain, accordingly mounted to that fancy's ability, of Wendell setting forth from the earth with stupendous great wings, outstripping the cornfields and the mountains, and rising up into the clouds like an enormous and beloved insect, with strong

29

hands upward and arched feet downward, and thundering male parts hung like a terrible anvil, whereon one beats out the resurrection and the death.

Whereupon the women turn to terrible carnage upon one another rolling down into the valley's bottomless depth:

> ... now she on top, now she, now she under, now she, and into the ravine at last, where between tall rank grasses the rubbish blooms.

The picture is so explicit in every psychic detail as to render any analyst silent before it. It is the whole psychic life story of Djuna Barnes.

Birds are shown in ecstasy in the heavens while Julie (Djuna) is still in a state of innocence, and later—a rare note of explicit feminism in her work—the wife and mistress go up to clean out the attic dovecote together and discuss the difference between men and women in society:

> —Their young are most gruesome, and die by the million! said Kate, as she pitched three out of the window. —And can you, she added, seating herself upon a log that Wendell had hewn for a perch, —tell me the reason that Wendell has fancies and we have the cleaning?
> —Most simple easy, said Amelia, piling up the dustpan with voidance and grain. —To man is the vision, to his wife the droppings!

Thus, briefly, does one argue for reading a primal psychic life-in-art, without guilt, for Djuna Barnes. Wald Barnes was a rarified example of the Spoiled Savage. He had "experiments" with Nature.

There is, however, another possible reading of the young woman Barnes, replete not only with anger unto patricide but also with guilt over murderous and incestuous desire. In Chapter Twenty-four of *Ryder,* "Julie Becomes What She Has Read," a strange girl named Arabella Lynn has a dream and moans: —*Accuse me not, it was not I, nor I, nor I!* It is the famous dream of Martin Luther that has been read. The Barnes solution to Luther's hysterical dilemma is a plot courtesy of Poe:

> —It is better, ah, far better, surely a thousand times better, that Arabella Lynn died while yet in bud! How comforting for her parents, the thought that this their daughter was snatched away into the great storehouse of heavenly tutelage before she had known stain of a baser world!

This was a real concern for Miss Barnes, as we are shown in another of her personal asides in an article on the Hippodrome Circus which she published in *The New York Press* in February 1915. She concludes with a description of the end of the circus:

> —As they came off to descend to the stables below I turned my head away. I'm glad my mother does not know as much about me as those elephants.

Miss Barnes hated her father. All the rest followed from that. Dr. O'Connor of *Nightwood* makes his first appearance in *Ryder*, and he, too, is offered as an alternative to Wendell Ryder. O'Connor is saved even though he is a man because he has the qualities of a woman. The Village affairs, the de facto marriage to Courtenay Lemon, her relationship with Thelma Wood, most of her friendships, all followed from this. Djuna Barnes believed two things: that women are not good; but men are much worse. She remained true to these beliefs throughout her life. The secretive nature of her apparently bold art and her decades of silence are explained simply enough. In 1931 she wrote in *The Theatre Guild Magazine:*

> —I like my human experience served up with a little silence and restraint. Silence makes experience go further and, when it does die, gives it that dignity common to a thing one had touched and not ravished.

iii

One could tell the story of Djuna Barnes, writer. But this can be done properly, I maintain, only with some background sense of the biographical context of her art.

She writes in four ways. The least important of these is her light journalism written between 1914 and 1940. The humorous short stories and the slight fictional sketches also enter into this category. If they are not of great value in themselves, they point to important characteristics which should not be overlooked when considering her more important writings. First among these characteristics is her sense of humour, which can be sly, delicate and bawdy. No other woman writer since Aphra Behn has had a better sense of humour, though its flashes must be attended to in the arch savagery that is always in the foreground of her writing. She loves the aphorism and the epigrammatic, whether it be frothy—I have an irresistible urge to be driven downhill in a cab—or more substantial—But to know

31

her is extravagance . . . or the lewd but powerful image of —What's a woman? A cow sitting on a crumpled grin.

A second thing which can be transported usefully from her light to her substantial writing is an understanding that always a portion of her work means nothing, is meant to mean nothing. That portion hangs as a disguising curtain before a tale that is as simple as it is terrible. The two Barnes stories are the effect of her weak and wild father on the Barnes family and the ill-fated love between Barnes and Thelma Wood. The other stories in early works are by comparison incidental, cadged from authors such as Strindberg or from anecdotes connected with the lives of friends. These stories are strange, with stark figures whose words are enigmatic and disconnected. The images presented by the stories are hyperbolic and loose:

> —He shouted, bawled, cracked whip—what did she figure she wanted? The kind of woman who can't tell the truth; truth ran out and away from her as though her veins were pipettes, stuck in by the devil; and drinking, he swelled, and pride had him, it floated him off.

T. S. Eliot, in 1956, upset Miss Barnes in his preparation of a publisher's blurb for *The Antiphon* with the assertion that her writing shatters the normal structure of the English language. He had something. Her images and her words and her very grammar float. That is why it is cracked whip rather than cracked the whip.

The reader should see Barnes' artistic units as independent cameos or portraits framed and hung. The always striking Barnesian unit is sufficient unto itself. What *does* it matter if we don't quite understand what —Sparkling with the fornications of the mint means? Or half the other lines of *The Antiphon* for that matter? It is curious that readers who have been schooled for years to appreciate the difficulties of Joyce and Pound and the delights of Stein should find the crystalline elegance and, after all, comparatively limited obscurity of Barnes (once the story is grasped) to be offputting. A part of it surely is that Miss Barnes' major work came after those writers at a slightly less historically advantageous moment. It is time to look again.

The acquisition of the *OED* and the heavy encrustation of her language both came after she returned to America. *Ryder* is more rich than difficult and more of an historic tour de force with parodies of Chaucer and bits of Joyce and turns of Restoration English. The short stories of *A Book* span across *Ryder* and the eighteenth-century-styled *Ladies Almanack* to meet the forceful prose of the later *Nightwood*. The richness of her relationship to the centuries of

English literature and her passion for words (equalled only by Joyce and Nabokov among the moderns) seem to derive from the fact that she never went to school and was instead read and spoken to in a great variety of styles by her grandmother, mother and father. Her originality has its taproot in this decision and informal education; Wald Barnes' withholding of his children from the school system was a commitment to exalted individualism—Mrs. Pankhurst had done exactly the same thing for the same reason. It worked.

So Miss Barnes writes in the several ways in which she was informally schooled at home. Nonetheless, there is a unifying principle that can be observed in all the four ways in which she writes: in the light journalism, the silhouetted stories, the parodic *Ryder* and *Ladies Almanack,* and the at once intensely simple and complex *Nightwood* and *The Antiphon.*

That principle, it seems to me, can best be defined in the fundamental meanings of the word "grotesque." Beyond the common meaning of monstrous distortion by which the term is almost exclusively known today, it is well to look to the origins of the word and its original connection with grotto, signifying the style of those paintings found in excavations of old Roman buildings.

This style of painting, which is the original meaning of the term grotesque, is not a naturalistic style. In fact, there is no desire to reproduce reality in a closely representational way at all. The style is, quite contrary to our modern sense of the term, frequently light and gay in character. The Roman grotto pictures are often untoward in subject and have human and animal forms fantastically intertwined. The ruggedness of the drawings with which she illustrated *Ladies Almanack* and *Ryder* also match the style of grotto painting. Grotesque is a sophisticatedly primitive typeface.

The best explanation of the grotesque in art is furnished by John Ruskin's definition of the style as —a series of symbols thrown together in bold and fearless connection of truths which it would have taken a long time to express in any verbal way. If we adapt this definition from painting to prose, Ruskin's notion of grotesque speaks to all the essential Barnes styles and includes the silences and verbal ornamentation which are so much a part of her way of writing through several stages which might otherwise give the impression of not being closely connected. To define her as a writer it is necessary to include her silences, her encrustations, her sense of humour, and her horror before life. A painterly writer then, a modernist and an ancient, an adherent of the grotesque with elements of Joyce, Eliot and Synge, but with a unique artistic voice that is immediately recognizable and unmistakable.

Miss Barnes has all the time in the world and no time. There is a sense in everything she has ever written not so much of timelessness, but rather of time out of repair and heaped up as in an attic. The effect is produced by her language and the way it swans about between centuries. Her conviction would appear to be that the past, present and future exist in one moment. In *Ryder*, Wendell believes in an afterlife but not in God, and when Sophia dies and leaves an obscene will we learn —In after-life, Sophia looked upon this document with amazement. It is intimated in Miss Barnes' last poems that both time and the afterlife are terrible reruns, so that life after death possesses even less sense than life before death:

> To Moses' empty gorge, like smoke
> Rush backward all the words he spoke.
> Lucifer roars up from earth.
> Down falls Christ into his death.

Is it then that Miss Barnes has taken up the rather comic blasphemous vision of her father and made it absurdly tragic, a tale told backwards by an idiot eternity? Wald Barnes in life recanted when everything fell down around him, remarried, became "normal." He even went to Florida. His daughter Djuna stood firm against the world she had received from him, and that and her art were the vengeance that was hers. Wendell achieves resurrection in the last lines of *Ryder*, but it is a meaningless event.

The conclusion to *Ryder* is the saddest imaginable return to Eden. Adamic Wendell has played fast and free with Nature, and so now rather than being cast out he will, in his daughter's backward mythology, be discarded *into* it:

> —In the wide field where the night was all among the grass and about the animals, Wendell went, leaning far back and yet stumbling.
> The black calf breathed against his side, and the dark cows breathed among themselves, and the horses, with no earth beneath their feet, trembled, as they slept and lay.
> And Wendell sat down among them and forebore to hide his face. Whom should he disappoint now?
> —Hee-haw! said the ass beside him, and he put his hand out and stroked the ass.
> Whom should he disappoint now?
> The horses whinnied as he touched their fetlocks, and the kine were shaken with the bellows of their breath, and he touched their new horns. The little mice of the fields fled about him, and he gave them his unchanged position, and the night birds murmured above and he

34

moved not, and the creeping things that he had not numbered or known, looked at him from a million eyes, and his eyes were there also, and the things in the trees made walking and running on the branches, and he spoke not.

Whom should he disappoint now?

And everything and its shape became clear in the dark, by tens and tens they ranged, and lifted their lids and looked at him; in the air and in the trees and on the earth and from under the earth, and regarded him long, and he forebore to hide his face. They seemed close ranged, and now they seemed far ranged, and they moved now near, now far, as a wave comes and goes, and they lifted their lids and regarded him, and spoke not in their many tongues, and they went a far way, and there was a little rest, and they came close, and there was none. Closing in about him nearer, and swinging out wide and from him far, and came in near and near, and as a wave, closed over him, and he drowned, and arose while he might yet go.

And whom should he disappoint?

That passage—it is Barnes at her best, though there are many other passages from *Nightwood* and *The Antiphon* which might have been selected instead—should be full and sufficient proof of the place of Djuna Barnes in modern literature, even though many histories give her only a line or two. Joyce, Proust, Kafka, Nabokov and a good many other writers have a much greater importance in the evolution of modern literature. Barnes, whom one can only call modern in a conditional sense anyway, has always stood far off to the side. Her theme is too strange and unique to become a universal story, though she almost does it. But how many have a book to outshine *Nightwood*? And who has dared to match the voices of Rabelais and Chaucer (her favourite writer) as she does in *Ryder* and the language of Shakespeare as she, yes, sometimes does in *The Antiphon*? And what is the perverse mechanism of fame that can have an artist be honoured as she has been by her greatest fellow artists and then be put on display in a dim hallway of contemporaneity like an heirloom that is too good to put away but does not merit frequent contemplation?

Miss Barnes herself did not help her own reputation much. She obdurately saved her life for the secrecy of her art. In *The Antiphon*, the mother blurts out her greatest fear: —*May God protect us! I wonder what you'll write/ When I am dead and gone.* The fear was correct, though the stigmatization was covert except for the actual members of the family and those who knew Barnes well. She would not have stated things plainly as so many other moderns do. When

35

Henry Raymont came to interview her for *The New York Times*, Miss Barnes roared back at his query about whether or not she ever intended to publish memoirs or journals:

> —Me, who won't write a biography, who doesn't want to be interviewed? How can you ask me such a question? Lillian Hellman's and all those people's memoirs are so disgusting—I mean, she's a nice woman—but they're all so terrible, why should I want to add to it?

She couldn't deny that she had said it—anyway, that was never the style of Djuna Barnes—but that remark would cause her considerable embarrassment because Lillian Hellman was one of a number of artists who had contributed to an informal aid fund that had been organized for her by Glenway Wescott. That was in the period, after her return from Paris, when she went as long as five days at a time with nothing to eat.

CHAPTER TWO

—*I'm not a lesbian. I just loved Thelma,* she told a close friend nearly half a century later and was essentially correct, though it had to be many years before that love, one of the most important events in her life and the seed of one of the century's striking works of literature, could be reduced and held in such simple suspension. They walked down 1922 and the boulevard du Montparnasse with their legs coming forward in perfect coordination as though they were one. They were dressed in black, and they did not stop until 1931. Thelma Wood was tall and gamin-like, but the thing you noticed about her on the street was the fact that her feet were extraordinarily large. Djuna Barnes, the elder of the two women, was also tall and very handsome. The most notable feature about her was the span between her upper lip and her nose, a facial characteristic marked in her New England family side from the eighteenth century, which made her look in sharp profile as though someone had bitten out the area under her nose. They walked like two countesses in one cloak.

ii

Djuna Barnes' most famous comment, fairly soon after she arrived in Europe, dismissed both America and Europe in one sweep. —*I came to Europe to get culture. Is this culture I'm getting? Then I might as well go back to Greenwich Village and rot there.* (That is the version of the remark quoted by Matthew Josephson. There is a variant reported by Robert McAlmon for the same year: —*Christ, we came over here to find culture, and, if this is it, I'll not take a second helping.*) When she returned to America in 1931 she wrote to a friend that America was a country that drove her into a state of imbecile childishness and that it was not a place to come for either love or happiness. Her objection seemed to be to the dangers of the American heedless freedom. —*With an American anything can be done,* says a character in *Nightwood.*

The revulsion against the "American way of life" in the period around World War I was so broadly based in many quarters of society that one cannot simply ascribe it to a certain artistic or bohemian

37

element. Good-natured Marianne Moore, who like Djuna Barnes was a slightly older and more reserved member of her generation, expressed one of the aspects of the problem in a poem in which she speaks of how America is a land with no proofreaders, silkworms or digressions, and also of how the language had reduced itself to plain American which even dogs and cats can read. It was a problem. Mark Twain's *The Mysterious Stranger* in 1916 and *The Education of Henry Adams* in 1918 gave serious voice to the idea that in all the subtle ways which alone constitute a meaningful life American democracy had failed.

America at the start of this century was still very much, for all its political independence, a provincial culture. It was also, even by 1900, quite an empty country. There were more than seventy million people, true, but they were spread out over enormous distances. When the century of troubled growth and cultivation drew to a close, the problem could no longer be evaded. It is a commonplace in all the discussions of the generation that came forth around 1910 that the greatest energy seems to have been located in the youth from the Midwest. Undoubtedly it was most lonely there. Many have spoken of how, only vaguely knowing there was another world outside their stifling and boring provincial towns and cities, they all the same knew that they had to leave and locate a cosmopolitanism.

The same seas of wheat that inspired Katharine Lee Bates' poem *America The Beautiful* a year after the birth of Djuna Barnes within the next generation inspired terror and revulsion. But this is not often said: The pattern of American life which the new American rebels and aesthetes fled from—some directly to Greenwich Village, others first to the Chicago lakefront—pressed hard up against New York and Boston. It is probably not sensible to make too much of a difference between any Ohio or Kansas town and, say, Springfield, Massachusetts, where the paternal grandparents of Djuna Barnes lived. The little rural town where Miss Barnes herself was born, Cornwall-on-Hudson, though it was within a day's drive by carriage from New York City, was only incorporated as a village in 1884 and had but a few hundred inhabitants in the 1890s.

It is for this reason that one should avoid an overly geographically determined view of the development of American writers at the beginning of this century. Though they lived and published in Chicago, Greenwich Village and Paris (and came from Cornwall-on-Hudson; Rockport, Maine; Oak Park, Illinois; and all sorts of other hamlets), each of the first twentieth-century American writers, to a greater extent than most writers in most other times and cultures, carried with him or her a determining portable spiritual municipality as they moved onwards and sometimes inwards in their flight from American boredom. It is a truism that scarcely any of them ever really escaped. Hemingway staring along the barrel of his gun. Fitzgerald, who despised the crass philistinism of his native Minnesota but sometimes managed to act the same way himself. The octogenarian Henry Miller playing Ping-Pong with naked Playmates in California.

Djuna Barnes, however, did escape, and yet she was the unluckiest of all the important writers of her generation. Her weak English mother, strong-willed American grandmother and spoiled American father were inept eccentrics. That was her misfortune, but it is the wellspring of all of her art. It is the sort of family story that could have played itself out in America, in Russia, or in any one of several South American countries.

iii

Matthew Josephson, whose expatriate magazine was titled *Secession,* noted in his 1930 book *Portrait of the Artist as American* that the pilgrimage of the Yankee spirit towards libertarianism and complete freedom of ideas resulted in highly individualistic artistic personalities (he cites Poe, Whitman and Melville, and one could add Djuna Barnes), but also it led often to a certain infantilism in the national character. Henry James had noted with horror how the Americans flocked to Europe and yet looked upon everything European with a stingy, defiant, grudging attitude. It was more complicated than mere provincial pride, however, because back at home those same Americans did not read American authors, and this was as true of those who were artists as it was of the common reader.

Matthew Arnold had long before cautioned, in speaking of Walt Whitman, of what would happen to America if it sought to follow Whitman's call for a bold culture wholly independent of the European movement. What Arnold feared did come to pass, ironically, when the Americans went to Paris in the 1920s.

The majority of the expatriates did not read European writers and did not have or use the opportunity to meet them, either. William Carlos Williams asked Robert McAlmon to present him to some young French modern poets when he came to France in 1924 and was puzzled when McAlmon replied that he didn't know any. At the same time they did not bring much native literary past in their intellectual luggage, with the altogether natural result that the American writer came to be a captive of his own present. Thus there began the first great modern period of referential writing in which the expatriates sometimes seem to be not novelists but biographers trapped together in a hall of mirrors with nothing to do but describe each other describing each other. Hemingway provides the span, from *The Sun Also Rises* to *A Moveable Feast,* and it is surprising that it has not been more widely noticed that there is an obvious verbal gesture to Djuna Barnes in the name of the hero of his first novel, Jake Barnes. The nice joke of the play on names is that Jake Barnes is horrified by "queers." Two years before he had made a similar passing wave in *The Transatlantic Review*, referring to Barnes with forked tongue-in-cheek as—that legendary personality that has dominated the intellectual night-life of Europe for a century, though he is quick to add he has of course never met her or read her books and contents himself with observing from afar that . . . she looks very nice. We know now from Hemingway's published letters that he admired Barnes as a writer. Hemingway used his contemporaries more than most (he boasted to his brother about it), but they virtually all did that sort of thing. In these same years, for example, Djuna Barnes herself was writing *Ladies Almanack* about the famed Paris salon of her friend Natalie Barney, a book in which every character has a real referent. In much the same fashion as Hemingway, she used the name Titus (the publisher of *This Quarter*) in one of her stories, with no special point at all except revenge. Lives and names of their contemporaries—it was all that all but a few of them really had. Scott Fitzgerald circling round the Murphys is the most extreme example. Hemingway and McAlmon come next to mind.

But Djuna Barnes had her family. Her father had correctly warned her that it was going to take a lifetime to unravel it all. She also had her own language. A few of the Americans did learn French— Matthew Josephson, Malcolm Cowley, Natalie Barney (whose command of the language was good but not quite as flawless as some of her American friends believed), Man Ray—while most set about to make an already reductive language simpler still. Barnes, as a casual friend who had been one of the ladies from *Ladies Almanack* complained bitchily behind her back several decades later, was the only one of the expatriates who chose early English as the one language she ever cared to learn.

That is true, but it was not affectation on her part. It all started with the unorthodox education that was given to the young Djuna Barnes in a very American way. Immersion in the rich history of the English language was not common among her artistic contemporaries, but there were some others who also tended in this direction. Matthew Josephson read deeply in the Elizabethans. Eliot is another obvious example. The dominant note, however, was still being sounded strongly on the eve of World War II when Henry Miller, to promote his young friend Durrell's first book, proclaimed —*I am against the English with all my heart. I greet Lawrence Durrell as "the first Englishman"! Down with Chaucer! Down with Shakespeare!* It was said of Cummings that he would never forgive the English for having had Shakespeare, who obviously should have been American. Barnes told me that Americans were antagonistic towards English usage because it is superior to American English.

The expatriates who went to Europe possessed a mixture of American arrogance and aversion for their native land. Greenwich Village was just a stopping place before the generation to which Barnes belonged faced what Waldo Frank termed —the classic debate of American culture, Should an American artist stay at home?

Ford Madox Ford, the Englishman with a predilection for the American Midwest, thought that the primary animus for the new literature had come from the Midwest because it had scarcely been touched by the War. The two mythical towns from which all the young writers came were Hot Fudge, Nebraska, and Agamemnon, Iowa, and there was a bit of truth in each part of the jest. An Eastern poet visiting Chicago, Alfred Kreymborg, recalls in his memoirs that at first he was offended by a poetic movement which took as its motto "Boost Chicago." The blowsy term never really went away. Pound used it in exhorting his fellow poets and countrymen to boost Eliot, and one of the last American journals of the Paris period—noted for its two-line anonymous poem: Out of the gorse/ Came a homosexual horse—was called *The Booster.* But there was so much freshness and amiability among the Chicago writers that Kreymborg was soon won over. Chicago had Sandburg, Masters, Lindsay, Anderson. There was *Poetry, The Little Review.* In time there was a fair back-and-forth between New York and Chicago. Barnes, for example, published several of her early stories in *The Little Review* in its Chicago days and submitted work to *Poetry.*

The youthful Chicago push had to end in New York, because that was where the publishing houses were and also because no wealthy altruistic boosters came forward, and so the work of publication had to depend entirely on the unmonied determination of people like Harriet Monroe, Margaret Anderson and Jane Heap. And perhaps, too, because Chicago was just a little too close. In a forgotten early play by Edmund Wilson the hero surveys the process of the intellectual's migration:

41

—When you're in Galesburg, Illinois, you want to get to Chicago; then when you get to Chicago, you want to make good in New York. Then when you do put it over in New York, what in God's name have you got? The thoroughly depressing companionship of a lot of other small-towners like yourself who don't know what the hell to do with themselves either!

Some chose to turn their backs on their empty and mean little towns forever. Berenice Abbott was one of these. She had followed James Light and Sue Jenkins to New York. They had gone to Ohio University from the same Pittsburgh high school as Malcolm Cowley. In Ohio she had helped them put together a little magazine called *Sansculotte,* and when she came to New York it was with only six dollars in her pocket. She wanted to be a sculptor—Nina Hamnett noted in her memoirs that that seemed to be the ambition of all young American girls of this period—but ended up as Man Ray's assistant in Paris and eventually as a photographer of international stature. More than half a century later she would still speak of Ohio with flashing indignation in her eyes.

Many, of course, tried to mine their little towns from New York and Paris. Van Wyck Brooks, working in a New York publishing house, has recorded how every week brought a new pile of *Winesburg, Ohios* and *Spoon River Anthologies,* and how very quickly it became apparent that this material was intrinsically limited. Among the more sophisticated younger writers, only Robert McAlmon continued to work this provincial ground as well as the expatriation scene far into the Paris years.

The male writers put layers of colour onto their backgrounds. Both Hemingway and McAlmon represented themselves as former cowboys, and Ezra Pound of Idaho boasted of how he had worked his way to Europe as a cattlehand on a boat. These harmless affectations would be met in Greenwich Village and Paris by their European equivalents, people of vague antecedents carrying box-tree family histories and titles. Many of the slightly younger aspiring writers and artists were either able to use their spirit of place more deftly, like Glenway Wescott from Kewaskum, Wisconsin, or else, like Charles Ford, a poet from Mississippi, or Thelma Wood, a sculptor from Missouri, they were somehow quite free of it. Miss Barnes was never tied by her place but would never be free of the shadow of her childhood.

iv

Djuna was not seduced or raped but "given" sexually by her father like an Old Testament slave or daughter. There was evidence in the unedited version of *Nightwood* which Barnes told Eliot in a letter was semi-autobiographical. Now it has been confirmed: Barnes was "given" to Percy Faulkner, 52, the brother of her father's mistress, in 1910 by Wald and Zadel. She went to Bridgeport with him from the Long Island farm to which the Barnes menage had moved, soon parted, and then came to New York in 1911.

In the unpublished manuscript portion the girl (she was not Nora then but Catherine) is initiated by an older man who had held her on his knee when she was a child and ate caramels and melted because she looked up at him and said, "Yes," and then he was frightened because she would not cry afterwards.

At this point in the manuscript there is an extremely odd iteration as the girl loses her virginity yet again, this time to her father after a ceremony at the Christmas tree in which the father has placed a ring on her finger. Time slips gear; the girl is on her knees to her grandmother begging her not to let it happen, and the grandmother's response is that it *had* to happen. And then she is back in the deflowering, brandishing a carving knife and made strong and blind by her father's feelings about women and love.

The mother has sprinkled flour in front of her door in the hope that there will not be footprints in it in the morning. The lover leaps backward out of a window and into the garden. It is a film run backwards and in double exposure, a theme too powerful to be put plainly and a ferocious fairy tale at best. It did happen, and the outrage was the shadow-play behind all her art. Afterwards, Elizabeth divorced Wald.

Chapter Five of *Ryder* is entitled *Rape and Repining!* It concerns the rape of the mother in her youth by a fourteen-year-old lad, and it is the occasion for the second voicing (the first appeared in 1923) of the great Barnes theme, which is time being sucked back into the vortex:

—What Nation has the Son first and the Mother second? What tree springs up before the orchard, saying, *"Orchard, Orchard, here is the tree!"* What infant gives Birth to its Parent, what Child crawls out of the cradle, that its Mother may have where to lay her head?

The answer to that incestuous riddle is simple—it is the writer recreating her past.

V

Young Djuna Barnes lived briefly with her mother in Queens and enrolled for drawing classes at the Pratt Institute. She then had a room of her own in the Bronx. Years later—she prided herself on her notoriously bad memory, the memory of Montaigne, she said— she could not even precisely recall the years of her attendance. It is made more difficult because she did not receive a degree or a certificate. As early as 1913 she had obtained a position as a regular freelance illustrator and columnist for *The Brooklyn Daily Eagle*. Her initial training in drawing had been given to her by her father, who purportedly (none of his work appears to have survived) was a competent watercolourist. She does manage to recall that she studied under Pratt's noted instructress Elizabeth Ely Lord, and that she had classes in still life and figure drawing. She accounted for a part of her tuition by posing, robed, for some of the classes. She also studied at The Art Students League in the fall and winter of 1915. At this time her address was 42 Washington Square South. At the League she studied with F. Luis Mora and Frank Vincent Dumond, the two most prominent teachers at the school. The main things she learned, she remembered, were the bones and muscles of the body. In the end, she simply drifted off to earn her living full time.

Newspapers flourished in the New York Metropolitan area—there were over twenty with reasonable circulations—and the competition to write for them was very strong. *The Brooklyn Daily Eagle* was one of the liveliest New York papers of the time, and one of the reasons for this was that young free-lancers were encouraged to submit "on space" and were paid rather well if their pieces were used. The advantage that Barnes possessed was that she could both illustrate and write, which she did with such gusto that she soon became a regularly featured columnist. By 1917, she told me, she was earning $5,000 a year, a most handsome salary for the time. In those days Miss Barnes was called Djuny by her friends, but because of her great reportorial energy she was referred to as Gunga Duhl by fellow professionals. She contributed twice-weekly columns to *The Brooklyn Daily Eagle,* and many of the contributions were accompanied by a drawing signed simply "Djuna."

Barnes did local-colour stories. She did a few murder and suicide stories and an account of the ordinary business of the Kings County Court with its strange permanent gallery of the shiftless who turn up every day to hear the stories. She wrote about the old and the poor at Coney Island, about orphanages and homes for the aged, about soapbox oratory around the Franklin statue in Printing House Square. There was an article about the decay of Chinatown and another ("Why Go Abroad? See Europe in Brooklyn!") about the foreigners and the atmosphere in Brooklyn's produce market. The tango was fashionable, and so there were articles on the dance and "the meaning of Tangoism" (a mere steaming up of America's decadent souls), on roof dances and roof-garden restaurants, and an interview-article with three drawings about Vernon and Irene Castle.

Many long-forgotten actors and actresses were interviewed, but she also interviewed major theatrical personalities of the time such as Diamond Jim Brady, Lillian Russell and Florenz Ziegfeld. She had a series called "Veterans in Harness" in which she portrayed a postman, a streetcar conductor, a waiter, a fireman, an elevator man, and so forth. She went to boxing matches and interviewed the champions Jack Dempsey and Jess Willard, who told her that soon girls would be boxing for a living. She wrote about Twingless Twitchell and his Tantalizing Tweezers, a show-business dentist who extracted teeth publically.

In the main the articles are very good. In 1917 she did an interview with a Negro theatre company, and it was explained to her that, just as they endeavour to choose poets to be their ministers (*—Do he be a man standing in a church or a church standing in a man?*), so the same criteria must be applied to the craft of acting. At the end Barnes says *—I shall try to remember everything.* The soft and quick response is *—You can't forget, Miss,* whereupon the theatre curtain drops suddenly, and many voices are heard crooning "Walk Together, Children" as she leaves. Several of her articles are cast in this sort of quasi-dramatic form. Evidently she did not take notes as she worked, because in one of her interview-articles of 1917, the actress Helen Westley interrupts her to ask if she has been taking notes and is told *—I don't have to. My memory always makes a paragraph out of a note automatically.*

We don't have much information about Barnes in the Bronx and Brooklyn. She did write one newspaper article supposedly recalling her Bronx days, but there isn't really anything autobiographical in it. There is a fleeting glimpse in another article of Courtenay Lemon at Fleischman's Café in the Bronx. She probably began to live with him in 1916. In any event, they separated early in 1919.

In early 1914 we see Barnes visiting the Fifth Avenue salon of Mabel Dodge to show her her pictures. Barnes' articles were appearing and she had had a few poems in *Harper's*—that may have owed something to her grandmother's connections—but she was quite unknown and deceptively shy. She dressed plainly. Her auburn hair

Newspaper drawings, 1914–1916

was swept back austerely. It seemed to her some years later to be a kind of transitional phase in her life when she stood poised between her old manner and a new personality that was about to unfold. It was the first time in her life that she had encountered monied people and what she termed the nonchalant classes, poet-revolutionaries, who casually pointed the way to the future —with an index finger that had previously been dipped in gold ink.

—These were my grateful days. I was grateful to Mabel Dodge, who let me eat as many sandwiches as my suburban stomach could hold. I was grateful to Carl Van Vechten for having written the introductory card that had given access to so much.

She thought she looked funny, perhaps out of place in that artistic atmosphere, all highly glossed white-enamel walls and white furniture and Venetian glass. Some people did pay attention to her, though she noticed that they tended to be older gentlemen. She worried about whether it was lack of sangfroid on her part or interest in her pictures which drew them, and she reflected on how the younger men seemed to have no interest at all in her, nor she in them.

Love had been a subject too intensely debated in her family. It was the atmosphere of art that she longed for and yet had never been able to feel as an actuality until she stood in the salon of Mabel Dodge:

—And yet I was in awe of no one. I attempted not to show the arrogance of my upper lip that would persist in an attempt to curl, probably because I wanted to cry and wouldn't, and I felt cold because I wanted so dreadfully to feel warm and hopeful and one with them.

Mabel Dodge held up one of her pictures, deciding whether or not to like it. Barnes would see Mabel Dodge again, on Cape Cod about eighteen months later. Barnes was a member of the Provincetown group, while Mabel Dodge was just beginning an affair there with the dark and intense artist Maurice Sterne, who was a few months later to become Mabel's third husband. When Djuna left Courtenay Lemon, he wrote to Sterne in great bitterness, accusing him of being the cause of the disintegration of the marriage (Lemon, for the record, refers to her in his letter as his wife), which Sterne denied was the case, but which does not in the least remove the probability that Mabel Dodge's husband did have a dalliance with the young artist. (Barnes thought that Sterne was a bit of a stinker. His own papers confirm this judgment: He boasts that he once succeeded in destroying a lesbian relationship by making love to both the women.) The picture, or the painter, didn't suit Mabel Dodge.

TRAINING SEALS IN STAGE STUNTS

BILLY SUNDAY A FIRE-EATER IN PULPIT
War, He Says, Has Been the Best Thing
for Religion in All the Last Century

MANY WANT BABIES
how about yourself?

A NEW YORK PRIZE-FIGHT

MY SISTERS AND I AT

BROADWAY THINKS IT IS ONLY STREET
IN THE WORLD, SAYS ATTERIDGE
IN ONLY CITY IN THE Smallest Town
It Is as Provincial as the Smallest Town
Found on Any Map in the Geography

COME INTO THE ROOF-GARDEN, MAUD
And, Maud Dear, Bring a Sense of
Humour with You, for the Place Has
None of It

INTERVIEWING ARTHUR VOEGTLIN
IS SOMETHING LIKE HAVING
A NIGHTMARE —

SATAN GIVES INTERVIEW
Admits It's Best Man
Has Done So Far
But Declares It Still Falls
Lamentably Short of Hell

Suggests Improvements

NO MORE BACHELORS:
Girls to Propose . . .

SOME DOUBT IS CAST
ON SUICIDE THEORY AT
CAHILL INQUEST

NOTHING EVER DONE WELL THAT WASN'T PLANNED IN BED

Newspaper headlines by Djuna Barnes

—Anyway. Go up to 291 Fifth Avenue and ask for Mr. Stieglitz and show him. Perhaps he can help you.

By late 1915 Miss Barnes was a resident of Greenwich Village. After Washington Square South she lived at 220 West Fourteenth Street, and her next address, in 1916, 86 Greenwich Avenue, was a room that she shared with Lemon. She had always been a free-lance, even when she was writing exclusively for *The Brooklyn Daily Eagle.* By 1914 her reputation as a columnist had grown secure enough that she was able to transfer her professional skills to Manhattan and write regularly for three major papers—*The Press, The World* and *The Morning Telegraph.*

It is not common for an author to have control over the headlines set to journalistic work, but we may assume that Djuna Barnes did have this control, since the flow-on title in nineteenth-century form infused with twentieth-century sardonic wit is met with regularly in various forms over a period of fifteen years in her work. *The New York Morning Telegraph Sunday Magazine* heading of November 26, 1917:

How the Villagers Amuse Themselves
The Task Is Sordid and Hard,
But It Must Be Done—
So After an Early Breakfast
Out Sets the Bohemian

flow on naturally enough into the 1928 *Ladies Almanack:*

showing their Signs and their tides;
their Moons and their Changes;
the Seasons as it is with them;
their eclipses and Equinoxes;
as well as a full Record of diurnal
and nocturnal Distempers

and is very much in evidence in the old-fashioned chapter headings of *Ryder:*

Chapter Forty: Old Wives' Tale,
or the Knit Codpieces

and trails off only in the early 1930s when Miss Barnes, returned from Europe, was employed to write articles for various journals, mainly *The Theatre Guild Magazine,* to which she gave titles such as:

Self-portrait by Djuna Barnes, 1914

Nothing After Midnight; An Interview with Gabrielle Chanel; With This Word to the Wise—the Women Who Seek Beauty, or Hamlet's Custard Pie—Giles, the Butler, Learns What Is Wrong with the Drama.

Miss Barnes went to remarkable lengths to obtain several of her stories during the period when she was striving to establish her reputation. In 1914 she gave herself over to a demonstration of fire rescue techniques at a fireman's training school on Sixty-seventh Street in Manhattan. She allowed herself to be rescued three times by three different methods: she came down on a rope ladder; had a small rope thrown up to her by which she had hoist up the more substantial rope on which she again descended; and a fireman descending from a storey above her had her hug him tightly as he brought them both down.

As she prepared for her first rescue she watched a man fall tautly into a man-encircled net far below. There were eyes in the windows of all the neighbouring buildings, and all pedestrians stood staring up at her. —It was, she wrote, the first time in my knowledge that I had earnestly desired to be sure of living ninety-nine years, a desire, which it happens, she was never to repeat. She also said that it was the first time in her life that she knew that she was a coward. In order to stem her feeling of incipient sickness as she dangled high above the pavement—in those years, of course, this sort of thing was very popular in films—she kept repeating over and over to herself: *There is one act that must be committed beautifully—suicide!*

One of her stories has sometimes been exaggerated in accounts by those who remembered or knew of her days as a reporter. I had heard several tales of how she had allowed herself to be hugged by a gorilla. It was a gorilla, but a young female one at the Bronx Zoo, then the only surviving member of its species in captivity. The animal weighed only forty-five pounds. The article, which appeared in *The New York World Magazine* in October 1914, is not one of her better ones. The gorilla, called Dinah, is given a mock interview by Miss Barnes, who asks her what she thinks of the United States and is told by Dinah that the taxi meter climbs faster than a chimpanzee and that she is most anxious to try chewing gum, that strange American delicacy that seems to keep so many faces in something like rotary motion beneath hats. Djuna was hugged by Dinah and found it somehow impersonal and condescending and yet strangely agreeable. She compared it to having a garden hose wrapped around one.

Barnes was far better describing a seal training session with one sanctimonious seal who continually prayed but stole fish from the bucket when the trainer's back was turned for even an instant, and then resumed praying while swallowing. There is a nice description of the intensely androgynous atmosphere of sexual awkwardness in the Dempsey training camp.

Sharply pronounced personal and social viewpoints are frequently evidenced. Some of her most interesting pieces from that point of view are the ones dealing with the Suffrage Movement. In spite of occasional sympathetic remarks or references to her sisters, it is quite clear that Djuna Barnes wouldn't be in it. In part, it was surely her intense individualism that would not permit her to conscript herself into any movement; in part, perhaps, it was the sad example of her grandmother at home who had been an active suffragist and whose personal life and career mocked the high expectations with which she had set out. Many of the values by which Miss Barnes lived in those years were precisely the ones which the Movement put forward, but Djuna Barnes had none of the middle-class security that had nurtured so many of the Greenwich Village bohemians and suffragists. She had come up the hard way and was still pushing onwards to her goal of artistic stature. There was no time at all for speeches on the subject and very little patience for listening to them for that matter.

One of the articles which she did for *The Brooklyn Daily Eagle* in 1913 was a Suffrage Aviation Meet which was held on Hempstead Plain. All of the women decided not to become aviatrixes, and, the highpoint of the rally—according to Miss Barnes—they succeeded in collecting one dollar fifty for the Movement. Her condescension shows through most clearly in a 1913 *Eagle* article on a school for suffragists run by a Mrs. Catt.

Djuna Barnes' greatest reportorial feat took place in 1914 when she allowed herself to be force-fed for *The New York World* in simulation of the force-feedings which the English suffragists were then undergoing. There had been press speculation about the possibility of force-feeding an I.W.W. agitator who had gone on a protest hunger strike in prison. Miss Barnes was placed on an operating table and attended by four men, one of them a doctor. Just before she mounted the table to begin the procedure, she caught sight of the yard of red rubber hose and also of her own face in a mirror, ghostly white. Three of the men pressed down on her ankles, hips and head, while the doctor painted her nostils with a mixture of cocaine and disinfectant and then examined her nasal passages and throat with a bright light prior to introducing the tube into one of her nostrils.

She wrote that she had determined beforehand to meet the trial professionally, since after all it had been faced by scores of women in England, but she found it to be an anguish beyond description. The hands holding down her head tightened like a vice and were answered by corresponding pressure from the other pairs of hands, while nerves the existence of which she had been totally unaware brought searing pain to her face and breasts. The pain flowed down her spine, gradually replaced by a dull ache that spread through her body from her shoulders. The doctor's eyes were constantly before her face. He held up the container from which the warm milky-coloured liquid which she could not taste flowed into her. The room floated. She was on the verge of fainting, but suddenly a tremendously powerful surge of resistance came to her and she felt her throat constricting against the burning flow of liquid. She wanted power to halt the hated infusion into her body. Her body was rent with shivers, and she was covered with cold sweat. She registered a voice warning her to relax her throat or she would choke, and she wondered whether the experiment might after all end in death. It was quite real.

> —If I, play acting, felt my being burning with revolt at this brutal usurpation of my own functions, how they who actually suffered the ordeal in its acutest horror must have flamed at the violation of the sanctuaries of their spirit? I saw in my hysteria a vision of a hundred women in grim prison hosptials, bound and shrouded on tables just like this, held in the rough grip of callous warders, while white-robed doctors thrust rubber tubing into the delicate interstices of their nostrils and forced into their helpless bodies the crude fuel to sustain the life they longed to sacrifice.

Afterwards she observed as if from afar the tiny red moustache on the soft face of the doctor as he removed his surgical mask.

vi

Between 1916 and 1918 the amount of time and energy which Djuna Barnes devoted to her columns lessened considerably. She was already a very well-known figure in New York and could take a certain amount of pride in the career that she had started to make for herself: There is always Stanley and his African adventure and so one cannot call her the founder of participatory journalism, and yet certainly no other woman journalist was doing the sort of things that she was prior to World War I. But she had never thought that this was to be her career. Sometime in the second half of 1918—we can date it by the last contribution which appeared in print—Djuna

Barnes drew up a list of sketches to make a book. She also wrote at least part of a preface for the book, which was never titled and never appeared, though we don't know whether it was ever put to a publisher or if she simply decided that a book of character sketches would represent a step back. Her first little book, poetry and drawings, had appeared in 1915. It had not earned her anything, but it had attracted some notoriety and because of it she was regarded as a serious artist in the Village. The sketches which she chose for the prospective book did not involve any of her own escapades. She was going to include Dempsey and Diamond Jim and Belasco and Frank Harris. Frank Crowninshield, the Editor of *Vanity Fair,* was to be in it. The sketches were often quite vitriolic. Barnes describes *Vanity Fair* as a magazine for a public that wants something French but has never been to Paris. In the office the telephone girl wears sables, the office boy has sideburns, there is a discreet tea served every afternoon, and special peppermints are kept in a little oak cabinet for the stenographer when she bursts into tears. Barnes had first gone to the office to sell Crowninshield a picture. He tried, she said, to see her garters, and, when he failed, he invited her to lunch where after ordering in French he leaned forward and said in a rather impersonal way: —*Now tell me all about your dear little life.*

A few of the sketches were to involve criminals and the police. Next to the name of Lieutenant Guadobossi on her Contents page Miss Barnes notes dryly that he denied everything that he said to her. There was to be a sketch—it never appeared in print and appears to have been lost—of the gangster's wife Mrs. Nicky Arnstein, Fanny Brice.

At least two of the sixteen sketches were of a nature which would not have allowed their publication by a proper publisher in 1918. One was about a slender young boy of uncertain sex who played the piano and kept the company of a fast crowd of opera singers. He was taken up by a tremendous singer who weighed twenty-one stone and had nostrils like a stallion. The lad tries to—creep into one of her crevices and make the experience have some meaning to her.

The other untoward profile was of a woman called Doris the Dope who had a small child named Douglas and claimed she was the discarded mistress of Lord Alfred Douglas. It is the strongest of the Greenwich Village sketches that Barnes wrote. Doris claimed that she worked in the "Secret Service" and showed Miss Barnes her black drawers the first time that they met. Barnes described her as lesbian in wartime, more or less normal in peacetime, a compulsive thief (but only of one's best clothing and rarest books), and an imaginative liar. She suffered from syphilis, was addicted to "snow," smoked continually, and was a follower of the arch mountebank Alastair Crowley. She invited people for tea and sometimes forgot to be there, sometimes greeted them sprawled naked on a mattress on the floor.

Miss Barnes lost a favourite nightgown to her when one night Doris appeared without the child, said she had nowhere to go, and asked to be allowed to spend the night in her flat. During the night she awoke and asked Djuna if she would have an affair with her. Djuna said no, whereupon Doris went back to sleep. She was gone in the morning, and the theft was explained with a note: —I liked it. Once Doris came to John Reed (Jack to Djuna) and told him that her boy was dead and she needed fifteen dollars to bury him. Some minutes later he chanced to hear her whistling in a nearby park and saw the boy emerge from a bush and go off hand in hand with her. The final anecdote in the sketch is about how Doris boasted to Courtenay Lemon that she could piss like a boy. A bottle was brought and set several yards away. Doris raised her skirts, firmly grasped either side of her *"petit* [sic] *soeur"*—even the most daring bohemian publisher would have backed away from printing a scene like this in New York in 1918—which she raised up not only to hit but actually to fill the bottle.

There were real bohemians, among the other kind, in those days in Greenwich Village.

Barnes and Lemon were both markedly more reserved in manner than almost all their Village artist acquaintances. Barnes always managed to be dressed in a svelte manner, though her means were rarely ample. I assume that the journalistic earnings about which I was told must have applied at best to a single year (Miss Barnes always made a fetish of truth, but she was also intensely proud), for we have the account in Peggy Guggenheim's memoirs of how Peggy was urged by her cousin Helen Fleischman (who subsequently married Georgio Joyce) to provide Djuna with some of her lingerie. There followed the first incident in several decades of awkwardnesses between the two women, for Barnes was given lingerie which was fine but not new, and indeed had been mended in places. The recipient was indignant; the donor, embarrassed, because her cousin Helen, she learned subsequently, had simply thrown open her own elegant cupboard and invited Djuna to select whatever she fancied. One item that she selected on that occasion was the famous cape—it was a substantial high-fashion lined cape—that she was to wear fairly regularly for fifteen years.

The Greenwich Village awkwardness was compounded when Peggy called on her unannounced one hot summer day and found her at her typewriter dressed only in the mended lingerie. The most singular thing about the way Barnes dressed in those years was her earrings. Pendulous earrings that sometimes approached the dimensions of tassels from a small bell-pull. But Courtenay Lemon didn't like earrings at all, and they quarrelled over them. Years later, according to Edmund Wilson, she gave that as a reason she had to leave Lemon.

vii

Courtenay Lemon was in his thirties when Djuna knew him; very thin hair, average build, with just a slight tendency to obesity. Berenice Abbott remembers him as being benign and pleasant, a "nice guy."

He drank a lot, mainly gin. He earned his living as a staff member on a magazine called *The New York American* and later worked in the copy room of *The New York Times*, where he also drank, from a paper cup. He was a Socialist and wrote pamphlets and articles on subjects such as "Free Speech in the U.S." and "The Class Struggle in Municipal Politics." Those that I have read are boring and cliché-ridden. His real interest was in writing a philosophy of criticism. He had been working on it for seven years when Barnes knew him, and she came to the correct conclusion that he was never going to complete it. Lemon pushed a great deal of Henri Bergson at the young Djuna, but without, she thought later, any real effect.

Lemon had in common with Barnes a quiet but mordant wit. The drama critic Harold Clurman, who worked with him some years later, recalled that he was quietly sarcastic and contemptuous in his attitude towards most people. As his first name indicates, he was descended from an old established American family. Barnes told Wilson that Lemon's fine mind and the breadth of his knowledge literally stunned and appalled her so that for some time she didn't know whether she was coming or going —*Oh, you couldn't pry me away from him,* she told Wilson, and then she was gone. Jimmy Light's wife, Susan, remembers that there was a period when Djuna snubbed Courtenay at 86 Greenwich Avenue.

If we leap ahead by a decade and judge by the reaction of Barnes to Thelma Wood's infidelity to her, we may guess that Lemon was unfaithful to her, perhaps even only once, because the whole relationship was cut off so quickly. Or it could have been the fierce temper of which Maurice Sterne accused him. There was, at any rate, the possibility of a reconciliation at first, because she wrote to him on July 28, 1919, telling him that she had not yet made up her mind when she would come back and asking whether he had read her poems. That is also the way it happened with Thelma. Djuna would stay in touch for a while (considerably longer in the case of Thelma Wood than Lemon), then she would make a lurch towards return, but there would be no permanent return. There is the following undated letter from Lemon to Barnes:

> Dear Djuna,
>   Forgive me—I can't help it. Please do not blame yourself—it is all simply an unfortunate accident, for which fate is more to blame than you or I. After all, what's the difference—I simply don't exist any more—and there's an end to it. Try to regard it simply as if I had been run over by a trolley-car. I would like to write more but I can't. Forgive me and forget—or remember only the happinesses you gave me before I returned to the nothingness where we must all go soon anyway. I no longer blame you for anything—you did not and could not know—and I wrecked everything by not making sufficient allowances. I love and bless you and trust to your strength of intellect to pull you through to the interesting and fruitful life that this false start should not be allowed to blight.

He did attempt to see her again, but was reminded of his promise not to trouble her anymore. The relationship, she told him, was torture for her. There is no record of what happened to their pet parrot, which had once nearly bitten off Lemon's nose.

Eighty-six Greenwich Avenue, where they lived together, was the plumb centre of intellectual and artistic life in the Village in those years. James and Susan Light had taken a seventeen-room apartment in an old triangular tenement, and they let the surplus rooms to friends and friends of friends who came along. Everyone was there, if not as an actual roomer then as a frequent visitor. When the building was ripped down, it was replaced by a movie theatre with a plaque commemorating the residence of Georges Clemenceau, who had lived there after the events of 1871, which is why it has passed into history as "Clemenceau Cottage," though it was never called that then.

James Light was working for George Cram Cook's Provincetown Players. He acted and directed and also painted and wrote for them. Sue Light was an editor on the *All-Story Weekly,* and it is there that eighteen of Barnes' earliest, less substantial short stories appeared between 1914 and 1919. Their protégée, Berenice, lived with them, too, very much the kid of the large grouping and totally devoted to

58

the Lights. She told me that, if they had asked her to hide the corpse, she would have done it without hesitation. Ida Rauh, the actress, lived there, and so, at various times, did Matthew Josephson, Kenneth Burke and Malcolm Cowley, and a promising actor and painter named Charles Ellis. The suffragist Dorothy Day lived downstairs. Floyd Dell, the editor of *The Masses,* and Eugene O'Neill both spent considerable amounts of time at Clemenceau Cottage.

Djuna and Courtenay's triangular room was at the end of a long corridor and thus somewhat apart from the other rooms at the broad end of the triangular building. People mixed when they wanted to, but no one intruded on anyone else. They were rarely seen to use the kitchen. Malcolm Cowley remembers that Djuna and Courtenay moved back down the hallway from the apex of the triangle to a somewhat larger room shortly before they separated and moved away. They were, he recalls, really the only quiet people in the rather large retinue.

Josephson felt that Clemenceau Cottage contained the most personable of the Village's New Women. Conversations there could be long and heated, but there was always an effort to spice them with wit. Sophistication was the standard to be raised against everything bourgeois. Barnes was fairly unusual for the way in which she expressed her sophistication in terms of striking fashion on limited means. Most of the other young women disdained cosmetics and tended to wear either masculine clothes or flowing robes.

The Clemenceau crowd would go upstairs to Christine's two little rooms with campstools. It was an inexpensive little restaurant close to Macdougal Street and was preferred over the Greenwich Village Inn (Polly's) on West Fourth Street which was the rowdiest and most popular of the bohemian places in the Village and a good foretaste of what was to come in Paris. Christine was a plump and demure young woman with, Barnes thought, lovely golden hair that could always be counted on to have lost all its hairpins by midnight. Christine's phrase was —*Life teems with quiet fun.* Polly Holladay was also a quiet young woman. Her offsider was a volatile anarchist named Hippolyte Havel, and his phrase was —*Hélas, bébé!* Barnes wrote one of her newspaper articles about Polly's. It was a place where the new ethic reigned strongly, and the women saw to it that they were allowed to pay their own way, which usually meant a full meal for thirty-five cents.

There were other centres as well. In addition to Mabel Dodge's salon and Stieglitz's gallery, there was the salon of Gertrude Vanderbilt Whitney, the sculptor, and there were the more radical political salons of Max Eastman and Mary Heaton Vorse's I.W.W. group on

West Tenth Street. In the Village studio of the then unknown Man Ray, Djuna first met Mina Loy and Marcel Duchamp. Albert Boni's bookstore on Eighth Street was an important place, because you could buy the work of the Imagists there and the installments of *Ulysses* in *The Little Review,* which were being avidly followed in the Village.

Barnes was seriously ill during the Spanish flu epidemic of 1919 and was taken care of by Lemon in the months immediately before the separation. Cowley remembers that they were still at Clemenceau in January 1919. There is a letter from Barnes to *The Little Review* in March 1919, written from 220 West Fourteenth Street.

Lemon did not join the general exodus to Europe that began in 1920–21. In 1919 the chief script reader for the newly formed Theatre Guild died. Barnes and Lemon knew many of the Guild members. (She wrote an article in 1916 about the founding of the group.) Lemon was offered the job of script reader and stayed in the position for a decade.

Lemon finally resigned with an angry letter to the Theatre Guild Board in which he protested against the Guild's growing commercialization —in line with the usual American idea of size being more important than quality. After this letter, Lemon's name disappeared from the following two programs, reappeared on the third, and then was gone. It is reasonable to suppose that he was fired, because his chief opponent was the head of the Theatre Guild, Lawrence Langner. Lemon remarried. For a time he had links with A. R. Orage's journal *The New Age.* He died of a heart attack at age fifty in April 1933.

After their separation, Barnes entered into a series of swift affairs. A few years later, in Paris, Barnes was discussing her dalliances with her friend Mina Loy, and Loy's attractive daughter Joella listened quietly off to the side while Djuna spoke scornfully of how she had had nineteen male lovers, most of them Americans, and then had finally given up and taken a female lover. There are many candidates for the list, but only a few who belong indisputably on it. One is Laurence Vail, and the authority for that is Peggy Guggenheim in her 1946 memoirs, where he is called "Florenz Dale." Another, according to Kenneth Rexroth (in *Conjunctions: I,* 1981–82), was Horace Liveright.

Vail had been raised in France and spoke English with rolling r's. His gold-streaked hair was very long and usually blew about in the wind because he wore no hat, which was not done in those days. Vail was one of the most dashing figures among the artistic men of the

Village. He was high-spirited and promiscuous. Peggy Guggenheim records her own fascination with Vail as being founded upon his total unpredictability:

> —He was like a wild creature. He never seemed to care what people thought. I felt when I walked down the street with him that he might suddenly fly away—he had so little connection with ordinary behaviour.

With time it would become clear that there were only two types to which Djuna Barnes was attracted: the wild and the indifferent.

Laurence Vail was the golden boy of the Village; Marsden Hartley was its grand randy figure. Prior to 1920 Hartley was much more famous than he is now as a painter, poet and critic. In 1916, Barnes described Hartley in an article in *The New York Morning Telegraph*. Because of his haughty manner, his piercing eyes and his beak-like nose, Hartley would invariably be compared to an eagle. He had a serious drinking problem. (Djuna Barnes' problem was just beginning.) Some years later, when his reputation had declined considerably but his manner had not altered at all, Barnes gave life to the cliché description by calling him an eagle without his cliff.

Hartley and Barnes were lovers. The seduction began with Marsden drawn up before Djuna coolly detailing for her like a patient salesman of celestial goods the superior dimensions of his sexual equipment and endowment. It worked, though we have no way of knowing whether that night was the one about which she told a friend she had worked all summer searching for an evening to go with her new nightgown. It was the manner of the times, most closely identified with Millay and, later, Dorothy Parker, but Barnes was very much her own lady years before that. To a would-be lover who made the mistake of asking if she was free that night, Barnes replied —*I come high!*

A tall and handsome young European down from Harvard named Putzi Hanfstaengl courted her most intensely in the days before her friendship with Lemon. A subsequent lover told me that Putzi once suffered an extremely painful burst blood vessel in his penis while dancing with Djuna. Decades later, in 1952, he sent her "greetings from your old seducer." She had had occasional word over the years about Putzi's role as Hitler's jester, which she detested. The romance with Putzi was serious, for one of the deleted portions of *Nightwood* deals with the heroine's first love, who is a German whose head has —the curse of madness in it. Their romance begins

Marsden Hartley

with a walk across the Brooklyn Bridge and ends three years later when the fiancé (he is not named) comes to her in a top hat to tell her that he can't marry her now because she isn't a German. She considers suicide, is dissuaded by an intuitive neighbour, and then rushes to offer herself to him. He, however, offends her with the calculated vulgarity of his response, when he suggests that she is trying to trap him into marriage by having a child. They end by quarreling bitterly and even physically. This affair with Hanfstaengl took place in 1914, and then, as the manuscript says, there were others. She described one of her lovers as looking like a disappointed horse; another, as scarcely larger than Tom Thumb.

Floyd Dell was a good friend and one of the earliest well-known critics of her work. In addition to his Marxism, Dell advocated a sort of bohemian vulgar Freudianism which consisted of concurrent psychoanalysis and total sexual freedom for all. Edmund Wilson, though at this time in the midst of a major affair with Edna Millay, was also friendly with Miss Barnes, who spoke to me with some warmth about him sixty years later. When Barnes returned from her first trip to Europe in 1922, she wrote to Wilson calling him a "nasty boy" for not responding quickly enough to a literary proposal she had sent to him a few days earlier. Wilson was one of the most driven and forceful young men in the Village. In 1918, Jane Heap of *The Little Review* had already identified him as foremost among those engaged in —*trying to steal up and sneak Matthew Arnold's old cloak off Eliot.* Wilson himself in *The Twenties* cites an opinion about him by Barnes which got back to him. McAlmon and Barnes were discussing Wilson. McAlmon said that Wilson worked harder than either of them, to which Djuna replied —*Oh no. He lives like a pet pony!*

Wilson proposed to Barnes. He took her to dinner at a Montmartre restaurant in the summer of 1921 and asked her to live with him, proposing that they go to Italy together. The romance failed because that evening Wilson was full of bulldogish enthusiasm for the work of Edith Wharton, and Barnes could not abide Wharton's writing.

Her first affair after the separation from Lemon was with Jimmy Light, who had separated from Susan shortly before. Malcolm Cowley remembers meeting Djuna and Jimmy at an Italian speakeasy. He sat down with them, and he and Djuna got into an argument on the relative merits of male and female sexual parts. Cowley held that men were superior because they could urinate standing up and write their initials in the snow, to which Djuna replied, —*I can make a period.* The conversation continued, and Cowley thinks he may have been objectionable and speaking bad French to boot. Miss Barnes made a cutting remark, to which Cowley, because he had heard that she was supposed to be forthright in her language, replied, —*Fuck you, Djuna.* She rose grandly and swept out of the restaurant, carrying Jimmy Light with her.

The greatest number of the men friends of Djuna Barnes were homosexuals or bisexuals. Silver Carl Van Vechten, who married the actress Fania Marinoff, was one of the closest of them. He was a man of great enthusiasms (one was for Firbank, whose work he introduced to America) and affectations. He wore rings and bracelets and a stony face, all of which quite compensated for his large buck teeth and the fact that he was from Iowa. He is recorded as once having complimented a young woman by telling her that she looked like a child of Sarah Bernhardt by a yellow panther. He called himself Carlo. It is extremely likely that Barnes had an affair with Van Vechten, and equally, like all the circumstances in our lives which do not entail a certain level of intensity—and that, of course, means many marriages as well as casual affairs—it is a matter of no importance at all.

Barnes and Van Vechten remained friendly for a decade, by which time he had moved from elegant aesthete and novelist to *New York Times* music correspondent and then went on to become a photographer whose archive provides one of the most complete records of artists of his time. He did Djuna in 1930, and she complained that she came out something like a freshly dug up mummy. In memoirs published in a Yale University journal, Van Vechten claimed that he had been Djuna Barnes' boss in her first newspaper job, but since she was always a free-lance, what he probably did was provide entrée for her.

Another of her soft friends, and one with whom she did not fight, for the letters which she wrote to him are without exception warm, was Allan Ross MacDougall. He, like Peggy Guggenheim, was one of the few friends who chanced to be in the vicinity of Barnes' life not only in the Village and in Paris, but also in England. Dougie was a minor poet, but his real place in literary history is as a friend of poets. Everyone seemed to like him, though once he was involved in a public fistfight with Tristan Tzara in Paris—neither of them was even slightly hurt. After her death he was chosen as the editor of the Millay letters. In Paris the only thing he wrote was *A Gourmet's Almanac* (1930), a literary cookbook with recipes. Barnes is thanked in the Introduction for some old chapbooks with drawings which she furnished for the book. She also contributed a drawing of her own. When he began to work for a fashion magazine, Barnes teased him: —*Ass, hair, and teeth out and writing for "Beauty."* Another of her

64

good bisexual friends was Harrison Dowd, who had also been very close to Millay. Barnes and Dowd remained friendly until his death. We know, too, that Barnes received some support from Lawrence Langner, who occasionally played at being a patron.

viii

There comes now, well, friend would surely be too hasty a word, and acquaintance would be quite inadequate, so let us say an important familiar of Djuna Barnes for several years beginning in about 1914. His original name was not Guido Bruno. He was born in 1884; died in 1942. He was very fond of talking about his origins, but they were rarely the same ones. To most he announced himself as an Italian, but to some he explained that he was really a Serbian, while to those he considered important enough he would confide the "real truth," that he was an exiled officer of the Hapsburg army. Only to the small circle of those who really were both important and close to him did he confide that he was an actual Bohemian, that is, a Czech. In Hugh Kingsmill's 1949 biography *Frank Harris* there is direct testimony that Guido Bruno spoke American with a German accent. The Bruno publications give evidence of a man who knew several European languages. He printed translations and renditions not only from German and Russian, but also from Montenegran folktales, and much of it was material not otherwise available in English. There were also little foreign turns of phrase in his English.

In an autobiographical essay, *The Confessions of a Self-Made American* (*Bruno's Weekly*, April 29, 1916), Bruno seems to be saying that he was born and educated in Germany, but he is very evasive about when or where. As he is taking out his American citizenship—before the clerk in a western city (again, there is no when or where)—Bruno recounts how his youth is reviewed in a flash in his mind:

> —I saw myself as a young boy singing patriotic songs. I saw myself as a youth in uniform with unsheathed sword swearing an oath of allegiance to my king. How terrible that oath was! "During day and night", the oath reads, "in water and on land, in peace and war, will I follow his leadership, will I be loyal to him. Even against my father and my brothers will I be loyal to him."
> And then I thought how I had been educated at his expense, being a

65

beneficiary of a stipendium, how I had to thank him indirectly for my college and for my university education. And I thought of my father and of his father and of all my ancestors, and I thought of my brothers who wore his coat and spent their lives in his service, and all this I thought in less than a minute, and I told the Clerk that I would come back on another day to sign my declaration of intention.

There is something troubling in all of this with its intimation of a tufted undergraduate, albeit on straitened means, tied by generations to the service of some baron or kaiser. Mind you, nothing is actually said of nobility, but it is there all the same with the uniform and the unsheathed sword. One hears behind it, or so it seems to me, the soft murmur of that peculiar German-Jewish self-hatred that is the primary motivation in Felix Volkbein, the minor character with whom *Nightwood* begins. For the father of Felix Volkbein is named Guido.

He was a towering man, six foot three, and quite broad as well—a regular wall of a man. In some accounts he is given blond hair; in others, dark. He produced an offputting impression because his very large face and hands were fat and always oily, and he did not put his stature to use, instead always standing slightly bowed and never looking anyone in the eyes. His costume has been described as rather hectic. He tended to wear a brown derby, checked suits and spats. Djuna Barnes described the entrance of Bruno into Greenwich Village in an article that she wrote in 1919:

> —This man seemed to have been born well-shaved. The first time I saw him, he stood in the centre of a large, high and dark room. In the middle of this room stood a teak-wood table, and on this table reposed an immense beruffled cake.
>
> The manicured and hair-dressed object from the confectioner's was a cup-cake. The presence was Guido Bruno.
>
> He said: —*Down here, I see, you have your back yards in the front. And your front yards, I perceive, you keep in flower pots.* He added: —*When the wind blows, the atmosphere is distracted with the plumage of swallows—in other words, your chimneys have learned how to grow old charmingly. This place has immense possibilities.*
>
> Thus one day Guido Bruno was among us. He did not nudge his way in, he did not rise in our midst, rather, one should say, he fell.

He was a pretender. In fact, Albert Parry in *Garrets and Pretenders* (one of the most important sources for literary and artistic life in the early Village) gives Bruno the laurel as the supreme pretender. He was an operator, there is not the slightest doubt, and in time he generated intense hatred and disgust for the way in which he hastened the conversion of Greenwich Village into a garish amusement park for the day-tripping bourgeoisie. Among the most bitter attacks on him are those in an excellent little magazine of the period, *The Quill.* He rented a large garret at 58 Washington Square, which, before Potter's Field became Washington Square in 1823, was the working premises and home of Daniel Megie, who was the gravedigger and coffin-maker for the city's poor. Bruno, who had a nice streak of natural curiosity and pedantry, had looked up the title records. He came to Greenwich Village in 1906 and worked in a mortuary while he learned English. He was the son of a rabbi. His name—really—was Curt Kisch.

The garret just happened to be directly opposite the Fifth Avenue bus terminal, so the people who came downtown in response to the leaflets and little magazines, which he had energetically distributed uptown, could see the garish signs pointing the direction to the garret on the other side of the ice-cream parlour as they stepped off the bus. Bruno's Village magazines had shifting titles, but they always retained the single anchorword "Bruno": *Bruno's Bohemia; Bruno's Review of Life, Love, and Literature; Bruno's Monthly; Bruno's Weekly; Bruno's Scrapbook; Bruno's Review of Two Worlds; Greenwich Village Edited by Guido Bruno in His Garret on Washington Square;* simply *Bruno's;* and the best-known series of them all, *Bruno's Chap Books.* This last title reflects the English and European inclinations of Guido Bruno, for it was taken from the title of a well-known English journal of Beardsleyesque inclinations, *The Chap Book.* When he was younger he had worn his hair long after the manner of Wilde. In his Greenwich Village period he would frequently be seen in a green felt hat preparing his chapbooks for the printer at a café table drinking Vichy and milk. When he published *Greenwich Village,* the first of his series, he lived entirely on leftover French pastries from a sympathetic baker on Fourth Street. Bruno claimed that *Bruno's Chap Books* at their height had a circulation of 32,000.

The first book by Djuna Barnes, really more a booklet with eight poems and five drawings, *The Book of Repulsive Women,* appeared as Number 20, Special Series, of the *Chap Books* in November 1915. It sold for fifteen cents at first, but its price was very quickly raised to fifty cents when it became clear that the chapbook was enjoying notoriety.

There was nothing in the poems or drawings that tempted the censor who was clearly nodding, for there is no American book published in the first twenty years of the century that would have been more susceptible to censorship. Censorship was to come next year for another book when Bruno was briefly arrested for his publication

Cover illustration, *Bruno's Chap Books*, 1915

of Alfred Kreymborg's tale of a streetwalker. It produced a great flurry of publicity that established Kreymborg's name and brought fresh waves of tourists to pay ten to twenty-five cents in order to enter the garret and observe a considerably large number of bohemians painting and posing for each other. At the hearing, Guido Bruno triumphantly waved a letter of support from George Bernard Shaw before the judge.

The atmosphere of Barnes' eight "rhythms" is quite in keeping with the book's title. We must remember that while this was a period in which the forces of European Decadence were still being very much felt, no less in the United States than in Scandinavia, Italy, Poland and Russia, there was certainly in all the English-speaking countries as late as 1915 an extraordinary reticence on sexual themes in literature. Oscar Wilde did not write his homosexuality; he merely practised it. *The Book of Repulsive Women,* a full decade before Radclyffe Hall's *Well of Loneliness,* was the first modern literary work in English to bring the theme of woman's "bitter secret" (it is never named) to the misty fore:

> Someday beneath some hard
> Capricious star,
> Spreading its light a little
> Over far,
> We'll know you for the woman
> That you are,
>
> See you sagging down with bulging
> Hair to sip,
> The dappled damp from some vague
> Under lip,
> Your soft saliva, loosed
> With orgy, drip.

One must assume that, in spite of the collection's title and the tell-tale word orgy, the Sumner committee was either incapable of recognizing or of articulating what that "vague under lip" from which the repulsive woman sags down to sip was. Barnes had boldly and deftly taken advantage of a public inability to comprehend what such images might portray. Thus there was an astonishingly easy if meaningless victory over censorship. Like Queen Victoria when her advice was sought on the legal position of lesbians, the American censors evidently couldn't even imagine the offense. Ironically, a court action was underway during these months over Theodore Dreiser's decorous novel *The Genius.*

69

The poems are written in rhymed, matched accentual lines of the sort that would in time come to be labelled Eliotic. They show a doomed woman or women (this sort of double exposure is very characteristic of Barnes) proceeding at an urban but stately pace through poverty and enervation to death. It has been the tendency in discussions of the Barnes oeuvre to relegate *The Book of Repulsive Women* to the bin of "early work," which these poems certainly are, and yet some of the best stanzas have the same anemic power of early Eliot and phrases that stick in the mind:

> Those living dead up in their rooms
> Must note how partial are the tombs,
> That take men back into their wombs
> While theirs must fast.
> And those who have their blooms in jars
> No longer stare into the stars,
> Instead, they watch the dinky cars—
> And live aghast.

The series ends with two short suicide poems, simple pictorial descriptions of women's bodies. The central figure of the cycle has — great ghastly loops of gold/snared in your ears. We can never be sure about whom the poet is speaking and so must settle for a generalized image of a damned everywoman. In an announcement before the poems appeared, Guido Bruno had called them —a chant which could be sung by those who are in the daily procession through the streets and highways of our metropolis. Various of the poems have street names for titles. *The Book of Repulsive Women* remained an underground work. It was to be more than half a century before it was even mentioned in print.

Guido Bruno was without doubt one of the most fervent activists in the struggle against censorship in pre-Prohibition America. He introduced the work of Beardsley to America (Barnes did some drawings à la Beardsley which were sold in Bruno's garret), published letters and odd works of Wilde, and materials by and on Richard Wagner, Lord Alfred Douglas and John Addington Symonds. He could boast not only the first substantial publication of Djuna Barnes on a subject no other publisher would have touched, but also the first publication of Hart Crane. He first staged *The State Forbids*, an extremely strong pro-birth-control play. Slightly later Bruno met Frank Harris and eventually became his literary secretary and most dedicated disciple. Of course, Bruno's garret was a farce and a travesty, but one must not forget that these were hard times for many young people—in the recently published memoirs of Malcolm Cowley there

Drawing from *The Book of Repulsive Women*, 1915

is an account of how he once fainted from hunger while walking the streets of New York. Bruno gave food and a place to sleep to his pseudo-artists on display, even if he did rather spoil that by advertising his garret with the subtitle *First Aid for Struggling Artists*.

Alfred Kreymborg recalls how he met Bruno at Polly's, first recited poetry at the garret in a weak voice and was given the entire proceeds of the evening (twenty-five people at ten cents a head) in a grand gesture, and yet, when *Edna* had been exonerated in court, Bruno immediately printed a second edition at a much heightened price and paid no royalties at all to Krimmie. A cunning rogue with literary pretensions then, but one must also take into account the fact that this strange man who seemed a potential successor in literature to P. T. Barnum still managed to remain a poor and bona fide confidence man of letters in spite of all the underhand dealings with which he was taxed and which ought to have made him a wealthy man.

His most important benefactor was Charles Edison, the son of Thomas Alva Edison. Later, after the death of his father, Edison would become Governor of New Jersey, but in those years he waited and played the Village bohemian. Bruno printed Edison's poem *The Mexican Boarder* as a separate booklet, and they collaborated in the running and promotion of The Little Thimble Theatre at 10 Fifth Avenue opposite The Brevoort Hotel. It specialized in phonograph shows and provided a showcase for musicians. For a time Bruno ran a little theatre company, The Bruno Players, there. Edison gave Bruno a lot of money, and he used it to print more chapbooks which he pressed on people to purchase as they left The Little Thimble Theatre to which there was no admission fee. Since Bruno's association with Edison began early in 1915, it means the *Book of Repulsive Women* was one of the books published with these monies. Edison in later years would maintain that Bruno was a most talented though unscrupulous man, and that in any case he had never given him much money.

The most unpleasant, persistent rumour about Guido Bruno was that he kept a covey of graphomaniac women with whom he slept and from whom he took money ostensibly to publish their verse. When the books did not appear, Bruno could usually frighten away the occasional lawyer with his calm assertion: —*I, Bruno, sleep with all girls.* (It was his custom to refer to himself as *I, Bruno.*) No woman was game to front up to such calm accusations about herself in a courtroom, but one came very close, and it is from her letters that the rumours are given some substance. Her name was Mary Fleming, an Irish widow or abandoned wife and poetaster with a child whom she was putting through Rutgers. She said she was in her later thirties, and prematurely grey. She lived in New Brunswick, New Jersey, where she had once worked as a legal stenographer but had come to enjoy some profits from land purchases. She had published a few poems in *The New York Evening Mail,* and Bruno, who had evidently heard that she was wealthy (after making a profit of $20,000 in a real estate deal, she bought herself some furs and jewels), wrote to her praising the poems and suggesting that he go to New Jersey to visit her. When he finally did go, but only after putting her off several times, he suggested that she sell her house and move to New York, where, he said, he would obtain a $75 per week job for her with the Munsey Syndicate. Mary Fleming telephoned the Munsey Syndicate (they published a magazine to which Djuna Barnes contributed some of her early work) and learned that the influential woman whom Bruno had named did not in fact work for them. In spite of this warning note, however, Mary Fleming did not draw away from Bruno. When her lawyer finally came to Bruno, he patiently explained that Mary had gone into partnership with him—it was a matter of some $1,500—fallen in love with him, and given him a good screwing. It was a regular pattern, Bruno said, for women to give him large amounts of money to publish their verses and then to copulate with him in his garret, and the result of this was that honour forbade his going into court and explaining this aspect of his publishing business. Both the lawyer and her priest advised her strongly against pressing the matter any further, but she would not give it up.

She thought that he was about fifty-five, although he described himself to her as being thirty-five. He also said he was a single man who lived a hermit-like life in a little 6 × 10 room in the Lafayette Hotel for ten dollars a week, and his personal expenses, he claimed, were only an additional seven dollars a week. He asked Mary Fleming to write some stories for his magazines, and he gave her a copy of Balzac's *Lily of the Valley,* a tale of the infatuation of a matronly lady for a youth, to study with the suggestive passages marked. She called him a satyr and a lizard and wrote to a journalist whom she knew:

—I have met all sorts of men, in many walks of life, but never one so low and depraved as this wretch. He's not really human, he's a sinister shape of hell, without shame or pity or feeling for anything except money. I noticed a queer thing about his eyes, but did not note its significance until too late to be of use. A yellow light came into them when money was the subject of conversation—a queer wildfire sort of light.

She claimed that she had been swept away by the munificence of his condescension.

Now she went about ferreting out information about Bruno. A Mr. Gilman of Brentano's told her, she said, that Bruno was a European-trained crook. She was told that he had tried to foist a number of fake Beardsleys on art dealers in New York, claiming that he had discovered them in Paris. She consulted Nugent Brothers, one of the printers he used, and discovered that Bruno had the entire firm living in hope of a takeover bid by what Bruno purported to be a syndicate of eight millionaires. She checked on their names and found out they were all in prison.

Mary Fleming found out that Bruno was in fact married, and that he had a daughter named Eleanor. In the Kingsmill biography of Harris someone remarks of Bruno: —Let it be said to his credit that whatever hole he was in or however short of money his family knew nothing of it and thought him a journalist. Fleming had an inaccurate theory that Bruno's wife was a woman named Antoinette Bureau, who had been arrested after hiring herself out as a Belgian maid to wealthy families who would then have artworks stolen from them shortly after she left their employ. Fleming claimed that Bruno had once supplied a Turner and a Whistler to the Anderson Gallery in New York, and that when she had questioned him about where he had obtained such valuable paintings, he had replied —Oh, at auction.

In Frank Harris Bruno had found a more perfect version of himself. Bruno called himself an anarchist after the model of Hippolyte Havel, who in his own turn had been secretary to Emma Goldman. That meant that the good one derives in life belongs in the first place to oneself, though it is to be shared with the world as well, and that to be an anarchist means to be an individual, "to walk your own way." Harris' personality combined elements of both aristocratic pretension and anarchism, for which reason he was commonly called the Tory Anarchist. Guido Bruno had all his life been striving to achieve fame and success according to just this awkward formula. Harris, when he arrived in New York as the grand English editor and man of letters to take over Pearson's Magazine, was no less a social pretender and calculating parasite than Bruno, but he could write— Bruno had the self-awareness to acknowledge that he himself could not—and he possessed the style to face the world with dignity, innocence, idealism and world-weary sadness, in whatever mixture was required by the given situation. That Bruno literally worshipped Harris can be seen clearly in the reminiscences *My Four Years with*

Frank Harris, which he published in *Bruno's Review of Two Worlds.*
In these memoirs he regularly makes comments such as:

> —In such moments a great man reveals himself and impresses us indelibly with his genius. We see the simplicity of a great mind, like the beauty of a sleeping child.

When Bruno was his secretary, the pink-cheeked Harris would lie in bed wearing a neck scarf and a tie with his pyjamas and genially abuse him as he conducted his business. Bruno used to lament his inability to keep Harris sufficiently in the background. They would conduct fortnightly campaigns of begging and cajoling letters designed to separate idealists and their money. Generally these campaigns were very effective, but it would sometimes happen that a prospective benefactor would call unannounced and discover Harris, attended by Bruno and a Japanese butler, sweeping around in striped trousers and waistcoat.

In the end Harris ruined *Pearson's,* which had had a large circulation when he came to it, though he replied with dignity to a reader who wrote in to abuse Harris for what he had made of the magazine
—Pascal says somewhere that all great work is written on a man's knees. What I have written on my knees, Mr. Macaulay calls sewergas. Frank Harris, it is clear, fits the pattern of the men friends of Djuna Barnes. She wrote an article about him in *The New York Morning Telegraph Sunday Magazine* in 1917 with her usual rolling headline:

> On Men of Genius—"I find Success More Easily Won Here in America than in England," Says Frank Harris, Author and Editor of *Pearson's Magazine* and the Man Who Made the Fortnightly Review Famous on Two Continents; "America is Radical at Heart, and If You Ever Get a Moses Americans will Follow Him into the Promised Land, Whereas in Europe Moses' Only Chance of Leadership Is to Become a Lackey of the Classes."

It was Barnes who first led Guido Bruno to Harris:

> —Djuna Barnes, a promising young artist, who, however, hasn't decided yet whether to become a great artist or a great writer, hailed me in a restaurant where I had dined.
> —*I have sold a picture!* she cried.
> —No . . . *Really?* I retorted incredulously. *Which one?*
> *My black, gold and ivory Buddha,* was her answer.
> I remembered it. A very weird picture. Ultra Djuna, which means more

75

unusual than all the Moderns of the extreme left wing united in a crazy quilt. All I had been able to discern in this picture was an enormous belly, and claws of gold on ivory white hands, hanging in the black space like the photography of a successful seance where hands had materialized hanging ghostly in mid-air.

—I didn't get much, however, she continued. *Only twenty-five dollars.*

—Only twenty-five dollars! I repeated in astonishment. *Who on earth paid you that price for that picture?*

—Frank Harris, she answered. *Do you know who he is? He is writing a life of Wilde. An Englishman, very aristocratic and all that. . . . He is very interesting. A great talker. Wrote lots of books. He must be very rich. He claims to be sixty-three, but he looks like thirty-five. Why don't you call on him?*

When Harris, finally caught up and out in debts and entanglements from which his winning personality could no longer rescue him, quit America for Europe, people were surprised that his tall but pudgy Sancho Panza did not go with him and also astounded at how Bruno all the same vanished. It may have been that his own affairs had also become dangerously unmanageable. Mary Fleming for one had sworn that she would never give up in her campaign against Bruno. There was a rumour, unsubstantiated, that he slipped off to Buffalo, New York, to run a secondhand bookstore, but in fact he went to Wisconsin where he worked for the Progressive Party and Senator Robert La Follette.

He was a terrible pretender, and yet, if we look calmly at the array of his publications and put all the anecdotage to the back of our minds . . . they are not too bad. They stand as an important monument to the "serious period" (usually reckoned to be 1912–18) of Greenwich Village.

Bruno was too calculating in his wildness and too transparently mercenary. He was swarthy and not at all handsome. All of these things would have been critical in the estimation of the young Djuna Barnes. She was a fiercely professional writer, and Bruno, for his part, would never allow the otherwise freely used name of Bruno to be used on those vanity volumes, such as Mary Fleming's, that he published. As a matter of fact, there was only one other woman artist besides Barnes whose work appeared in the proper series of Bruno's publications. She was the artist Clara Tice, who specialized in sketches of breastless nude females and who once had a show of over two hundred caricatures of Village personalities in Bruno's garret. Her work was singled out for attack by the Society for the Prevention

76

of Vice. In 1915 Bruno held a mock trial in one of his Monday night "Cabarets Bruno" in which Clara Tice was tried for murdering art.

There were certain difficulties in store for anyone who was associated with Bruno. His reputation was so bad that bookstores would not stock his publications and newspapers would not usually review them. Kreymborg describes in his memoirs how conscious he was that he was courting literary antagonism by having his works published by the bohemian sensation-monger. And even within the pages of his publications his own authors were mocked by him. Mary Fleming records that Bruno selected the worst of her poems for the book and then, when he showed it to her, taunted her and said that the reviewers would laugh at it. Clara Tice was saluted in verse: O Clara Tice,/ You rhyme with mice. And Djuna Barnes was the subject of a little squib in *Bruno's Weekly* (April 22, 1916) which begins with praise and ends nastily:

> —Djuna Barnes, who designed the front cover of *Bruno's Weekly* this week, retired to a sedate and quite private life. After a rather exciting career of a few years of newspaper work (drawing and writing) she decided to do some real work unhampered by editorial (sic!) influences. A series of war pictures and among these her uncanny gripping "*The Bullet*," are not only the work of a promising artist, but one of one who started really to fulfill promises.
>
> As well as in drawing and painting she has a style of her own in her literary adventures. Her poems and her short stories cannot possibly be called otherwise but adventures. She feels the rhythm of her inspiration and she struggles along as good as she can to make us feel it too. Her inspiration is flirting constantly with her creative desires. But Djuna Barnes ia a bad match-maker. The little things in life make for tragedies. Spelling, punctuation, syntax, lack of concentration, are such little things. They are every-day tragedies in Djuna's life.

Bruno is referring to the fact that, because Barnes never attended a school, her spelling and syntax have always been somewhat chaotic in spite of a vast vocabulary and deep verbal and imaginative resonance. Bruno's own syntax in this little note is so much worse than his usual standard that we must assume either that he is mocking her first drafts in the passage or that he was drunk when he wrote it. In either case, it is clear that there was some grudge behind it.

Bruno disappeared and Djuna Barnes went to Paris, but elements of the strange man remained in her mind, and a transposed shadow of the man slipped into *Nightwood*, which opens with an account of Guido Volkbein, a Jew of Italian descent who invents an Austrian ancestry for himself complete with progenitors who had never existed and a coat of arms to which he has no right. Volkbein had managed, by means of denying his Jewishness as well as by money changing and trading in old masters and first editions, to obtain a plausibly noble house in the centre of Vienna. He dies of fever six months before his sole son, who is named Felix, is born. It is this Felix who seems modelled in certain respects after Guido Bruno. (Another model named Deutschbine was mentioned by Peggy Guggenheim in her memoirs, but he contributed circumstance rather than character to the Barnes portrayal.) Both Volkbein and his son, Felix, share with Guido Bruno one particular characteristic, a natural propensity towards genuflection, bowing down before a person of any plausible importance or nobility. The physical description of Felix is precisely that of Guido Bruno: he is both tall and heavy, and he has a long, stout, oval face with a melancholy expression. He dresses somewhat oddly so that he gives the impression that he is in part dressed for the day, in part for evening. He wears spats, knows seven languages (which is the number Charles Edison attributed to Bruno), is an expert in folklore, and he possesses a very strong natural pedantry which causes him to pause before bridges, graveyards, churches and castles.

The sketch of Felix Volkbein is done with sharp and bold line. It provides a strong opening for the novel, but it is unconnected with the further development of the story. Baron Felix Volkbein does introduce the theme of bowing down, but in quite a different form than that in which it figures for the other, major characters. Years later Berenice Abbott asked Barnes why she had chosen to open the novel with this strongly etched portrait of someone who turns out to be so unimportant in the novel. She answered quite directly that it was done simply to confuse and draw some attention away from the lesbian love between Nora and Robin that looms so large in *Nightwood*.

In *Nightwood*, Volkbein is married to a woman named Hedvig (she dies giving birth to Guido) who subliminally doubts Felix's title, though on the surface she accepts the fact that she is a baroness without question. When Felix marries Robin Vote in the novel, he says to her —*You are a Baronin now.* The reference is to another of Djuna Barnes' most unusual acquaintances, first in Greenwich Village and then in Paris, the Baronin Elsa von Freytag-Loringhoven.

Like Guido Bruno, the Baronin was of uncertain antecedents. Janet Flanner called her a great Danish lady. The more commonly accepted version had it that she was German, the wife of a wealthy

78

German businessman who had lived in luxury at the uptown Ritz Hotel until the war, when he returned to Germany and soon committed suicide, while she moved to Greenwich Village. A 1921 book by Charles Brooks, *Hints to Pilgrims,* contains a chapter which is a lightly disguised sketch of Hart Crane and the Baronin, who figures there as the Countess Sillivitch. She is described as being from Bulgaria or Estonia, or somewhere. The title belonged to the last of an indeterminate number of husbands, and even its form is unsure because in her early years in Greenwich Village she is recorded as having used a double particule (von Freytag-von Loringhoven). The first poem that she submitted to *The Little Review* was signed Tara Osrik, which might even have been her actual name but was not. Her real name was Ploetz. Her father was a builder in North Germany. Her mother was Polish.

The Little Review, or rather, the Misses Jane Heap and Margaret Anderson, followed a literary line which amounted to high art ascending to aesthetic anarchy. In life *The Little Review* group was inclined to lesbianism. It was managed with considerable restraint, when one considers that the freedom of the cruder bohemia around them in the Village had already gone as far as a flourishing lesbian brothel. James Joyce and his splintering prose was their pride; Baronin Elsa von Freytag-Loringhoven and her madly stuttering, trumpeting poetry was their fancy. They let it be known to the cognoscenti that she was the greatest woman artist of her time. She was at the very least the freest.

There was always an air of gay desperation about her. She was very poor. Djuna Barnes wrote well about the delicate interplay between poverty and eccentricity in the old Greenwich Village:

> —The Village exists as such, because it *is* threadbare. Put a fur coat on it, and it will be merely another block or two of Manhattan.
>
> There will always be someone to laugh at poverty, as there will always be a pinch of poverty for someone to laugh at.
>
> The fact that the Village is poor, makes the rest of the City smile: that the rest of the City smiles, makes the Village conscious—and that is all.
>
> Now when poverty *plus* ideas is made conscious, the world becomes gay.
>
> When one is conscious in a good cause, or in a bad one, the reaction is—defiance. The defiance of the artist is not expressed in the abrupt— *You choose the weapons, Sir!* a glove thrown down in the dark, a sobbing of swords as they leap from the scabbards. No indeed; the duel is one that is all thrust and no parry. This dusty, threadbare person suddenly plunges home the clever dagger of surprise, shock, what you will. . . . The Village doesn't know it any more, but in every one of its

alleys, its short blocks, its old houses, there is a spirit of *holding out against* the rest of the city, an antagonist keeping off an antagonism.

There was no closeness of manner between Djuna and the Baronin, but their disposition to think of themselves as artists fighting gaily with their backs to the wall is unmistakably the same.

It is odd. There exist no real descriptions of the Baronin, although she has a passing page in all the memoirs. Margaret Anderson did mention that the Baronin had hair the colour of a bay horse, but everyone else mentions only the times that she shaved and shellacked her head. That she wore postage stamps on her cheeks (the two-cent American stamp for ordinary letters in those years was pink, and she had filched five dollars' worth from the offices of *The Little Review,* for which she was forgiven). That she wore battered and worn metal tea immersion balls on her breasts as jewelry. That her hat collection at different times included a coal scuttle, a peach basket, a velvet tam-o'-shanter with feathers and spoons hanging from it, and once a cake, replete with lit candles. That she wore stuffed birds. That her lipstick was black, her face powder bright yellow, and, when her head was shaven, she sometimes painted her skull purple. She had a patchy old fur coat and a Mexican blanket and would regularly walk the streets of the Village from five to six with nothing else on, which occasioned a few wild forays with the police. It is said she could throw a rather good punch and run well. Yet, in spite of such regular self-exposure, there is considerable confusion on the part of memoirs even about the basic contours of her body. One source has it that she had a lean masculine figure, while another claims that she possessed a perfect torso. Apart from her paraphernalia, scarcely anyone except for those in the close circle of *The Little Review* seems to have seen her at all.

The best story about the Baronin concerns her courtship of the handsome young poet-doctor from New Jersey, William Carlos Williams. He made the mistake of asking to meet her after seeing a piece of her sculpture, which he describes as waxen chicken guts under glass in the flat of Margaret Anderson and Jane Heap. He was told that she was mad, noble, and a great admirer of his poetry. At the time she was under arrest at the Tombs for the theft of an umbrella. Williams met her upon her release from the prison and took her to breakfast on Sixth Avenue near Eighth Street. She struck him as being in her fifties—she was actually in her early forties when he met her—and he thought that she had perhaps once been a beautiful woman. She made a strong impression upon the doctor, and he made a fatal error at a subsequent meeting with her by gallantly telling her that he loved her, because, he wrote later, she reminded him somewhat of his "gypsy" grandmother.

She advised him that what he needed in order to achieve greatness was to contract syphilis from her and thereby wholly free his mind for serious art. The syphilis was inherited through her father, who had infected her mother on their wedding night. The marvellous story concerns a sortie which she made to Rutherford, New Jersey, in pursuit of Williams. He happened to be dining with Robert McAlmon that evening but was lured away from the house by a fake call to tend a sick baby. As he started to get into his car, a woman's hand grabbed his left wrist. It was the Baronin. Then, goes the story first put forward by Matthew Josephson, she threw open her fur coat, revealing her nakedness and exclaimed: —*Villiam Carlos Villiams, I vant you!* Alas, —and thus it nearly always is with these stories— Williams himself recorded that she merely said —*You must come with me,* and when he didn't comply, thwacked him on the neck with all her not inconsiderable strength.

Another person who suffered badly through kindness to the Baroness was Berenice Abbott, who offered her a room in her flat. She wanted the whole flat and called Berenice a common person and not a "gentleman" when she wouldn't give it.

Wallace Stevens was for years literally afraid to set foot below Fourteenth Street after one meeting with the Baronin for fear of encountering her again. One source has Hart Crane, who lived on the floor above *The Little Review,* fleeing at the sight of the Baronin, but the Unterecker biography records that Crane used to do detailed imitations of her, and that once, going to retrieve his typewriter from her, he decided instead to buy another one himself. A Village artist named Bill Zorach went to bed one night only to have the Baroness scrabble out naked from underneath his bed and chase him out of his own apartment.

Dr. Williams had a second encounter with her in New Jersey, but he had in the meanwhile taken some boxing lessons and so knocked her down when she attacked him. She promised from the local prison that she would never do it again. Williams continued to maintain that he was really crazy about the woman, but he gave her two hundred dollars to get out of the country. It ended by being four hundred, because the first lot was either stolen or was purported to have been stolen.

Whatever her past might have been, the Baroness lived very close to real poverty in Greenwich Village. She worked briefly in a cigarette factory, but she so infuriated her fellow workers that one of them had knocked out two of her teeth. Later, she sold newspapers and stole food. When she began to print in *The Little Review,* she was earning a scant living by posing as a life model for artists such as Glackens, Henri, Bellows and Genthe, many of whom rendered her in non-representational fashion. She did, however, manage to keep two little dogs with her in her two tenement rooms. It had once been three dogs. Later, when she went to Paris and Berlin, she had only one little dog, and it was with her when she turned on the gas in 1927.

Elsa von Freytag-Loringhoven began her friendship with Djuna Barnes awkwardly. She told her: —*I cannot read your stories, Djuna Barnes. I don't know where your characters come from. You make them fly on magic carpets—what is worse, you try to make pigs fly.* It was, of course, a very good way to start a friendship with Djuna Barnes, who at first did not like her, then gave her wild poetry grudging respect, and ended by championing her art and being her main source of support in the final two years before her death in much the same way that she had supported her grandmother Zadel in the last years of her life a decade before. She kept her photo on her mantle. Djuna Barnes chose to let the Baronin write her own obituary, which appeared with a terse prefatory note in the form of extracts from letters written to her in *transition* in February 1928. The letters are undated, but all have the character of an autothrenody:

—We must look the monster in the face that is my life. I am badgered about as if I had been a culprit, having been robbed, bearing the empty title of that poor dead, swindling miserable suicide, my last husband. Djuna, I cannot see it any more otherwise. There is no perspective. I will probably yes, yes, yes, probably have to die. When life is not, one has to die. That is simple, terribly simple! I have to die, and I beg you to keep away all bitterness for the hurt I must give you. It is not my fault, should I not otherwise help I can't and in a little time you will be almost relieved to be rid of my eternal troublewhine between life and death, as I certainly will be myself. I hope sweet, I will wonderously enjoy myself after! I deserve it, and so I will get it, think of that though. I, oh how much I should like to enjoy myself and you still on earth, but if it is denied? You would not wish me to be always a miserable wretch, such things are impossible for sensible people like you and me. I write you this as a last farewell letter, not because of melodramatic taste but I find it my duty not to leave you stealthily.

The prefatory note by Barnes hints that the actual death was not suicide but —a stupid joke that had not even the decency of maliciousness. There were rumours that she had not turned the gas on herself, but the letter seems to deny that possibility. The suicide note was, in any event, the ideal genre for her unique sensibility and language.

The two women were opposites in certain ways. Elsa would seize on an idea and worry it to death. Djuna never passed the time of day with an "idea," but she had a special pocket of respect for those like Courtenay Lemon or the Baroness whom she judged to have deep intellectual power. There were other essential ways in which they were exactly alike, however, and one passage from the letters of the Baroness might in every phrase have been uttered by Djuna Barnes herself:

> —I never lie, because it would violate the psychological picture of life's cause and events. Only mediocre sentimental authors lie. All persons who are ruthlessly lonely—by inner rendering of outer circumstances—must be mad within commonplace lifemesh for: they are single—singular—absolute. I have always been thus.

The Baroness, who counted herself an ardent American, did not play as large a part in the café life of Europe as she had on Macdougal Street. That was due in part to the fact that her energy and confidence had sagged with time. It was also probably true that she had less to offer the Europe that had produced Duchamp and Tzara but was now occupied with the evolution of an artistic style that would be called Surrealism, than she had had to offer a less sophisticated Greenwich Village which was stunned by her antics. If Dada existed in America, it existed largely in the person and poetry of Elsa Baroness von Freytag-Loringhoven. In Europe, where she was institutionalized twice, she was simply a poor, mad lady. Elsa was an ally in desperation, and years later Djuna would say that her words would come back to her when no one else's did.

There were strong and strange women in those days in Greenwich Village. One was Rihani, a tall and lean woman with a Greek boy's face, who danced on her knees swaying rhythmically from the waist. But Greenwich Village also had the luxury of a fairly large number of women who were individuals and often beauties in a way that transcended the silliness of the false bohemian or the aridity of the dreaded bluestocking. The most well known of the bluestockings was Henrietta Rodman, a high school teacher and radical protester on behalf of women's rights who bobbed her hair and wore a loose shift and brown socks. It became the bluestocking uniform of the Village, but not too many wore it. The names of many of the Village beauties who were at the same time in every way their own women have almost been washed away by time: Mary Pyne, Renee La Coste, Edna Kenton, Ruth Pickering and Mary Davies, who gained fleeting fame as a rhyme-a-dance girl because she once wrote some words for a poem on a partner's cuff as they tangoed.

The natural rivals for primacy among these ladies of Greenwich Village were Djuna and Edna St. Vincent Millay. The popular success came easily and swiftly to Millay, whose poem *Renascence,* signed E. St. Vincent Millay, Esq. (her mother had wanted a boy and throughout her life her closest friends called her Vincent), which she had mailed in from Maine, won the $500 first prize—an unheard of sum for poetry—for the 1912 anthology *The Lyric Year.* There had been nearly ten thousand entries. Master Millay swept into Greenwich Village and turned out to be a red-haired elfin creature with an entourage of attractive younger sisters. Norma became an actress with the Provincetown Players, while Kathleen became a writer. They all lived with their mother, who has been described as a puzzled little hen whose progeny had turned out to be nightingales rather than chicks, in a top-floor apartment at 25 Carlton Street. In the evenings what amounted to three separate salons were conducted, but during the day the Millay home became a serious artistic academy for the three sisters. Edna was not beautiful, but it always happens that a grouping of sisters can blur that distinction slightly, and she more than compensated for that with the charm of her frankness and her romantic tomboyishness. Wilson, who knew them both rather well, thought that Barnes was jealous of the success of Millay.

Djuna and Edna had more than a little in common. They both came from broken homes. They both had a passion even as young women to dress and present themselves in a distinctive fashion, which they had to accomplish on very limited means. They both had a well-developed sense of humour. The difference was that Millay's humour was light and sharp while the Barnes humour was dark and tearing. Both women carried themselves as superior beings.

Edna Millay had a brief incident of lesbianism in France shortly before she got married in 1923. That affair was with the main love of Djuna Barnes, Thelma Wood.

Millay was never a poet's poet, though she was loved in the Village for her aura of enchantment and her warm insouciance, but she very quickly became the most popular female poet in the country and, eventually, simply the most popular poet in the history of the country. Young women poured into New York after her to hold the world close enough, burn their candle at both ends, and fail to recognize the men with whom they had had a dalliance when last they met. It

Edna St. Vincent Millay

would be more than fifty years before young women would be seen passing through international airports in their Djuna capes and triangular hats and a Djuna bookstore would open in New York. Djuna tried very hard to force the feminist bookstore not to use her name.

For many of her first years in the Village, Djuna Barnes wore solid black from neck to ankle with a touch of white here and there. It is remembered that she would sweep through Washington Square on her way up Fifth Avenue followed by hordes of youngsters whistling and howling with laughter. She wouldn't turn her head or bat an eye.

ix

Djuna Barnes and Edna St. Vincent Millay came to know one another through their work for the Provincetown Theatre. Millay wrote three verse dramas for Jig Cook and the Provincetown, one of which, *Aria da Capo,* was extremely successful.

The Provincetown started in the summer of 1915 on the Cape Cod porch of youthful and prematurely white-haired Jig Cook and his wife, Susan Glaspell, as a speculative idea that was suddenly carried forward in much the same way that the Washington Square Players had been formed. To a certain extent the Provincetown was formed in reaction to what was seen as the stodginess and latent commercialism of the Washington Square group. The creation of a Provincetown wharf theatre for staging one-act non-commercial plays during the summer season was a brilliant stroke. Artists and writers had been summering there for three seasons already as a result of the proselytizing on behalf of the region which had been done by Mary Heaton Vorse, both personally and in her *Harper's* articles. It was cheap to live there and to stage plays. It became the summer capital of Bohemia.

The Provincetown Theatre was a playwright's theatre, but even that fact has to be put in the context of a merry all-hands-and-trades atmosphere that gave the undertaking its exuberance and force. The playwrights were frequently also actors—Djuna Barnes took minor parts, and so did Edna St. Vincent Millay along with her sister Norma, who was a serious actress and had major parts—and they also helped to construct and paint the scenery. The Provincetown Theatre constituted a family of some forty-odd artists. Even Christine Ell, who was literally the chief cook and bottle washer, for she ran a little restaurant over the theatre, would slip downstairs to deliver a single line in many of the plays, an entrance which would always bring the house down with gleeful laughter. Two very handsome Village eminences, Max Eastman and John Reed, whose wife, Louise Bryant, was one of the theatre's playwrights, simply walked onstage and modelled rather than acted. Against this gay pandemonium struggled Nina Moise, the stocky stage director who could stop but not subdue the rehearsals by hoarsely shouting: —*Where do you think you are—at a tea party?*

We know that Djuna Barnes would occasionally serve as an usherette, and perhaps it is not apocryphal that she hawked programs even after the curtain for her play *Kurzy of the Sea* had gone up. It was part of a double bill with Eugene O'Neill.

Because they were not really friends there is no correspondence between Barnes and Millay, but the character of their acquaintanceship is well conveyed by a passage from a letter which Millay wrote to her sister Norma from Paris in March 1921. It concerned a play, *The Lamp and The Bell*, which she had just finished writing and had sent to her sister. It is in *The Letters of Edna St. Vincent Millay*. Millay wanted her play to be kept out of the hands of the Provincetown Players for as long as possible, and she particularly singled out Djuna Barnes. Millay's sister Norma told me angrily that I was wrong in seeing any lack of friendship in that letter. However that may be, when *The Lamp and The Bell* appeared in print, Barnes did damn it with faint praise in a review. No one was spared the Barnes haughtiness, not even the star playwright of the Provincetown Theatre, O'Neill, who was very deferential towards Djuna. She did a fine ink sketch of him. O'Neill had insisted to Djuna that she was a better playwright than he, and there is an undated O'Neill letter, probably written in 1923 or 1924, which seems to speak of a promised collaboration between them:

> —Can't you let it rest until Fall when I will be around for three months—and in the meantime hook your editor for an advance on the strength of my assurance of cooperation?

In August 1924, O'Neill wrote to Barnes in Berlin:

> —I'll look forward to reading the new play. When are you coming back to us? Never, I suspect you hope. But aw, come on over! . . . I treasure your book. It is great stuff . . .

But in spite of those friendly overtures the connection with O'Neill and the Provincetown was never taken up again, and she retained a

Portrait of Eugene O'Neill (courtesy McKeldin Library)

low opinion of O'Neill as an artist over the decades. We know from the Gelb biography that O'Neill thought very highly of *Nightwood*, but was actively discouraged from expressing this admiration by his wife.

The summertime success of the Provincetown enabled it to be set up as a year-round theatre in a converted stable on Macdougal Street next to the Liberal Club. The stage was so small that there was scarcely room for more than six actors on it at any one time. The Provincetown in Greenwich Village still had the odour of horses about it. It had been a stable, and a stable it would be again, it was said, after the failure of the Provincetown Theatre. Djuna Barnes wrote of her participation in the venture in *The Theatre Guild Magazine* (January 1929):

> —We used to sit on the most uncomfortable benches imaginable in that theatre, glad to suffer partial paralysis of the upper leg and an entire stoppage of the spinal juices, just to hear Ida Rauh come out of the wings and say—*Life, bring me a fresh rose!*
>
> Our private lives were going wrong in all directions; we did not eat for days that we might save up to dine at the Brevoort; we sat in the Hell Hole and became both foreign and philosophic.

It is interesting that in this same article she says of her work for the Provincetown —I wrote out of a certitude that I was my father's daughter. Though the Provincetown Theatre was very American in all important respects, especially in its repertory and its membership, an attraction to European culture was a strong facet of the Provincetown's collective personality. It suggested the European migration that was shortly to come for American writers.

The first New York Provincetown season in 1916 with O'Neill's *Bound East for Cardiff* followed by plays by Floyd Dell and Louise Bryant made the enterprise financially viable and quite well known. The Provincetown opened its 1919 winter season with Barnes' short play, *Three from the Earth*. Its main action concerns three deceptively simple country lads who have come to retrieve some letters written to an elegant lady by their father, who has committed suicide. The play's main feature is an ever-promising, never-easing inscrutability. It was the first step in a direction that would become the central characteristic of Barnes' art. The dialogue turns sharply, but there is never anything around any corner in the play but another corner:

> KATE —*How's your father? I remember—he was always mad—he used to wear a green suit and carried around white rats, all over his shoulders. Ah, yes, your father—he was a barber, wasn't he?*

89

HENRY —*No, chemist.*
KATE (uneasily, laughing a little) —*I have a bad memory after all. And your mother—a prostitute, I believe?*
HENRY (calmly) —*At times.*

The play was warmly reviewed in *The New York Times* (November 9, 1919) by Alexander Woollcott, who followed his review with a parody of the play's manner called *Free from the Birth: a Malthusian Sardonicism in One Act.* Woolcott's perception of the play is of lasting worth because of its relevance to *The Antiphon* nearly forty years later. Woolcott wrote of *Three from the Earth:*

> —It is really interesting to see how absorbing and essentially dramatic a play can be without the audience ever knowing what, if anything, the author is driving at and without, as we have coarsely endeavoured to suggest, the author knowing either. The spectators sit with bated breath listening to each word of a playlet of which the darkly suggested clues leave the mystery unsolved.
>
> This trick of hinting at things which are never revealed, of charging an act with expectancy never satisfied, of lighting fuses that lead to no explosion at all is a trick used occasionally to intensify a scene. It is a trick which, played often, would enrage an audience.

Woolcott was wrong in thinking that the "inscrutable authoress" did not know what she was driving at, but such a conclusion is understandable, for indeed the audience is granted nothing but the considerable dramatic tension generated by the secret situation. *Three from the Earth* was the first of many *tableaux vivants* drawn from the strange childhood of Djuna Barnes. The dramatic effect of mysteries with no solution and fuses which burn backwards into silence are effects which all too easily in some artists lead only to pretension and preening, but which can in artists like Barnes and Albee (dismissed many years ago by Barnes for the "vulgarity" of *Who's Afraid of Virginia Woolf*) produce a very special and powerful sort of dramatism. It is reasonable to speculate that an O'Neill-Barnes collaboration would have been something like Albee's *Tiny Alice* in character.

All of which is simply to say that from the beginning Barnes showed herself to be a special sort of dramatist, one capable of effects denied to more straightforward dramatists but by that very fact incapable of evoking universal involvement in an audience. She wrote many short plays in her early years. They are more like sketches than closet-dramas. A few of them such as *An Irish Triangle* (*Playboy*, May 1921), which was her third play staged by the Provincetown, are the weakest things ever written by her. Barnes' very first dramatic efforts had been mini-plays written for *The New York Morning Telegraph Sunday Magazine* in 1916–17. Her first proper play was *A Passion Play*, which appeared in the Kreymborg journal *Others* in February 1918. Between 1918 and 1923 Barnes did a series of ten playlets, some of them under the pseudonym Lydia Steptoe, which appeared in journals such as *The Parisienne, Vanity Fair, Shadowland* and *Smart Set*. The Lydia Steptoe idea was probably taken from Bruno, who used to write frivolous pieces under the names Mildred Meeker and Maude Martin. Two of the Lydia Steptoe pieces were labelled "Ten Minute Plays." One of these, *Madame Collects Herself* (1918), flutters above the rest and is remembered.

A Madame Zolbo has put her hairdresser in such a jealous rage that he gives the order to his assistant, Fifine, to kill her. Madame Zolbo is murdered by a hot curling iron which is thrust through her heart. She had made the hairdresser, who was a former lover, jealous by asking him to take care with a lock of hair belonging to another lover. It develops that she comes apart in sections like an orange, for every part of her belongs to some other lover. In the end there remains only a canary at her centre, but even as the hairdresser gloats over what he has done, the little bird begins to swell to gigantic proportions. This surrealistic jest was written when Ionesco was only a little boy.

Barnes' ten-minute plays coincide with the time when she was under strong Irish, Scandinavian and Russian literary influence. It was the first period when the peripheral literatures were having a great impact upon European culture, and this inclination was also very much present in Greenwich Village. In one of only four interviews ever given by her, in 1959, she explained to a Swedish reporter how, when she was young, she had read *Miss Julie* and raced off to write the short story that was her first major success—it won an O. Henry Prize in 1918—*A Night Among the Horses*. *The Beauty*, one of the Steptoe ten-minute plays, is a bright farce about how two aristocratic Russians, Ivan and Katrina, cope with boredom. The playlet is Dostoevsky but, again, Dostoevsky out of Firbank:

> IVAN —*I cross myself and I say: "Is it possible, Ivan Volovain, that you suffer so?" The sleigh bells only exceed the sleighs coming and going, and women from here to Moscow turn to the arms of their lovers. I, I alone, live solitary and desolate in this country that has but one Katrina, and but one beauty.*
> KATRINA (lying back, lighting another cheroot) —*Our psychologies are almost too rich for this world, are they not, Ivan?*
> IVAN —*Absolutely.*
> KATRINA —*We must be careful. I am brain-weary. You may kiss me.*

The Irish playlet of the following year, *An Irish Triangle,* is a surfeit of Synge. It contains what we may call the basic Barnes triangle (in which the wronged woman is proud and indifferent), but unfortunately the mock Irish rings false:

> —*Sure it's a happy creature I am, and right proud of the glory and beauty of my limbs, and the independent way of my breasts, and the little canny lights of my two eyes that do be striking fire and blazing this way and that.*

There were several other Barnes plays written in the early 1920s, *The Dove, To the Dogs, Anna of the Portuguese* and *The Biography of Julie von Bartmann,* which was evidently the play Barnes was going to send to O'Neill. *The Dove* was produced by the Studio Theatre at Smith College in 1925 and then played (unsuccessfully) in The Little Theatre Tournament in New York in May 1926. Norma Millay acted in it. Several of these early plays were in the trunk of her Paris papers which vanished during World War II.

X

Miss Barnes had only somewhat greater success as a poet than a dramatist in her early career. Her poems were traditional in form and rarely, with the exception of those in *The Book of Repulsive Women,* exceptional in subject. Of thirty-nine published poems between 1911 and 1923 only six were collected by her in the 1923 *A Book* (later re-titled *A Night Among the Horses* after its prizewinning lead story), and all the poems were post-1918. The others, published in *All-Story Cavalier Weekly, Smart Set, The New Republic, The Dial* and—many of the earliest ones—*Harper's,* are simply cameo pieces. Barnes is correct in her preference that these poems and most of her early stories be allowed to rest in their piecemeal publications.

One of the best of the early Barnes poems—included in *A Book*—is *Antique,* which was first published in 1918. Its old-fashioned austere attention to line partakes at least fleetingly of that New England personality that her contemporary Robert Frost (she knew him slightly and once sketched him) was to make his own. The poem, we may gather from its title, probably refers to an old portrait, but the braid "of amber stain" could indicate that it is a self-portrait in an antique frame, or a portrait of a close, red-haired friend.

A lady in a cowl of lawn,
  With straight bound tabs and muted eyes,
And lips fair thin and deftly drawn
  And oddly wise.

A cameo, a ruff of lace,
  A neck cut square, with corners laid.
A thin Greek nose, and near the face
  A polished braid.

Low, sideways looped, of amber stain,
  The pale ears caught within its snare.
A profile like a dagger lain
  Between the hair.

    The same austerity and understatement also characterize the best of the early Barnes short stories. They have very little in the way of plot, or perhaps far too much, whole lives and decades telescope into a few pages with very casual allusions. The Baronin was perhaps not far wrong, for the Barnes characters seem to fly out of nowhere, and their very strangeness, European and yet not European, takes the place of narrative in many Barnes stories. This is the predominant feature of her early writing. Of all the writers of her generation in America she made the greatest, and most successful, effort to see the world with European eyes and to record it with a European sensibility.

    The best of the early Barnes stories are characterized by a vaulted passage at the beginning and at the end of each story, and this gives them a well-made shape and pleasing symmetry, the more so as each narrative arch is supplied with a prior or subsequent false arch, the shadow, as it were, of the substance. The 1920 story *Oscar*, for example, begins with idyllic pine trees and garden paths before, after three very short paragraphs, arriving at: —Strange things had happened in this country town. Murder, theft, and little girls found weeping, and silent morose boys scowling along in the ragweed, with half-shut sunburned eyelids. This passage, in fact, provides the direction leading to the murder with which the story ends. And when the murder does occur (the main character's son unexpectedly slices the throat of his sweetheart) the action trails off and is ready to be replayed as Oscar's mother comes to find out what the reader has just been told: —They stood and stared at each other so long that presently Emma grew nervous and came down the garden path to hear what it was all about.

    This thematic device actually furnishes the title of one story, *Be-*

yond the End (1919), which was subsequently changed to *Spillway*. The entire action of the story, the return of a woman to her marriage after an absence of many years with a child by another man, is superfluous. When a shot is heard at the end the woman thinks of her husband: —He has quick warm blood. The primary sense of "spill" is its meaning of waste and death, but the end of the story does not actually give this death. Her husband has a shooting gallery in the loft of the house, and the reader knows no more than his wife as she gets up stumbling in her dress upon hearing the shot, which could be nothing more than target practice. Certainly the best of the story lines which play themselves out "beyond the end" is the 1920 story *Mother* about a little Englishman and his unattractive tall, middle-aged mistress who suddenly dies. The title of the story is really a footnote to its last two sentences: The lover, realizing that he is feeling the full force of his passion for her for the first time and that it is a passion somehow, —in the presence of a relative, throws himself down on his face like a child and goes to sleep that night with his knees drawn up. The title *Mother* then becomes the story's essential word, since it explains the relationship between the man and his mistress which is otherwise not commented upon at all.

xi

This much is self-evident in the early work of Barnes: she has been reading—*Dubliners*, the short stories of Chekhov, the plays of Strindberg and Synge, the novels of Dostoevsky—and the signs of influence and apprenticeship are everywhere. Where Barnes fails badly are those places where philosophical themes run amuck. In *Oscar*, for example, the mother and one of her attendant suitors talk about life at some length:

> —*You must, however, warn yourself, in fact I might say arm yourself, against any sensation of pleasure in doing good; this is very difficult, I know, but it can be attained. You can give and forgive and tolerate gently and, as one might say, casually, until it's a second nature.*
> —*There you have it, tolerate—who wants tolerance, or a second nature. Well, let us drop it. I feel like a child.*
> —*It's difficult not to feel like a child.*

Such dialogue is best when—in the same story—it reaches sardonic absurdity in the same way that it does in *Three from the Earth*:

—No, no!
—Yes, yes, he said gently, softly, contradicting her.
—Yes, evil, and pitiful and weak; he seemed to be trying to remember something. *—What is it I have overlooked?* He asked the question in such a confused voice that she was startled.
—Is it hate? she asked.
—I guess so, yes, I guess that's it.
—Kahn, try to think—there must be something else.
—Madness.

Such philosophizing is not native to Miss Barnes; some intellectual digestive process converts thought into peculiar and rather charming, but meaningless, stylization. Several friends throughout her life were to comment that she was the very opposite of an intellectual but that a strong show of intellectualism was one means by which her haughtiness might be slightly subdued. It was a time of deep and passionate talk, and, even though her own style was the aphorism rather than the discourse, there is at least a little evidence to show that she collected and sifted some of the Greenwich Village high style into her prose. In his memoirs, *A Victorian in the Modern World,* Hutchins Hapgood records how Barnes took the phrase "remorse is the path by which the evil spirit takes possession" from him and used it in *Oscar.*

The spirit of Chekhov is felt particularly clearly. *The Dove* is essentially a parodic *Three Sisters.* There are only two sisters, Amelia and Vera, who are spinsters with a longing to live perversely, but the third woman is supplied by a young woman, the "dove," whom they have met in a park. The play is a battle over the definition of perversity, and the red-haired dove is attempting to draw the two sisters not to Moscow but to life and away from perverse inhibitions. The play's finale gropes for its proper violent expression with an unfulfilled promise of death by sword, but the explosion instead occurs when The Dove —bares Amelia's left shoulder and breast . . . and sets her teeth in and then marches offstage where she fires a pistol—this is all very reminiscent of Chekhov's *Ivanov*—and returns with a pierced picture which she holds aloft, proclaiming: —*This is obscene!* The assertion is not flung against art or its destruction but at those who content themselves with experiencing nothing more than pretty pictures. One may draw many parallels, but with a difference, between the women of Chekhov's short stories and those in the stories of Barnes, who are also slightly comic provincials but stronger and more proud. So many little details, like the cotton wool which the undertaker had forgotten to remove from the ear of the corpse in *Finale,* are pure Chekhov.

The Barnes characters live near death and violence; this and not sex is her true subject, though frequently the fact is well enough concealed. The triumph of death, which is beautiful by contrast to the messiness of life, is, of course, the primary theme of the proud *crepuscolari* or poets of the cave who had flourished many years before in Europe (D'Annunzio, Sologub, Villiers de l'Isle-Adam). The only proper American forebear is Poe. Miss Barnes wrote an article which was in part about Poe's Fordham Cottage in the *New York Sunday Tribune* in February 1919.

Many of the Barnes deaths involve animals. The two most dramatic of these are the stampede of horses in *A Night Among the Horses* and the conclusion to *No-Man's-Mare*, where an age-weakened wild horse being used to carry a corpse in a funeral procession suddenly bolts for the sea, and the action of the waves appears to bring the corpse to life as its arms are tossed about while the two sink from sight. She dreamt about animals. All the time.

The very first of the major Barnes stories, *The Rabbit*, which was published in 1917, is about an Armenian suitor who strangles a rabbit stolen from a neighbourhood butcher in order to prove that he is a hero and can do something, as his imperious girl friend had demanded of him. (Seven years later, Isaac Babel would write one of his most famous short stories, *My First Goose*, on a remarkably similar theme.) Sometimes the death is not dramatic at all but merely introduces an element of peace or heightened beauty. Death in these early Barnes stories is rarely frightening.

Guido Bruno wrote an article about *Three from the Earth* in *Pearson's Magazine* in December 1919 ("*Fleurs Du Mal à la Mode de New York*" was the title), to which was appended the first literary interview ever given by Barnes. When Bruno told her that her writing was too morbid, she retorted: —*Morbid? . . . You make me laugh. This life I write and draw and portray is life as it is, and therefore, you call it morbid. Look at my life. Look at the life around me. Where is this beauty that I am supposed to miss?*

xii

The Little Review where many of these stories appeared was a perfectly natural home for them. Djuna Barnes made her name in *The Little Review*, and certainly she was regarded very highly by the journal but her terrible defensive pride and haughtiness precluded any real warmth and partisanship on her behalf. There were reasons enough to have expected that Margaret Anderson and Djuna Barnes would understand one another. Anderson had shown that same sort of fierce independence in the early Chicago days of *The Little Review* when she had refused the financial support of Amy Lowell, who had arrived with her servants and the intention of taking over the journal's poetry section. Miss Anderson preferred, instead, flea-ridden Chicago hotels and, once, a tent in order to keep her journal her own. There can, however, be little hope of friendship between two people who are mortally afraid of receiving condescension from one another. The famous Barnes reply to a 1922 *Little Review* questionnaire could not have failed to injure.

CERTAIN MAGAZINE

PLEASE COPY

We love danger but we are a little tired of being our only victory. We not only supply the guns and the target but we are also called upon to design the grave clothes.

TO THOSE WHO RING
DOOR-BELLS

Yes, we love fanatics: they usually have something interesting enough to keep them occupied while we are having a little fanaticism of our own. . . .

DJUNA BARNES
(for the L.R.)

The emotional draft for that text almost certainly existed from 1918 when *The Little Review* came to Greenwich Village. The friendship simply was not to be. In her memoirs, *My Thirty Years War*, Margaret Anderson wrote:

—Djuna and *The Little Review* began a friendship which might have been great had it not been that Djuna always felt some fundamental distrust of our life, of our talk. Her intense modernity covered the resentment for the first year or so. . . . To the more important luxuries of the soul she turned an unhearing ear. Djuna would never talk. She would never allow herself to be talked to. She said it was because she was reserved about herself. She wasn't, in fact, reserved—she was un-

97

enlightened. This led her into the construction of self-myths which she has never taken the pains to revise.

It embarrassed her to approach impersonal talk about the personal element. It embarrassed us to attempt a relationship with anyone who was not on speaking terms with her own psyche. Her mind has no abstract facets. She is impatient of such facets.

The specifics of Miss Anderson's complaint are wrong—the Barnes oeuvre may be said to be one of the best instances of deep auto-analysis outside the Freudian canon in modern English literature—but the social geography showing the place of Djuna Barnes among the artists and intellectuals of the Village is all the same a very accurate one. She mocked Anderson and Heap for being so fastidious that they washed the soap before using it.

Decades later Margaret Anderson wrote in a private letter:

—In our young years I never thought her very good-looking, as many people did, but now she is beautiful—I mean it, really. Her serious face is beautifully tragic, and her smile has the loveliest, most touching, charm.

What Margaret Anderson always admired, and it stayed the same, was Djuna's voice, which, when she did deign to talk, was stately and grim until suddenly, after a quip, it burst into short but explosive laughter and then carried on as before.

In 1918 Barnes was the centre of a little incident at the Spring Fete which was held to benefit *The Little Review* at Christine's.

The party was given by the Souls in Revolt (an "unorganized organization"), and they managed to attract about a hundred people at two dollars a head. A reporter for the *New York World* described the assemblage as consisting mostly of attractive young women and ugly men. The evening featured songs with Allen Tanner at the piano and a speech by the Japanese-German-American writer Sadikichi Hartmann (his other claim to distinction was that he had known the elderly Walt Whitman), a writer featured prominently in the Guido Bruno publications. Hartmann, under the mistaken impression that it was to have been a costume party, had come dressed up as a character in a well-known contemporary play. He spoke for rather a long time until Hippolyte Havel shouted out —*Sit down, Kichi!*, which he did, but something made him arise again in a few minutes, and in doing it he knocked a plate of chicken à la king into Djuna's lap. A long-haired youth leaped up to avenge the injury to Djuna. A space was cleared, but no blows were struck. Hartmann was declared the winner for the quality of his abuse and the elegance of the way in

Henry Budington, 1857 (courtesy
Wesleyan University Library)

Zadel Barnes Gustafson and
Axel Gustafson, London, 1888

Mary Pyne (photo courtesy Special
Collections, the University of Maryland
Libraries, College Park)

Djuna Barnes with Putzi Hanfstaengl,
March 1928 (photo courtesy Special
Collections, the University of Maryland
Libraries, College Park)

Polly's, Greenwich Village, pre-World War I

"The Dome," drawing by Nina Hamnett, 1924

Djuna Barnes, 1914

Djuna Barnes being force-fed, photo from *New York World Magazine*,
September 6, 1914

Djuna Barnes, photo by Man Ray, 1920s (copyright Juliet Man Ray)

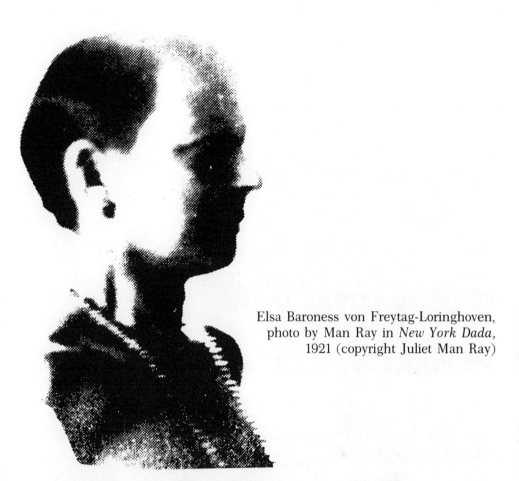

Elsa Baroness von Freytag-Loringhoven,
photo by Man Ray in *New York Dada*,
1921 (copyright Juliet Man Ray)

Caricature of Guido Bruno (bald figure) in his garret,
from *Fragments from Greenwich Village*, New York;
published privately by Guido Bruno, 1921

Publicity photo of
Marguerite d'Alvarez
(Vocalion Records/
The Aeolian Co.)

Drawing of "Kate Careless"
in *Ryder* (courtesy
St. Martin's Press)

"All Because of Wendell?" Drawing from *Ryder*

Matthew O'Connor, drawing from *Ryder*

Djuna Barnes, by Man Ray (copyright Juliet Man Ray)

which he backed off whenever the fight seemed in danger of becoming real. In the end the combatants threw their arms around one another and made up. A good time was had by all except Djuna Barnes.

Margaret Anderson was probably correct in citing 1918–19 as a turning point in the Barnes manner. It had something to do with failures and disappointments in her personal life, surely, but another way of looking at it is to see her vivacity in the period between 1915 and 1918 as simply a temporary ploy for survival.

xiii

She was serious, but there were not yet many people to take her seriously enough. If she was loved in these years, and she was, it was because she was unmistakably, like Edna Millay, a genuine artist in a Greenwich Village swarming with young women who were not quite. It wasn't easy to be a woman artist in the first decades of this century. Maxwell Bodenheim, the first among the great characters of the Village and a man of considerable critical discernment, expressed respectful boredom about her work in *The Little Review* in 1919, and yet in just four years he was to write of her:

> —She is the only good writer of my knowledge who does not yield to the minutiae of poetic sentimentality and atone for it with hours of misled harshness. Even de Gourmont and Dostoevsky are not entirely guiltless in this matter, but Djuna Barnes does not waver. Human beings to her are no more than small differences in anatomy and bulging, enclosing the claw that tears itself through the medium of ripping at other objects, and numbly falling to the ground after the crushing pressures of meretricious thought. Her nouns and adjectives are ever-changing nerve centres for this animosity.

But whether it was her singular savagery and mounting disinclination to peddle her own wares as they became more and more valuable, or merely a more neutral bad luck, the whole of Djuna Barnes' reputation was never to equal the mounting sum of such extravagant praise from her peers over the years. She would manage to enjoy simultaneous fame and obscurity, boasting in the 1960s that she had become the world's most famous unknown writer.

After the appearance of *Nightwood*, Edwin Muir wrote in his excellent history of early modernism, *The Present Age from 1914*:

> —Miss Barnes's prose is the only prose by a living writer which can be compared with that of Joyce, and in one point it is superior to his: in its

richness in exact and vivid imagery entirely without that prettiness which so readily creeps into an Irish style. There is not in her use of language, as there is in Joyce's, the faint suggestion of a possible distinction between the thing said and the way in which it is said, the feeling that one could have said it another way if one had liked. A style which is inevitable and inventive at the same time is the most powerful of all styles; for it both removes our opposition to it and takes us with its novelty. Miss Barnes has this gift of style.

But when she had been in Paris only a few years, H. L. Mencken could condescendingly ask his readers: —*Who now can remember Djuna Barnes from the old Greenwich Village days?* Who indeed.

CHAPTER THREE

—*I'm not a lesbian. I just loved Thelma,* she said much later, at a time when she looked with resigned dismay upon what she had done, although never upon who she was and what she had written (*Nightwood*). They walked together, tall and attractive, and their colour was black. You could not fail to notice them on the streets and in the cafés of Paris where the Americans used to congregate in the 1920s. But it would happen, too, that they went out separately, mostly at night, only rarely during the day. Then Thelma's mouth was thin and hard and her manner was ferine. Her bright silver earrings and bracelets were dangerous at night. A long and malicious toss of her wrist could draw blood across the cheek of a hapless male who thought he saw a spectacular evening before him. Sometimes, when Thelma had been drinking enough, she might go off with a fellow, but she was really hunting other women. Barnes would be drawn after in a blind and desperate search for her.

Djuna Barnes lost all of her imperiousness as she searched frantically for Thelma from bar to bar. There were many evenings when Thelma was not to be found, and then Djuna would stop and drink and drink. On one such occasion, it is recorded, she fell down drunk in the gutter as she was leaving a café, but fortunately there were friends there to pull her up. Far more often, when Thelma was found, it was Thelma who had to be propped up and led home.

ii

The love of women, like the lined black cloak, came from Greenwich Village. It wasn't Thelma Wood, it wasn't Paris. Her mother, when Djuna had returned to New York after it was all over—the love affair and the last American expatriate grouping of her generation—blamed both. Her mother told her that she could never expect to live down that city. The 1940s back in New York against her will were the first days of cloistered silence for Djuna Barnes. —*It's Paris! You needn't tell me. Don't I know what that place can do? I accepted your father under the Arc de Triomphe, and look at us now!*

We know that she had had a great love for another woman in the

101

Greenwich Village days. The only witness to that love is a short passage in the 1952 memoirs of the artist Maurice Sterne, *Shadow and Light*:

> —I had dinner with Djuna Barnes, the avant-garde writer, occasionally. She ordinarily spoke very little, being more interested in observing the people she was with. One night at Polly's Restaurant in Greenwich Village, Djuna suddenly exclaimed that she saw someone she knew. She took me over to a table where a mousy girl was dining with some friends. Djuna began hissing, —*I hate you, I hate you, I hate you* over and over again. The tan mouse smiled sweetly but there was an electric spark in her smile and they had an ominously quiet, violent fight before Djuna stalked out with that long stride of hers.

The "mouse" was Margaret Anderson, and the matter concerned her lover, Jane Heap. In Paris, Barnes told Charles Ford that she had had a deep crush on Jane Heap for many years. Letters that Djuna wrote to Emily Coleman in 1938 call Jane Heap a shit, and may indicate that they did have a passing affair. The tricornered hat made famous by Djuna in Paris was exactly like the one that had been worn by Jane Heap in the Village. In his memoirs, Sterne continues:

> —Djuna's most intimate friend was the loveliest young woman in the Village, a Titian-haired beauty who was fatally ill. When Mary Pyne died I found Djuna sobbing painfully, her head buried in her arms, saying over and over that she would never get over the loss. These were the only times I had even a glimpse of the true intensity her controlled facade covered.

Twenty short poems are distributed among the short stories of Barnes' first major work, *A Book* (1923). Taken separately, they are simply poems on various themes. One of them is *Antique*. But if eleven of them are taken out and read sequentially they constitute a story in themselves. It is a love story passing from bliss to ever-growing pain as the sickness and death of the loved one is described. The cycle concludes with poems describing the grave and the transmutation of the corpse into a garden with hawthorn and

> . . . beneath her armpits bloom
> The drowsy passion flowers of the dead

There is little direct emotion in the poems. Rather, the grief and the love are made abstract and Christian:

> The only pattern in the mind
> Is the cross behind the Christ.

102

The final short poem, *Finis*, concludes *A Book*, and the phrase *when we are dead* promises a lifelong commitment to the love and the memory, which is in accord with the continuum of life which is stressed throughout the cycle.

The longest of these poems is divided into six parts and is called *Six Songs of Khalidine*. They are dedicated *To the Memory of Mary Pyne*, and it is on the basis of this dedication, taken with the Sterne memoirs, that we may presume to speak of the love of Barnes for Mary Pyne. The *Six Songs of Khalidine* were written shortly after Mary Pyne's death and submitted to Harriet Monroe at *Poetry*, but they weren't published. One of the drawings in *A Book* has been identified as being of Mary Pyne by Charles Norman in *Poets and People* (1972). The picture is not of a beauty, but then that sometimes happens to people when they are drawn by Miss Barnes. The poet attends the dying woman in a night-long vigil. The two women kiss in mad despair at the death they both see all too clearly.

Two of the previous five-line poems, *Hush Before Love* and *Paradise*, seem to speak of consummated love. The first line of the second poem is

—This night I've been one hour in Paradise

and yet this consummation is shadowed by betrayal—there is reference to the cock that crowed three times when Peter disavowed Christ and also to the Judas kiss.

Mary Pyne was, like Djuna, a red-haired poet, though she published scarcely any of her work. Harry Kemp had found in her his Ideal Woman. Kemp styled himself the "tramp poet" of Greenwich Village, a role in which it must be said he took a decided second place to the better-known Bodenheim. Kemp and Barnes didn't get along. Mary Pyne has been described only in passing in biographies of Eugene O'Neill, because she was friendly with him and concerned about his drinking. She had a part in his early play *Before Breakfast*. Pyne is described as gentle, soft-voiced and mystical, always off in a world of her own. There is a brief description of Barnes and Pyne at the *New York Press* in *The Street I Know* by Harold Stearns (1935). One of her poems, called *Grieve Not*, appeared posthumously in *Bruno's Weekly* (August 28, 1915):

> . . . For in thy heart is naught of bitterness
> And all is well; play thou but on and on
> Until some time when, bending low thy head
> In reverence in humility,
> Thou seest about thee in the Silences

Rapt, list'ning faces where before were none;
Not men—ah no, but more—the Souls of Men.

It can be assumed that this poem was placed for publication by Miss Barnes and also that it was addressed to her.

iii

Djuna Barnes went abroad for the first time on commission for *McCall's* magazine and the Scripps-Howard Syndicate. It is also recorded that her fare was provided by Peggy Guggenheim and Helen Fleischman. The commission for *McCall's* was probably a loose one, since Miss Barnes' first piece was published there in 1925. The article was about American women who had married European nobility and their feelings about living in a foreign culture.

Her letters of introduction were put to use. In 1920 the high priesthood of expatriate culture consisted of James Joyce, Ezra Pound, Gertrude Stein and T. S. Eliot. Miss Barnes wrote to Miss Stein and asked for a photograph from which to do a sketch of her, but when they did meet there were no prospects for a friendship. Apart from Alice Toklas, who effectively controlled the terms of all friendship on the rue de Fleurus, there were no regular female members in the Stein circle. Years later Miss Barnes recalled with indignation the way in which Stein cut her:

> —D'you know what she said of me? Said I had beautiful legs! Now what does that have to do with anything? Said I had beautiful legs! Now I mean, what, what did she say that for? I mean, if you're going to say something about a person . . . I couldn't stand her. She had to be the centre of everything. A monstrous ego. Her brother—what was his name?—Leo. Leo Stein. Poor thing. He was a nice boy. She simply ate him up!

In a book review of Stein's *Wars I Have Seen*, which she wrote for the *Contemporary Jewish Record* in June 1945, Barnes calls Stein a matron who has written a primer and her style —a sort of static flight— she can be nudged, she cannot be hurried. She mocks Stein's lack of modesty or connection with common sense or real life.

Barnes was introduced to T. S. Eliot in a Paris café in 1921, but she did not really come to know him until the publication of *Nightwood*.

Miss Barnes had some help from Pound, the great helper, in her

Gertrude Stein

first years in Paris. Writing under the name Old Glory, Pound sent a letter to Ford Madox Ford's *Transatlantic Review* commenting on its first five issues. The letter began —"April number good. Especially Hem. and Djuna." Pound then dressed the perfect Parisian aesthete—or, better, the outsider's idea of the perfect Parisian aesthete—with wind-tossed hair, velveteens and open shirt collar with a loose tie flowing back over his shoulder. He was at a high pitch of anti-Americanism, but even so he was far and away the most American of the Americans in Paris. For many his stature as a poet had to be balanced against what they saw as a compulsive and bad cowboy act. Ford Madox Ford's companion at that time, the Australian artist Stella Bowen, wrote of him:

—To me, he was at first an alarming phenomenon. His movements, though not uncontrolled, were sudden and angular, and his droning American voice, breaking into bomb-shells of emphasis, was rather incomprehensible as he enlightened us on the Way, the Truth, and the Light, in Art. He desired us to teach him to dance, and quickly evolved a highly personal and very violent style, which involved a great deal of springing up and down, as well as swaying from side to side, which caused him the greatest satisfaction although I am bound to say that it reflected little credit on his teachers.

Attractive women were all courted by Pound in a way that was amiably intense and yet ineffectual. Bryher describes the process well in her 1962 memoirs *The Heart to Artemis:*

—He got up swiftly and put his arm round my shoulders. It was a most uncomfortable position, an Elizabethan would have screamed or snatched up a dagger but I decided to be wary and calm.
—*Nice hair . . . nice hair . . .* he pecked chastely at a cheek. I wondered what in the world I was supposed to do and decided to gaze at him abstractedly and in silence.
We stared at each other for what seemed a very long time. Then he asked, with some solemnity: —*Have you no chocolates?*

Barnes went through this same sort of awkward ritual because she noted decades later, on reading of this incident related by Bryher, that much the same thing had happened to her with him: —*It seems he tried on us all.* In Venice in 1967 Ezra Pound made one of the breaks in his much-publicized silence (and rather exaggerated, as Barnes wrote to her elderly friend Natalie Barney) to recall his very brief courtship of Djuna Barnes: —*Waall, she weren't too cuddly, I can tell you that.*

They liked each other well enough, though. Pound actively promoted her 1928 stylized *jeu d'ésprit Ladies Almanack* by word of mouth. Four years later Barnes wrote to him to thank him for his efforts after she had been reproached for her failure to do so by Mina Loy. She invited him to visit her when he next returned to Paris. She had not sent him a copy of her first novel, *Ryder*, and wondered in her letter if he had chanced to see it. Later she did send him a copy (he was *Ezra, my dear*) and admonished him to —*Like it, you brute,* but there is no record as to whether or not he did.

They seem to have seen each other only at parties and on special occasions. Pound invited her and sat with her at the famous and wildly raucous private performance of George Antheil's *Ballet Mécanique* at the Théâtre des Champs Elysées in 1925, a performance distinguished for the constant fighting and shouting in the theatre and the industrial fans which began whirring onstage towards the end of the performance and chilled and thus quietened somewhat the rowdy audience. Eliot and Hemingway and Joyce attended this evening of *musique américaine.* Barnes and Thelma Wood were also present at a dinner party when Pound embarrassed himself and the party by jocularly suggesting that Joyce's demure English patroness Harriet Weaver was drunk because she had been persuaded to sip half a glass of wine.

Pound's reputation for energetic concern on behalf of writers and poets whom he sometimes scarcely knew and whose art could be quite antithetical to his own is one of the things for which he is famous. But it must be noted that, even though the loose Bel Esprit group which worked to raise money to free Eliot from his bank was formed by Pound together with Natalie Barney, there happened to be no female artists in the roll of the many whose reputations were significantly buoyed by Pound in that decade. Gertrude Stein professed to like him but felt herself incapable of seeing him:

> —All he has to do is to come in and sit down for half an hour. When he leaves, the chair's broken, the lamp's broken . . . Ez is fine, but I can't afford to have him in the house, that's all.

As regards Barnes, Pound ended by having no sympathy for her work at all and, in fact, thought that she enjoyed an overinflated reputation in need of deflation. In a letter to Eliot in 1937, Pound composed a limerick about Barnes:

There once wuzza lady named Djuna,
Who wrote rather like a baboon. Her
Blubbery prose had no fingers or toes,
And we wish Whale had found this out sooner.

Pound explained the jibe (the "Whale" is a reference to Ford Madox Ford) by telling Eliot: —This exaggerates as far to one side as you blokes to the other.

Joyce was the most important writer in Paris as far as Barnes was concerned. The statement was, of course, true for most other expatriate artists as well, but the degree of her devotion to Joyce's talent was greater. Barnes was celebrated for her remark, which she made when *Ulysses* first began to appear in *The Little Review:* —*I shall never write another line. Who has the nerve to after this!* It is extremely unlikely that the remark would not have been conveyed to Joyce by someone, perhaps even before she presented her letter of introduction. The fact that she was overawed by his art and yet not inclined to be deferential before him (or anyone else) would have suited Joyce. He had comparatively few literary friendships. Djuna got on very well with Nora, too.

There is no written record of their friendship, just a series of warm but formal invitation notes to visit at his dark and stuffy flat.

There is one incident which proves conclusively that Barnes herself stood high in the estimation of Joyce. For Joyce presented Miss Barnes in 1923 with one of the original editions of *Ulysses* containing many annotations. Some years later Barnes, when she needed money because she was taking care of someone (probably the Baroness), sold it. Many years later she muddled the story somewhat when being interviewed by James Scott, the author of the first academic book about her writing, for she told him that Joyce had given her the manuscript of the novel. (The annotated book is now owned by Harvard's Houghton Library.) Miss Barnes was very old when the interview took place, and the event had occurred forty-seven years before. Still, the presentation of Joyce's own hand-corrected copy of the novel (there were few copies in the first printing) is a sufficient sign of his strong friendship.

Miss Barnes happened to be a witness to a dramatic scene in Joyce's life just before the publication of *Ulysses*. The tale is told by Burton Rascoe in *A Bookman's Daybook* (1929). Barnes was walking with Joyce and his wife, Nora, across the Bois de Boulogne when a stranger brushed by them and muttered something to Joyce which Barnes could not understand. Joyce turned pale and began to tremble. When Barnes asked him what had happened, he replied: —*That man, whom I have never seen before, said to me as he passed, in Latin: "You are an abominable writer." That is a dreadful omen the day before the publication of my novel!* It is virtually certain that the stranger was Irish and the incident was staged. Joyce was revered by the Americans and many of the English writers, too, but not by his fellow countrymen, at least in part, it must be said, because of the haughtiness which he showed them. Recalling Yeats, he told Barnes: *—A good boy and a fine poet, but too proud in his clothes, and too fond of the aesthetic—as for the rest of them—Irish stew!*

Two of the few journal or newspaper character sketches written by Barnes during her Paris years were of James Joyce. One was published under the austere title "James Joyce: A Portrait of the Man Who Is, at Present, One of the More Significant Figures in Literature" in the April 1922 issue of *Vanity Fair*. The other was published as part of an impressionistic sketch of Paris called "Vagaries Malicieux" in *The Double Dealer*, also in 1922. Barnes had then known Joyce slightly less than two years. She described him as *—A quiet man, this Joyce, with the back head of an African idol, long and flat. The back head of a man who had done away with the vulgar necessity of brain-room.* He was living, she thought, *—in a sort of accidental aloofness,* and when he smiled he showed *—strangely spoiled and appropriate teeth.* The articles recount Joyce talking about Synge, Tagore, the origin of Greek names, Greek mythology, and an old woman who presented Joyce with some pornographic plates which had belonged to a lover of hers years ago. One of Joyce's best-known pronouncements on art is in fact cited in the *Vanity Fair* article from a conversation which he had with Barnes: *—A writer should never write about the extraordinary, that is for the journalist.* True to that article's title there is absolutely no awe in her tone in either piece, and she tells the reader that her attention wanders as Joyce talks to her, because *—He drifts from one subject to the other, making no definite division,* until finally she has *—lost all connection with this man, sad, quiet, and eternally at work.*

iv

The outlines of Joyce's artistic development shadow down upon Barnes' own artistic strategies, and it is not too much to say that you must know something about Joyce to know certain things about Barnes.

The American poet Jack Hirschman touched upon some importaŋt specifics in the influence of Joyce upon Barnes in a doctoral thesis (Indiana, 1961). He first noted that the verbal intricacies and the imagery of *Ladies Almanack* are quite clearly influenced by the portion of *Work in Progress* that appeared in *transition* in 1927. The saint's life and calendar forms, too, may be attributed to Joyce's friendship with Barnes, for he was well known to be inclined to both. Some of the parallels found by Hirschman do not admit of any doubt whatsoever, as, for example, Barnes in *Ladies Almanack:*— And saying riddle me this, or meddle me that, contriving the Potion as ever you may, hiccup hic jacet, as contrasted with Joyce's passage in *Finnegans Wake*:—Latin me that, my trinity scholard, out of eure sanscreed into oure eryan. Hircus Civis Eblanensis! Joyce read from the *Wake* for her. She laughed. He was delighted.

Above all it is in her extension of the limits of literary language that Djuna Barnes stands on common ground with Joyce. Joyce's earliest work was in Elizabethan form, and Elizabethan and Jacobean language is important in the work of both writers. Of the early twentieth-century English writers, few can be said to pay more persistent attention to layers of language and difficult historical allusion than Joyce, Eliot and Barnes. Joyce gave a new form to the novel. Eliot gave a new tone of voice to English poetry. Barnes was comparatively disadvantaged because her main narrative cargo was her rather singular family experience—a great and painful gift for her as a writer, to be sure, but a gift of less than universal appeal and currency—and also because she was a woman and a most unusual sort of woman at that.

The parallel development of Barnes and Joyce—she, of course, following shortly behind—is striking. Both have musical roots which fed their art. Both have a passion for the past and arcane language, which are applied to a present not very far removed. Both moved sharply from classically plain artistic expression to the invention of new mixed genres. The celebrated Joycean epiphanies, trivial moments of high emotion and significance, are matched by similar moments in the major early short stories by Barnes (though in her case the moments of intensity tend to be fixed at either the opening or the closing of the stories), many of which were written before it is likely that she would have been familiar with *Dubliners*. As Joyce moved from the early poems of *Chamber Music* to the short stories of *Dubliners*, so, too, Barnes moved from the poems of *The Book of Repulsive Women* to the short stories of *A Book*. Then both artists shift to the novel form, and the two "novels" of each writer both seeth with parody and travesty and wear the very term novel only with difficulty. Both writers play with drama left-handedly, and neither of them attaches much importance to narrative in the traditional sense. Hirschman goes too far, however, in suggesting that this entire period of Barnes' art is essentially imitative. There is to be sure a strong imitative current in her early art, but apart from certain places, such as her overly Beardsleyesque drawings before 1920, there is a much stronger vein of unmistakable originality in all that she did in her first decade as an artist.

After 1928 there follows nearly a decade of silence which ends with the appearance of her masterwork, *Nightwood,* in 1936. It is certainly true that that novel, though not without influences, speaks basically in its own unique voice. There is no shadow of Joyce. But it is equally true that the major Barnes work which followed after two decades of silence, the poetic drama *The Antiphon* (1958), is more Joycean than any other Barnes work for its apparently impenetrable density of language and intent. Both Djuna Barnes and James Joyce share a strong disposition to verbal encrustation. They both seek to conceal more than to reveal or "communicate," and in each writer one must learn to accept this manner if one is to be able to participate in the writer's poetic intensity. This important aspect of Djuna Barnes is natural to her and not the result of any influence. *The Antiphon* of 1958, though different from *Three from the Earth* in every other way, shares this broad characteristic, astutely noted by Alexander Woollcott, with the 1919 play, and both works hold it in common with *Ulysses* and *Finnegans Wake.*

There is, beyond the tactical and stylistic parallels between the art of Joyce and Barnes, also a similarity in the way they lived, not immediately apparent perhaps, but nonetheless quite real. Both writers were exceptionally reserved except when, too frequently, they drank excessively. Each writer had a rather unusual (for those expatriate times, that is) preference for a simple and ordered domestic situation. Joyce was successful in this, while Barnes failed, but that was a matter of fate.

V

Barnes has described her sailing to Europe in late 1919 or 1920:

—It was a one class boat—to those without discrimination. The cargo was chiefly disappointed teachers from the Middle West, who sat on deck eating gift fruit sarcastically. In the evening they turned into the

111

salon, drinking triple sec and trying to win at cards. A few of them thought they were being continental when they submitted to foreign embraces.

She shared a cabin with a Frenchwoman and passed most of her time with a sentimental and boastfully amorous French professor in his forties who was returning to Paris after many years in America. She and the professor sat at the captain's table, and she felt that her laughter, unusual in its timing and rather forceful, made her the object of the dining room's attention and speculation. When they landed at Le Havre she went to Paris with the professor on the train, and she evidently spent a number of days in his company acting somewhat distant and supercilious. He took her to visit the home of a purportedly elegant Frenchwoman whom he knew, but Miss Barnes, though impressed enough in some ways (—How many years of my life had gone into picturing just such a room!), affected to be put off by little touches of bad taste and pretension. As she left the drawing room the woman's teenage daughter showed her to the door and re-marked in charming English: —I hope you will suffer prettily in Paris. The professor paraded all the ornaments of Paris before her, and, she recounts, they all failed to make any impression. She ex-cepts only the French attitude towards perfumes and cosmetics, Cluny, the churches, and the way the French walk —with a cer-tain respect for the way their legs are fastened on . . . This note of American condescension before Paris and French culture is balanced slightly by complaints that the Parisian cafés are quite spoiled by women who talk in English to men who answer in American.

She liked the churches best and visited them often from her first days in Paris. She was not then or ever a communicant, though she later acknowledged herself to be essentially a religious person, but that was probably not the reason for her visits to the cathedrals of Paris. It is clear from a brief passage in her "Vagaries Malicieux" that the cathedrals are a metaphor of herself, and the grand yet sad aloofness which they possessed was also shared with her:

> —And so it was I came to Paris, and a few hours later was leaning out of my window in the Rue Jacob, and thinking in my heart of all un-known churches, and so thinking, I put on my cloak and went to Notre Dame in the sad, falling twilight, and wandered under the trees and thought of another city, in a truly traitorous fashion, until, coming upon an old woman selling oranges, I thought how bitter and quick the odour was, and how charmingly unnecessary it was of them to be like that—and on this unnecessity I came into my own.

But Notre Dame somehow leaves you comparatively untouched, you may not remember her for fear of intruding. She is a lonely creature by preference. She is not disturbed by those devotees who fall into two classes; those going toward, and those coming from, faith. She is in the centre condition, where there is no going and no coming. Perhaps this is why, for me, there was something more possible in the church of Saint Germain des Prés, the oldest church in Paris. It is a place for those who have "only a little while to stay"—it too is aloof, but it has the aloofness of a woman loved by one dog and many men. And here one takes one's tears, leaving them unshed, to count the thin candles that rise about the feet of the Virgin like flowers on fire.

You did not meet the Americans in the churches. There one found only a sprinkling of native Parisians and an occasional Russian or two. They were the only real émigrés in Paris at this time, and many of the Russian artists and intellectuals in particular divided their time between the cathedrals and the Bibliothèque Nationale because it was difficult for them to afford the luxury of even one franc for coffee and croissant at the cafés too often. The noise in Paris in 1920–21—it subsided slightly after that but still lasted a decade— was predominantly that of the Americans in the cafés. There was not one-tenth the number of cars in Paris that there are now. In 1921 Matthew Josephson wrote home to a friend in New York: —The cafés at the corner of the Boulevards Montparnasse and Raspail are *thick* with Americans. They cling to each other so closely that one tends to forget all the French one has learned in the United States.

Djuna Barnes was very much a part of this crowd, it is true, and that is how she appears in memoirs such as the McAlmon *Being Geniuses Together*. But it would be absurd to suggest that that is how she spent all of her time, although many of the expatriates, including Barnes, were inclined to affirm this myth. Of the expatriate memoirists, Alan Tate, like Hemingway, gives proper weight to the more unromantic truth about the serious writers of that "gay" time. Barnes, like the other fewscore accomplished and seriously aspiring expatriate artists in the army of poetasters and gawkers, spent most of her time writing. She wrote in bed, and particularly in the mornings. Her breakfast was brought to her every morning by an overworked young chambermaid with a stiff little broom clasped under her arm as she held the tray. The chambermaid was fanciful and had a story, and Miss Barnes must have become an audience for it, since she wrote later that she had passed many a difficult hour with her.

The Hotel d'Angleterre, located at 44 rue Jacob, was a small and rather run-down hotel, but it was one of the key landing perches

113

Silverpoint drawings
by Thelma Wood

for the Greenwich Village people coming to Paris. (The other favoured hotels for the American artists were the Hotel des Écoles and another on rue Chaumière.) Alfred Kreymborg was in the lobby when Djuna Barnes arrived at the Hotel d'Angleterre, and so were several other young Village writers grouping together in *Broom,* which had been left in the New York hands of the intense Australian poet Lola Ridge and was in the process of being editorially extended to Europe by its publishers Harold Loeb and Matthew Josephson. According to Kreymborg, Djuna Barnes walked into the lobby, saw the *Broom* writers, and exclaimed dramatically: —*So this is Paris!* Man Ray, Berenice Abbott, Sherwood Anderson, Marcel Duchamp, and Marsden Hartley—glossy from a New York auction of some of his paintings which had netted him $5,000 just before he sailed— were all at the hotel.

Thelma Wood was not at the Hotel d'Angleterre. She was a permanent resident at the Hotel Récamier and had likely also come to Paris during the summer of 1920. An illustration of a sculpture by her appeared in *Gargoyle* in 1921. It was said that she had a small and regular private income during all her years in Paris, which may have been the case since she was one of the Americans who had her own car, a dashing red Bugatti from which she had had the muffler removed. She supposedly drove magnificently but like a madwoman in this roaring car. We don't know precisely when Djuna Barnes met her, or where, probably in the American crowd at one of the cafés. We do know that Barnes met Thelma Wood on her first trip to Paris, though she returned to New York on publishing business and then came back to Paris again in 1923. Soon afterwards they were living together.

By the time she had returned to New York (it was a bad crossing) the first six weeks of Paris no longer seemed so horrible, and she was able to speak of life there as altogether charming. At first in Paris she, like many other of the Americans, had lived mainly on omelettes, because, without any French, that was all she could order. She was interviewed in *The Greenwich Villager* on her trip and said that La Rotonde was like the Brevoort, not only in its American clientele but even in its decoration, complete with American pictures. — *It's awfully hard to work in Paris,* she said. —*Edna Millay was doing more than the rest of us. Everyone just sits around and says, "Gosh, isn't it great to be here!"* Miss Barnes noted that, while the cost of living was half that of the United States, —*of course you spend everything you save on clothes.*

The cost of living for the expatriate bohemians soared when summer came because tariffs were raised in response to the further waves of Americans. Many of the Villagers moved on to Germany, where it was possible to live in the grand manner on the foreign dollar. Barnes went on a round that passed briefly through Budapest and Vienna before ending in Berlin, where she stayed for several months at the end of 1921. There is a photograph of her with Putzi Hanfstaengl and Charles Henri Ford in Vienna on a subsequent trip made circa 1931. She saw Putzi for the last time in 1938 in London and must have been among the very first to learn Hitler's secret from him, for she remarks in a letter to a friend that she has heard Hitler hasn't a mouse's rations in his trousers.

There is some record of Berlin because Barnes had written to Robert McAlmon urging him to join them and then, thirty-five years later, the aging and sick McAlmon discovered the correspondence in a trunk and wrote to Barnes from Sarasota Springs recalling their Weimar experience. She chided him for the way in which he seemed to throw himself forward with every step he took in Paris. He countered by recalling her overly dramatic cape-throwing gesture in Berlin. She had taken a room at In den Zelten 18. When he came, towards the end of September, McAlmon took a large room there, too. Others living there or in a neighbouring house included Marsden Hartley, Berenice Abbott, Thelma Wood and Harrison Dowd. Dowd was at that time suffering from jaundice and had, Barnes told McAlmon, turned bright yellow, one of her favourite colours. Isadora Duncan and Charlie Chaplin, whom Djuna Barnes knew from a visit he had paid to the Provincetown on Cape Cod, were in Berlin in 1921 and spent some time with this little group. Barnes and Chaplin had lunch and went to the hospital together to visit Dowd. The visit was recalled with joy by Chaplin because for the first time in many years no one seemed to register either his name or his face, and he ended by embracing one of the Sisters in jubilation before they left.

Hartley was the doyen of the Berlin group of friends because he had many prewar acquaintances in Berlin from his period as an Expressionist painter, and so had the contacts to organize interesting theatre and nightclub outings. Barnes went to the theatre often. There was a lot of drinking and sipping tea with absinthe at the Adlon Hotel. Once an old woman who was also having tea fixed her lorgnette on Miss Barnes, who picked up a fork and ogled back at her through it. Hartley would hold court before a passing parade of well-born and starving Germans to each of whom he would give marks which were only worth a few American cents to him but could buy a day's food.

Djuna used her sudden economic advantage to buy brocaded velvet, and she also bought a lot of old Russian jewelry and some iron

117

necklaces and bracelets. There is even a reference in McAlmon's 1952 letter about Berlin to —your trodding on orchids. The dollar in Berlin had about twenty times the purchasing power that it had anywhere else. People were for sale at bargain prices, and all sorts of sexuality and dress could be seen any evening along the Unter den Linden. It was depressing by most memoir accounts. Barnes said that she didn't see much suffering. According to McAlmon's memoirs she spent most of her time in her room writing. It may have been in Berlin rather than in Paris—it is not entirely clear from McAlmon's letter—that Barnes made her remark about not taking a second helping of European culture.

The expatriates straggled back to Paris, and Djuna Barnes went with them. She remained always with some grouping of the American colony of writers and artists throughout her period of European expatriation. We know that she made a short sortie to Freiburg to write an article on twilight sleep, but it was not printed. Until everyone started to leave, however, she declared her intention to remain in Berlin as long as her money held out, though she also told McAlmon that she felt that she *must* see London and especially wanted —to speak to the bank clerk.

vi

The 1920s were the first time of Djuna Barnes' hysteria, though its manifestations were withheld for some time. The mask continued to fit her tightly, but she was drinking in earnest and occasionally smoked marijuana. She complained to friends that from time to time she suffered from a terrible sinking feeling in the pit of her stomach, and she would sometimes stare fixedly into space. She spoke to close friends about an intense horror at the prospect of growing old.

Paris was, it has been simply said, a good address for an artist in the Twenties. Djuna Barnes had few illusions. If her wit was noticed, so were her incredibly long silences in the cafés. That, too, had begun in New York, when she would sit in the café of the Brevoort and stare —sulkily and scornfully at the crowd. An obscure journalist named Calhoun, in the California journal *The Argonaut* (1923), recalled of her Brevoort vigils: —Many admired her, but probably few expressed it, for she met all advances with a defiant vulgarity that confused utterly, for who could guess that it grotesquely masked a spirit full of delicacy, imagination and poetry? John Glassco records just this sort of introduction to her in Paris in his fine *Memoirs of Montparnasse* (1970), where Djuna Barnes figures as the novelist "Willa Torance."

When he was introduced to her as coming from Montreal, she sneered at him in pallid imitation of Dr. Johnson: —*Why?* and, though she was in a large company of ladies, young Glassco was made awkward by the heavy silence. In fine weather she would sometimes appear early to sun at the cafés, and there are many who remember how she would sit by herself with a growing pile of saucers.

It is about this time in her life, 1922, that the first unflattering portraits are drawn of her. A piece in *The Chicago Literary Times* described her face as:

> —A face whose high cheek-bones suggest veiled fists beneath the chloroformed pity of large eyes: a face that is as white as a signal of terror, save for the scarlet martyrdom of full lips that have never become accustomed to life. There is a Chinese emaciation attached to Djuna Barnes' face that makes the last struggle of her youth seem unreal, and it has been desecrated by too many battles with Occidental worldly widsom.

Djuna Barnes was only thirty-two when that description was written, and the age of the person doing the sketch would have to be taken into account, but it is clear that the face was both turning and being allowed to turn into a semblance of one of her own merciless sketches.

John Glassco, who admired her as a writer but found the writing emotional to the point of hysteria, saw her as a person exuding faded asexuality and distinctive in spite of —a badly fitting sleazy purple dress and a shapeless Napoleonic hat. This impression was produced in 1928, one of the dark years in the destructive love affair between Djuna Barnes and Thelma Wood.

vii

Where did all the women come from? Malcolm Cowley does a sum of 236 writers born between 1891 and 1905 in an appendix to a later edition of his saga of the 1920s, *Exile's Return,* and he notes that only forty-four of his prominent names are those of women, thereby deciding that women born in this period probably had less chance of developing their talents than those born either before or after, and

119

were particularly deprived because not many of them had the opportunity to participate in the Great War. It is the one fundamental tactical error in a fine chronicle.

If one widens one's criteria of selection just slightly, that is, to extend beyond America, one may find a trio in Colette, Woolf and Barnes, who might in time sit more comfortably on the Parnassus of their time with Proust, Eliot and Joyce, than many writers of the time whose works already show clear signs of becoming period pieces. Millay. Mary Butts. Katherine Anne Porter. Akhmatova. Nelly Sachs. Tsvetaeva. Frances Newman. Christina Stead. Bryher. H. D. No, it was not a bad time for women artists. There has, really, not yet been another time quite like it.

One of the most notable things about women in the arts in those years was the part played by female patrons and their salons. Everyone knows the way in which Margaret Anderson and Jane Heap braved the censor and the courts to publish Joyce, and then there was the support of Joyce and the publication of *Ulysses* on the part of Harriet Weaver and Sylvia Beach. Shakespeare & Co. was the parliament of the expatriation. Other ladies of the Paris expatriation who supported unknown writers both with funds and publishing help were Stein, Natalie Barney, Nancy Cunard and Peggy Guggenheim. There were numerous interesting minor salons such as the one consisting of Gurdjieff disciples run by Jane Heap and Georgette Le Blanc, Maeterlinck's companion. One has only to read the memoirs of Bravig Imbs, aptly enough titled *Confessions of Another Young Man,* to see the way in which expatriate art at all levels did flow through the formal and informal salons of these women. It was a factor much more important than the cafés and bars, which were public and often very rowdy, and provided the only strong threads in the expatriates' social fabric.

The expatriate salons may be easily defined by contrast. The New York salons, such as they were, mixed society money and serious writers. You were not, except at the salon of Mabel Dodge, expected to say strange things. The French salon strived towards brilliance but rested on stable social relations. These salons were frequently directed by husbands and wives and strove for ease between the sexes as well as between minds. The English parlour salon was much more a matter of class and society ritual; wit waited until country weekends, among friends. The expatriate salon or clique was in a much more desperately central position, for these salons had to be not only a centre for the exchange of ideas and styles, but also a surrogate country and family as well as a justification for a particular way of life.

120

The oldest and finest expatriate salon of Paris belonged to Natalie Clifford Barney. It began in 1919 and continued on for a decade. An heiress of a Cincinnati fortune, Barney was unusual among the American women not only for the early date at which she began her salon, but also for the extent of her ties with French society. She was not welcome in certain quarters but was warmly accepted by many leading French artists of kindred disposition such as Pierre Louÿs, André Gide, Marcel Schwob, Paul Valéry and Colette. She was particularly friendly with the writers of the *Mercure de France*. There were three gateways through which French and English-speaking writers encountered one another: Shakespeare & Co., because of Sylvia Beach's association with Adrienne Monnier; the literary agent William Aspinall Bradley because of his French wife, Jenny; and the Barney salon. Her salon was by far the most important of these three because the regular Fridays were always carefully planned to include a good mix of celebrities and the interesting new.

Natalie Barney was not ambitious and had none of the Stein bluff and push about her. She boasted that no one reigned in her salon, and she least of all, which does seem to be confirmed by all accounts. Many years later Gertrude Stein lived rather close to her, and the two of them would sometimes walk Gertrude's poodle together, but they were never close friends. Barney was one of the expatriates who never went back, though she would often speculate on what it would be like. She dabbled in literature, aphorisms, memoirs, poems, mostly in French, but she tended either not to print her works or to print them in very small editions. One of her best aphorisms was that being famous was simply being known by people whom one would not want to know.

Her little attached house in the heart of Paris on rue Jacob with a spacious wild pavilion and the Temple à l'Amitié in the garden had been in part constructed during the period of the Directoire. The strange little temple dates from just before the Revolution; the garden had once belonged to Racine. It was a proper salon bubbling with real and not contrived intellectual excitement, though there were dramatic days, too, such as the appearance of the Nobel laureate Rabindranath Tagore in his robes or the notorious Mata Hari. No liquor was ever served, just tea and special little chocolate cakes.

Natalie Barney was a hedonist. Her lovers were beautiful women artists, though she enjoyed the social company of elegant men, too. The two great loves of her life were the poet Renée Vivien and the English painter Romaine Brooks, with whom she lived for most of her life. Brooks was also a good friend of Barnes.

121

Natalie Barney could evidently be terrible in her passion, for it is she who is the unnamed shadowy background figure in Colette's reminiscences of Renée Vivien:

—*I'm going away, she said.*
—*Yes? Where are you going?*
—*I don't know. But I'm in danger. She will kill me. Or else she will take me to the other side of the world, to countries where I shall be at her mercy. . . . She will kill me.*
—*Poison? Revolver?*
—*No.*
In four words she explained how she might perish. Four words of a frankness to make you blink. This would not be worth the telling except for what Renée said then.
—*With her I dare not pretend or lie, because at that moment she lays her ear over my heart.*

But away from the boudoir Natalie was as soft in manner as she was in face. It does not seem that there was anyone who hated her, though Barnes did call her a shit. That notwithstanding, however, Barnes wrote and dedicated a poem titled *Love and the Beast* to Natalie in August 1924.

Djuna appeared drunk at one Barney Friday but was forgiven for it, for she was one of the favoured figures in the Barney retinue. When a poet was reciting at a Friday, he or she would stand in a semicircular alcove, which stood to the side of the drawing room. In the alcove there was an antique tapestry above which was hanging a plaster frieze which had been presented to Barney by the man who had been Proust's model for Charlus. The drawing room was furnished in an understated manner. Barney was fond of saying that her mother had left her with the pieces that she herself thought not good enough to take back to America. There were four harps positioned in various corners of the room. Most of the furniture had a faint air of tattiness.

In 1927 Natalie Barney decided to have a special series of salons devoted to women writers in order to introduce French and Anglo-Saxon women writers to each other. In order to do this it was necessary to prepare little translation extracts for recitation together with the readings. It was difficult when it came to be Gertrude Stein's turn. Colette played a scene from *La Vagabonde*. Other women writers in the series were Mina Loy, Lucie Delarue-Mardrus, Rachilde, and the Anglo-Australian poet Anna Wickham. Barnes had her day on June 3, shared with Rachilde. She was introduced by Ford Madox Ford.

Barney wrote a portrait sketch of Barnes in a book titled *Aventures de l'Ésprit,* which she published in 1929:

> —Djuna Barnes, intègre, intacte et fruste, de son coin pâlissait sous cet outrage d'honneur. Si quelqu'un eût la faire sombrer avant qu'elle n'en arrivât "aux rives lontaines," c'est elle-même. Je n'ai jamais présenté un auteur plus gauche et plus incapable de servir sa propre cause. . . . Celle que revêt Djuna Barnes est d'une franchise et d'un humour qui rejoignet Rabelais en passant par Cervantes. Curieux mélange chez une femme d'une trentaine d'années. Elle a un type physique qui est aussi très à elle: un nez aiguise comme un crayon Eversharp; une bouche irrésistible au rire et des cheveux auburn qu'elle serre sous un chapeau à la Manet, dont elle semble une des esquisses les plus réussiés. On voit que ses grandes mains osseuses ont conduit des chevaux, et personne mieux qu'elle—et Degas—ne les décrit. Elle est grande et mince, et ses vêtements se cassent à angle droit sur des jambes robustes . . .
>
> Elle est capable of great friendships et les limite à deux ou trois êtres qu'elle voit sans cesse, et avec lesquels elle oublie même de craindre le reste de l'universe.*

Barney was one of those two or three great friends of the Paris period for Djuna Barnes, and we may assume that she said something very like this when introducing Ford and Barnes to her French guests in 1927. Natalie and Djuna had a brief affair the first summer Miss Barnes was in Europe, and they remained close friends ever after. The composer Virgil Thomson put the matter improperly in a 1972 interview in which he said: —*Djuna was a kind of charity of Natalie's, and I think Natalie gave her money.* Though she did, like Peggy Guggenheim, give Djuna some subsidy, they had a genuinely close relationship.

In at least one respect Barney was indebted to Djuna, for it was she who found Berthe Cleyrergue, who served Miss Barney all her life. Berthe was an extremely good cook and the only person in the

*—Djuna Barnes, upright, unsullied, unpolished, grew pale at the insolence of honour being accorded her. If someone was going to make her sink before she arrived at the "other shores," she would be the one to do it herself. I had never introduced an author more awkward and less capable of serving her own cause. . . . Djuna Barnes possesses a candour and a sense of humour which passes through Cervantes and goes right back to Rabelais. She is a curious combination of characteristics for a woman only in her thirties. Her appearance is most singular: she has a nose as sharply angled as an Eversharp pencil; her mouth has an irresistible laugh, and she squeezes her auburn hair tightly under her hat in the manner of Manet, resembling one of his most attractive sketches. One can see in the bone structure of her large hands that she rides horses, and no one has portrayed them as well as she and Degas. She is tall and slender, and her clothes fall at sharp angles against her powerful legs. . . . She is capable of great friendships and limits them to two or three people in whose company she is endlessly and with whom she sometimes even forgets her fear of the rest of creation.

Barney circle with a husband. In later years Janet Flanner reported that Berthe's greeting was always and invariably —*Et Mademoiselle Djuna, que fait-elle maintenant? Ah, quelle femme!*

Natalie Barney's first fame came as the result of the dedication of a series of letters to her by the elderly Remy de Gourmont, and then from her depiction as Valerie Seymour in Radclyffe Hall's *The Well of Loneliness.* But by far her major role as a literary character is in *Ladies Almanack,* which Barnes published anonymously under the pseudonym A Lady of Fashion in 1928.

It's a queer little book. The story it has to tell in calendar and zodiac form does not really move in time, even though it chronicles and celebrates the life of the central character Evangeline Musset until her death at ninety-eight (a reasonably prophetic guess since Natalie Barney did in fact live to ninety-five). The book does nothing more than describe without duration or action the circle of women over which she presides. Natalie Barney was delighted with the satirical frolic. The tale doesn't really present recognizable characters. They are rather more like old-fashioned humours with no need at all to be more than two-dimensional, though there were signs enough for those who were within the satirized circle.

I was shown Natalie Barney's own copy of the book in which she has neatly marked all the characters in the margins for history. Patience Scalpel, who alternates with the narrator of the tale, is Mina Loy. Señorita Fly-About, One of Buzzing Much to Rome, is Mimi Franchetti, the black-sheep daughter of a noble Italian family, and she is linked with Doll Furious, actually Dorothy or Dolly Wilde, who also called herself Oscaria and was Wilde's niece. (She also had a remarkable facial similarity to Wilde.) The two British Women of the month of March, Lady Buck-and-Balk, with a monocle, and Lady Tilly-Tweed-in-Blood, with a Stetson, are Lady Una Trowbridge and Radclyffe Hall. They believe in marriage but only of women to women and would do away with Man altogether. Bounding Bess, the woman hunted by Dame Musset and the members of her Sect in order that she be —well branded, i' the Bottom, Flank, or Buttocksboss, is Esther Murphy, who was a great champion of the superiority of women and would on occasion stride about with a rather large whip. Cynic Sal —she dressed like a Coachman of the period of Pecksniff, Dame Musset's final choice in love, is Romaine Brooks, who wore a man's top hat. Among the flitting characters are Natalie's sister Laura, who is Sister, and —one dear old Countess, who is Ilse Baroness Deslandes, an old lover with whom Natalie had regular fiery quarrels. The page figures who bob about in the text are Janet Flanner and Solita Solano, who lived together for several decades. Of all the ladies who figure in *Ladies Almanack* only Janet Flanner publicly pointed to her presence in the book, with considerable pleasure, years later in her *Paris Was Yesterday.*

The entire artistic expatriation knew about the book, and yet, very like *The Book of Repulsive Women,* it remained well hidden from literary history for over forty years until in 1972 Barnes, who was concerned that the anonymous work might be subject to literary piracy (there had been a pirated edition of *The Book of Repulsive Women* a short time before), allowed it to be reprinted in a facsimile edition by Harper & Row.

The original edition was privately printed by Robert McAlmon at the Darantière Press in Dijon. Maurice Darantière had been the printer of *Ulysses* in 1922. McAlmon had the money to be very active as a publisher, and this is why he was unkindly called Robert McAlimony by some, a reference to his tangential marriage to Bryher, who was the heiress to a British shipping fortune. He received fourteen thousand pounds in settlement from his former father-in-law, with which money, deployed generously, he became the leading expatriate publisher of Montparnasse. His first important edition was the *Contact Collection of Contemporary Writers* in 1925, an anthology which included Barnes, Joyce, Ford, Pound, Stein, Hemingway, Butts, and also Norman Douglas and Havelock Ellis. McAlmon published Stein's *The Making of Americans,* and he also was one of the early publishers of Hemingway and Nathanael West.

Ladies Almanack appeared in an edition of 1,050 copies. It has twenty-two pen and ink drawings, and the first fifty numbered copies were hand-coloured by Barnes herself. Her illustrations are drawn with no perspective or depth and are modelled after some old French albums which Barnes had picked up in the bookstalls of Paris. —*I really shouldn't give away my secrets like this,* said Miss Barnes as she showed me one of these French albums which she had kept over the years. *Ladies Almanack* was to be distributed by Edward Titus, but he withdrew in fear from the project, so it was merrily and effectively hawked along the Left Bank by bold young women.

We are fortunate to have record of the moment of publication from John Glassco in *Memoirs of Montparnasse,* because the young Glassco was introduced to Djuna Barnes as the galley sheets of the book were being passed around in the Falstaff Café. There is an odd contrast in the sullenness of that scene as Glassco conveys it and the gaiety of the book itself.

It is a lusty little book, but it is quite possible not to see this aspect of *Ladies Almanack* too clearly because of its convoluted language. Both *Ladies Almanack* and her novel of the same period, *Ryder,* are full of Joycean wordplay. The influence is clear. Barnes herself had written in one of her 1922 articles on Joyce how he had impressed upon her that all great talkers spoke in the language of Sterne, Swift and the Restoration. Her own description of *Ulysses* as a —great Rabelaisian flower also suits *Ladies Almanack*. The language is a tossed salad of uncertain ingredients. It has largely the vocabulary and diction of the seventeenth and eighteenth centuries, but there are neologisms and usages to make any linguist frown, and there are strangenesses in the punctuation as well:

> —Now this be a Tale of as fine a Wench as ever Wet Bed, she who was called Evangeline Musset and who was in her Heart one Grand Red Cross for the Pursuance, the Relief and the Distraction, of such Girls as in their Hinder Parts, and their Fore Parts, and in whatever Parts did suffer them most, lament Cruelly, be it itch of Palm, or Quarters most horribly burning, which they do oft occur in the Spring of the Year, or at those Times when they do sit upon warm and cozy Material, such as Fur, or thick and Oriental Rugs (whose very Design it seems, procures for them such a Languishing of the Haunch and Reins as is insupportable) or who sit upon warm Stoves, whence it is known that one such flew up with an—*Ah my God!* . . .

This opening note of arch sexuality which likens the woman's sex to the intricate pattern of a Persian carpet design (and concludes with —the consolation every Woman has at her Finger Tips . . .) is sustained as a leitmotif throughout the short work. A woman's genitals are compared to various flowers and then to a garden of Venus. They are also described as whorls and crevices, an escutcheon, a nook, a path, a hollow tree, a furrow and numerous other things. Many of the descriptions are decidedly bawdy: a toll-gate, an empty hack, a cow's trough, her Jollies, a Sword with no Rust, and her Nothing. Women in their periods sit —on a stack of Blotters. But many of these descriptions nestle in long and intricate sentences, which are as firmly neutral and flat as the drawings which illustrate the book.

The work, in fact, presents itself as a protest against the indelicacy of sexual manners of the time. Dame Musset is presented as a pioneer woman, and she laments the way in which shyness and privacy have given way to vulgar brazenness. The narrator may from time to time be heard sadly to disapprove, and her companion, Patience Scalpel, more firmly disapproves and fails to understand. Mina Loy was accepted as the token heterosexual among the Barney women.

There are whimsical passages in *Ladies Almanack* which are strangely and sadly moving, such as the conclusion to the month of

126

April where the major Freudian premise about women becomes a wry poetic silhouette of the unawakened Everywoman for whom death is but the second castration.

> Such can be counted on at all hours, and
> are buried when dead, with the look of the good Clock which has
> been never slow or fast, but has tolled the
> exact hour for the duration of Mortality, and
> is silenced only and unrecording, for
> that the Lord put forth his
> Shears and cut down
> the Weights.

The finest portions of *Ladies Almanack* are about melancholy, and the words anatomy and melancholy occur frequently enough to force us to think of Burton's *Anatomy of Melancholy,* a title which is literally personified in some of the drawings where parts of the female body are presented to us as floating truncated sections of a corpse. *Anatomy of Melancholy* was one of her favourite books.

viii

Barnes used the freedom afforded by printing in English in France only after her novel *Ryder* had been subjected to censorship in New York. She had told friends —*I am writing the female Tom Jones.* She and Charles Friede, an editor from Liveright, had had to work over the manuscript together in Paris deleting passages (and several pictures) relating for the most part to bodily fluids. She was furious and insisted that the deleted portions be clearly indicated in the printed text, which they were. The original manuscript was also among the papers which perished in storage in World War II. She prefaced the novel with a chilly reproach towards American censorship and a boast to the reader that by means of the asterisks it would be possible to see where sense, continuity and beauty had been damaged and to obtain at least some sense of what a real work of literature might look like rather than the reconstructed versions that were being foisted on people by the —havoc of this nicety. One of the censored pictures was of a soprano reaching for a high note and, it could be clearly seen below her skirt, wetting herself with the effort. That censored theme was, however, used by her for the month of April in the *Almanack,* and she restored the picture of the peeing opera singer for the 1979 reprinting of *Ryder.* But she didn't restore

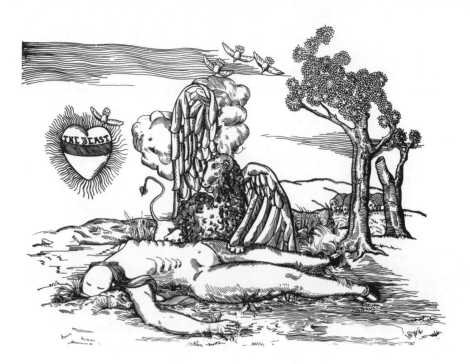

One of the censored pictures from *Ryder* (courtesy McKeldin Library)

the strongest picture, which is of a woman with an animal's dugs and a horse's legs. That picture furnishes powerful evidence of her father's bestiality and the never-resolved "Oedipal complex" behind her hatred of her father.

ix

There was a steady back and forth from America on the part of the expatriates. That was where the dollar had to come from directly or indirectly for most of them, and so it was never out of mind even for those, like Barnes, who sometimes fancied that they would never return on a permanent basis. Before her final return Miss Barnes went back three times.

The first return trip was in the interest of her forthcoming collection *A Book*, but she used the occasion to further her journalistic ties as well. In August 1922 she appeared for the first time under the pseudonym Lydia Steptoe in *Vanity Fair,* a nom de plume that would serve her for light and inconsequential journalism in several magazines. (Years later she used the name again when writing for *The Theatre Guild Magazine*, but by then it was Lady Lydia Steptoe.) In 1922 and 1923 she wrote mostly for *Vanity Fair*, humorous pieces such as an article in which chic forms of suicide are suggested, and on drama for *The New York Tribune*. She formed a link with *Charm* magazine for which she was to do many interviews and articles. Kiki and Mme. Lanvin were two of her more interesting subjects. She appeared on the stage, too, in a bit part in Tolstoy's *The Power of Darkness* and as one of the nuns in Claudel's *The Tidings Brought to Mary*, a special Christmas production of The Theatre Guild in December 1922.

The second trip was to prepare for the publication of *Ryder*. She sailed at the end of 1926 and returned to Paris in April of the following year. She received a cable from Liveright informing her that the novel had made the best-seller lists, but that pleasure was thoroughly spoiled by a second one warning her that there was a grave danger that even the expurgated text of the novel was going to be suppressed in the manner of Cabell's *Jurgen* a decade earlier. There was a brief hope of best-sellerdom. —*It will make you famous,* a reporter told her, to which she replied: —*I don't care about fame. I want the money.*

When she returned from this trip she wrote one of her Steptoe articles for *Charm*—"On Returning from Abroad." It is a mischievous article:

—The very smell of my native land was so different! The rubbish in the streets and along the gutters spoke of a greater, better descent. This was my city, it called to me, as from one horror to another. Paris had only purred like a cat that was not my cat . . . I had been long, too long from home! I yearned for a soda . . .

Although the article is facetious, it is fair to say that it also expresses her real views. Her third trip back to the United States had quite a different character. She was following Thelma. They stayed nearly a year, first at 45 Grove Street, then at 62 Washington Square South (next door to the well-known "house of geniuses," so called because Willa Cather, O. Henry and Theodore Dreiser had lived in it at various times). This was when Barnes had a job as a regular columnist for *The Theatre Guild Magazine*. Barnes went back to Europe by herself in September or October, 1931.

If you were not a dramatist it was quite as practical to conduct a literary career from Paris as in New York in those years. Indeed it may have been easier. The well-known incident of the acquisition of

Hemingway's *In Our Time* by a Liveright cable which glided in comfortably ahead of Scribner's more genteel offer by letter led naturally enough to the stationing of editors in Paris. Far more interesting authors were living in Paris than in New York. No actual offices were maintained, but there was a steady rotating presence of senior English and American editors, often including the publishers themselves, in Paris. They clustered together in the aristocratic Île Saint-Louis flat and office of William Bradley. One of the prime chroniclers of English-speaking Paris, Sisley Huddleston, looked about him and saw Alfred Knopf dining at the Trianon, Jonathan Cape at the Chaumière, Thornton Butterworth at the Coupole, "Harper" Wells, Jefferson Jones of Lippincott's, Harcourt, Liveright. He wondered whether the population of Montparnasse was not now chiefly composed of publishers and their representatives.

Djuna Barnes was published by Liveright. Of the New York publishers, Alfred Knopf had the most solid list, with a somewhat conservative and classical disposition, whereas Liveright led Scribner's in terms of contemporaneity and exciting young authors. Horace Liveright, who had left a successful Wall Street career when he was forty to join the Village bookseller-publishers Albert and Charles Boni in the firm Boni and Liveright, was a gambler who operated close to the line, which eventually led to the downfall of his empire. But within a very short time, while the going was good and before he began to back Broadway plays, Liveright assembled a rather dazzling collection of authors: Dreiser, Faulkner, Sherwood Anderson, Bertrand Russell, O'Neill, Eliot, Pound. And there were many others of only slightly lesser eminence. The Modern Library had begun at Liveright—Liveright had been forced to sell it to his young editor Bennett Cerf in 1925 in order to satisfy some of his debts.

It is probably pointless to speculate on the difference that really energetic backing might have made in the career of a writer whose manner and tone of voice were both so uncommon as those of Djuna Barnes. It happened that she was always to have distinguished publishers—later Faber & Faber and New Directions, and, subsequently, Dial, then, Farrar, Straus and, finally, Harper & Row—but somehow never one which was able or inclined to do more than let her work seek its level. She would remain her own lady but poor through the years and would grow extremely irascible when the very word publisher was mentioned. Which did nothing at all to help her literary career. In several instances known to me it almost certainly harmed it.

X

There were not many Frenchmen in those cafés. One wag said that one had been seen but that was during the Second Empire. Busloads of Americans would draw up to the Rotonde to stare at the hundreds of young American artists, mostly in the hope of a glimpse of Scott Fitzgerald. They were usually rewarded instead by a volley of profane abuse from Flossie Martin, a former Zeigfeld Follies girl who had lost her figure but still had impressive golden hair and pink cheeks and who hated America. Hemingway described the scene disdainfully in an article written in 1922, when he was still a reporter for *The Toronto Star,* as being rather like going —into the bird house at the zoo. He and most of the other serious expatriates kept away. —They have all striven so hard for a careless individuality of clothing, he wrote, —that they have a sort of uniformity of eccentricity. In other days Lenin and Trotsky had sat at the quiet Rotonde.

Some painters did still frequent the Rotonde, and there would always be a fair number of Scandinavians, but most of the artists would tend to go to the bars and cafés of the Boul' Mich' where they could happily blend in among the Sorbonne students and prostitutes. The majority of the cafés had extended their terrace chairs and tables in response to the massive influx of foreigners. They are still there today, of course, and the foreign presence in them is still considerable, but their period of renown as a centre of expatriate literary activity is usually reckoned to extend only from 1922 to 1929. On the corner opposite the Rotonde was the Dome and next to it, the Coupole. The Dome, which had a sort of spill-out from the Rotonde, was also predominantly American. The Coupole was more international in character. For a brief time in the Twenties there was something like a little guerrilla war between certain of the Americans at the Dome and the management of the Rotonde. The tempestuous Laurence Vail had had a fistfight and been thrown out. Cowley was also hostile to the place—he thought it was run by a police informer—and was arrested in a brawl there. Other interesting bars were the Jockey, which was managed for a time by a friend of Barnes', Hilaire Hiler, an American jack-of-all-arts (he did murals at the Jockey and worked for many years on a cultural history of dress and costume), and the Deux Magots, which did manage to remain a neighbourhood café and at the same time an international meeting place. Later Djuna Barnes would go to the Flore, because it was (but only temporarily) less frequented.

Robert McAlmon was another of the Americans who was particularly rowdy. He used to go to the Select, from which he was barred for a short time over a glass-breaking incident. A few of the café incidents found in the memoirs of those years are colourful; most are simply boorish. Once a mock fight was actually staged for the benefit of an American newsreel cameraman. A representative incident, from Nina Hamnett's memoirs *Laughing Torso* (1932), concerns a carpet seller who hawked small carpets, coats, necklaces, and sometimes very beautiful things for almost nothing in front of the cafés. There were many such vendors. A truculent American told him: — *Go away, I don't want any of your goddam stinking carpets,* to which the Moroccan replied in a pained voice: —*Sir, it is not the carpets that stink, it is me.*

Hemingway would frequent the Dingo, a previously French bar which had been converted into an expatriate place by a Canadian barman, who had in turn been succeeded by the Englishman Jimmy Charters, who became the most famous barman in the city. In his chatty memoirs *This Must Be the Place* (1934), which were ghostwritten by Morrill Cody, Jimmy the Barman calls Djuna Barnes one of his good friends, who brought him many clients, and someone who was —very much a lady and well-liked. Jimmy goes on to describe what he says Hemingway used to call his —greatest socking exploit on Montparnasse. It involved Djuna Barnes and Thelma Wood.

It was Jimmy's night off at the Dingo, and he dropped in very late for a drink before bed at the Select. Apart from Djuna Barnes and Thelma Wood, who were drinking with another girl whom he does not name, he recalls that the only other customers in the Select were McAlmon and a friend. And then, according to Jimmy, an —internationally known American newsman burst into the bar roaring drunk. He lunged over to the three women and sat down without ceremony next to Miss Barnes, whom he began to paw and maul. The journalist was one of Jimmy's best customers. He managed to get him to another table, where he bought him a drink and tried to distract his attention from Djuna, but without success. Jimmy asked him to come out on the terrace to have a mock session of fisticuffs, calculating that by this means he could both mollify Djuna and Thelma and draw the journalist away from the café. Unfortunately, Miss Barnes followed them outside and offered a commentary on her assailant's character, whereupon he slipped quickly out of Jimmy's hold and flattened her with a well-placed punch on the chin. The two women and McAlmon and his friend were also knocked down, but McAlmon sprang up and knocked down the journalist and sat on him. He made solemn promises to behave, but as soon as McAlmon got off him he began to swing again. Then Jimmy Charters waded into the fight. He had to knock the journalist down three times before he was finally subdued, with a gash that required three stitches.

This incident may bear some relation to strange and rather nasty little snippets that occasionally appeared in the gossip columns of New York newspapers, under the byline Walter Winchell. In one, Winchell reported that "femme writer" Djuna Barnes could hit a spittoon at thirty feet. In another, in 1932, Barnes went to a fashionable Paris nightclub, Le Boeuf sur le Toit, which the Americans and English had gradually taken over from the French and turned into an expensive drinking hole. She was reported as having saved her male companion —from the tougher waiters. What had happened, evidently, was simply that Barnes and Charles Henri Ford, who had both been drinking, slipped and fell on the dance floor. There had had to be a few sorting-out words with a waiter in order to establish that they were merely inebriated and not disruptively drunk.

Barnes did not often go to the homosexual dance halls and bars which are immortalized by the photographer Brassai in *Le Paris secret des années 30*. Hilaire Hiler and Hart Crane were two of the Americans who regularly went to those bars on the rue de Lappe. These bars could be dangerous. Once Berenice Abbott and Gwen LeGallienne were carried off in a police raid. Henry Miller, who hated the Dome and the Coupole, went to working-class bars and was in ecstasy whenever he was mistaken for a local worker. The Sapphic bars where women went in the 1920s were, according to Brassai, quiet and discreet. The boldly open bar Le Monocle and the female bordello for women Le Sphinx began only in the Thirties, when the Barnes–Wood relationship was in its state of final disintegration. This aspect of Paris life was not connected with their affair.

It was the drink rather than artistic or intellectual comradeship which makes the cafés and bars so central to this story. Before World War I, the English and American artists and expatriates didn't drink very much at all, or, if they did, it was mostly light French wine. Everything changed after the war. Absinthe, cognac and Pernod became the accepted things to drink among the expatriates, but they did not drink them as the French do. Pernod was the particular favourite of the American women, who sometimes gulped them down in succession like soft drinks. Joyless drinking without much conversation had become the rule rather than the exception by the mid-Twenties. It was fortunate that, when the pub crawl became the pattern, the distances between the drinking places were not great.

There was an element of caricature in the life the expatriates led, particularly in regard to their sexuality. For most of them, sexual freedom came too suddenly, and the puritanism from which, in dif-

133

ferent ways, both the Americans and the English were fleeing left them ill-prepared to cope with the freedom of Paris. The stage set was magnificent, but most could not master their parts. Those who had lived through the Greenwich Village period were probably better off. It is ironic that Djuna Barnes was virtually unique among all the expatriates in that she was playing out a life story which *began* in conditions of terrible freedom.

xi

—*I'm bisexual myself, like Michelangelo, and I don't give a damn who knows it,* bawled McAlmon, happily drunk, and hurled his glass onto the footpath where it shattered in front of an elderly Frenchman passing by. He was the ringleader of what he called The Crowd, and indeed people did tend to follow him from café to café, and in other ways as well. He had posed before art classes at the Cooper Union in New York, where he had been among the first male models to pose naked in America. He met Bryher there. She needed a husband, according to the terms of a will, in order to come into an inheritance, and she asked him to participate in a marriage of convenience.

He wouldn't take time with his writing and was one of the first of the modern Americans to confuse self-advertisement with creation. Joyce, who used to drink with him, told the Canadian writer Morley Callaghan that he thought McAlmon did have talent but that it was too disorganized. His manner reeked of superiority. Sometimes he was too drunk to move from his café chair. He had cutting or dismissive words for everyone, including Joyce, the artist about whom no one else in the expatriate colony spoke badly. And yet he rather got on with Djuna. Their friendship began, like Djuna's friendship with the Baroness, with a slight against Barnes' style when McAlmon wrote a letter to *The Little Review* in which he asked why it was that the Barnes stories were at one and the same time so Russian and so Synge-Irish. He claimed that Jane Heap used to wave the letter at Barnes to keep her at bay, and that she formed the opinion that he didn't like her as a result of this. Barnes quipped that the one thing one could be sure of about *Contact* (McAlmon was the prime mover in its publication) was that no contact would come of it.

She accused him of hating her when he asked her to dance in 1922, but years later she told him that it was precisely the way he

134

stood off from her that she liked. McAlmon was both active in her behalf as a publisher and bitchy about her talent in his Paris memoirs *Being Geniuses Together*.

The friendship of Barnes and Hemingway was very much like her relationship with McAlmon: it was real enough but essentially tangential. It tends to be forgotten now that in the early Twenties Hemingway allowed himself certain gestures of artistic bohemianism. The most famous of them was probably his one-line poem:

—The Lord is my shepherd, I shall not want him for long.

One of his early stories, *Sea Change*, is one of the first expatriate descriptions of lesbianism. A man and a woman are having a parting conversation in a bar (the barman is Jimmy Charters), and the subject is mostly allusive. The bulk of the narrative clearly lies outside the frame of the sketch:

—I'm sorry, she said.
—If it was a man—
—Don't say that. It wouldn't be a man. You know that . . .

There is one incident in the life of Djuna Barnes in Paris which made a much more indisputable contribution to Hemingway's *The Sun Also Rises* than the fact that her name may have been used for the character Jake Barnes. Hemingway himself was not involved in the incident, which took place in the Hotel Jacob, but he certainly knew about it because it concerned Harold Loeb, an acquaintance whom he used as a model for Robert Cohn in *The Sun Also Rises*. The story is told in Bertram Sarason's *Hemingway and The Sun Set*, in which the part played by Miss Barnes is ascribed to an unidentified woman novelist named June. Djuna had befriended a young woman named Frances from the New York staff of *Broom* who was also staying on rue Jacob. She was to have been Loeb's secretary in Europe and shared a cabin with him and the Kreymborgs during the crossing on the S.S. *Rotterdam*.

There are two versions. One has Frances determined to trap Loeb, who was rumoured to have a lot of money, either into marriage or a compromising position. The other—given some confirmation in an interview by Sarason with Loeb—has the young woman either compromised or humiliated by Loeb on the *Rotterdam* where Loeb (he admitted to Sarason that it happened, but claimed that it was all a hoax) made love to the girl in the cabin in front of the Kreymborgs.

As Loeb had dismissed Frances from the promised position shortly after they landed in Europe, there were grounds for a real grudge. They were both, in separate rooms, at the Hotel d'Angleterre. He purportedly had given her five dollars of unpaid wages, as a result of which she was stranded in the hotel virtually penniless.

Djuna Barnes took up the case of her wronged friend and laid a plot to have Loeb caught in Frances' room. The girl would scream for help, according to the plan which Barnes is supposed to have arranged, so that they could be discovered together, whereupon Frances would declare herself pregnant and demand that Loeb marry her.

The account which follows was given to Sarason by another *Broom* staff member, who was not a friend of Loeb's. Frances evidently lured Loeb to her room, and Djuna waited for him with a raised club at the landing. But the person who appeared on the staircase and very nearly became her victim, so the story goes, was melancholy Marsden Hartley.

Loeb did recall that Frances lured him to her room twice: the first time she indeed locked the door and made a row; the second, he said, he prudently stood in the doorway and refused to enter the room, suspecting some sort of plot. This incident, whatever precisely did happen, was incorporated into *The Sun Also Rises,* where the woman is also named Frances. She relates how the novel's Robert Cohn had brought his secretary from California and abandoned her in Provincetown.

The acquaintanceship of Barnes and Hemingway was limited to those first years of the Twenties and characterized by mutually respectful light disdain. When *A Moveable Feast* appeared in 1964, she remarked to Peggy Guggenheim in an almost Hemingway tone that the lad had finally given himself away.

One must take care not to press flat what was vital and original about expatriate Paris. There were real artists and true free spirits among the poseurs, not many perhaps in all, but still a greater number than are found in many other decades. One of the editors of *Gargoyle,* Florence Gilliam, over ninety and in a state of final frailty when I met her in Paris, sparkled with the recollection of Nina Hamnett's extemporaneous café poems and gay ballads which she would sing accompanying herself on the guitar. Florence Gilliam raised herself up on a toothpick arm to recite several stanzas with gusto: — We went down to Buenos Aires/ Where all the men are fairies. Hamnett played at the Dingo and at an Italian restaurant across the street from it. She would be seen in the company of princes and counts, but when the U.S. Navy had large contingents of men on leave in Paris she would don a sailor suit and good-humouredly play the part, and do the work, of a French coquette.

xii

Djuna Barnes would sit quietly and watch and listen, mostly at Le Flore in St.-Germain-des-Prés. She and the English writer Mary Butts—the poet Edouard Roditi was the first to remark on this—were the two great expatriate solitaries, although both were capable of occasional sorties of gaiety. (Did sombre James Joyce *really* dance a jig one tipsy evening in a Paris bar?) The one great café friend of Barnes was the freest spirit of all the Paris expatriates. He was not a weary meteor like Harry Crosby or Nancy Cunard. He was a self-preserving if tortured auto-caricaturist. Barnes spent many hours listening to him, and in the end she made out of him her single greatest literary character, the eloquent, outrageous and metaphysically pathetic Dr. Matthew-Mighty-grain-of-salt-Dante-O'Connor.

We are speaking now of the legendary Dan Mahoney.

Djuna Barnes used him twice, first in *Ryder* and then in *Nightwood*, where his poetic and philosophical monologues occupy by far the greater part of the novel, though he remains essentially a minor character. Mahoney passes briefly through *Being Geniuses Together*, where he is unnamed, and also *Memoirs of Montparnasse*, where, John Glassco told me, he called him Maloney because he knew what a litigious person Mahoney was. He is first named, as —Doc Mahoney, the wittiest man in Montparnasse, in Jimmy Charters' *This Must Be the Place*.

McAlmon was indignant at the Barnes portrayal of Mahoney, which he claimed was both untrue and unfair:

> —In her *Nightwood* she has a well-known character floundering in the torments of soul-probing and fake philosophies, and he just shouldn't. The actual person doubtlessly suffered enough without having added to his character this unbelievable dipping into the deeper meanings. Drawn as a wildly ribald and often broadly funny comic, he would have emerged more impressively.

Dan Mahoney himself, however, positively revelled in the portrayal by his good friend Djuna and dined off the depiction in Paris for years

137

after. When a neighbour, a wealthy old lady with whom he had quarrelled, began to give away pointedly marked copies of *Night-wood* in order to damage his reputation, Mahoney wrote gleefully to Barnes about it and laid plans to augment her supply of copies so that the book's distribution in Paris would be improved. It was his way. Whenever an acquaintance or friend died, Mahoney could be counted upon to exclaim: —*Goody!* It was not merely that he enjoyed becoming a Barnes character. When *Nightwood* was being prepared for publication there was substantial editing being done both by Barnes herself and T. S. Eliot, her editor at Faber's, and one of the sections marked for exclusion concerned the childhood of Dr. O'Connor. Mahoney wrote to Djuna begging her not to excise that portion. I know of no other instance of such correspondence between author and character in literary history.

McAlmon's indignation wasn't pure. He himself had earlier depicted Mahoney in his 1923 short story *Miss Knight,* which appeared in the collection *Distinguished Air.* The story is about a transvestite, but John Glassco, who knew McAlmon very well in this period, confirms that the character is based upon Mahoney. The story is justly forgotten now, but McAlmon himself had a high opinion of it and hopes for it when he wrote it.

We are presented with a striking contrast in the three representations of Mahoney. McAlmon's queen (his story is set in Berlin) uses several of the stock Mahoney coarse phrases invariably recounted by anyone who ever watched him in action in the cafés. He would say things like —*I didn't know he was blind meat* about one-night stands with uncircumcised men. In *Miss Knight,* the man-woman says precisely that: —*You know I hate—well, you know—blind meat—you know what I mean.* In *Memoirs of Montparnasse* he is described as being in ecstasy over an assignation with a grave digger, the triumph of vice over death, he claimed. Many of Miss Knight's speeches, according to Glassco, were also drawn from another sexual eccentric in the Berlin-Paris nexus, a man named Barber, but the monologues are in the main very much the way that Glassco remembers that Mahoney spoke:

> —*I'm so glad I'm a real man,* she shrieked across the room or café every now and then to relieve the tension of ennui that might, and does, settle upon all atmospheres at times. Properly she believed herself appointed as a camping comedian, ready to earn a right to her presence by keeping seriousness from making dullness exist through an overlong period.
>
> If a man in uniform, a policeman, soldier, or young cadet, passed her gaze she would call out to or after him unless the uniformed man's face

was an austere one. —*Come, get your supper, dearie, now come on,* she'd comment, while jerking her head coquettishly.

—*I was talkin' to a guy—one of these here high-brows, you get me, just scientifically interested and all that, you know—and he sez to me, "did you get queer in the army?" and I sez to him, "my god Mary, I've been queer since before you wore diddies."*

The McAlmon character hates refinement most of all and always speaks in an aggressively rough American way. Dan made the American papers in 1933 when a Frenchman knocked his front teeth out in a café for demanding that France hurry up and pay her war debt to America.

There is no comparison between that McAlmon Mahoney, and the soliloquies of the first Barnes O'Connor of *Ryder:*

> ... for when I'm lost in my bowels like a little child crying against the great darkness of myself, I think of that glorious Moll, and the incense going up like birds unto the seat of all thanksgiving, and a great peace is in me and my tears are caught up in light and heat and expectation, and my feet go with me, saying Matthew O'Connor, you'll come to no bad end, for I'm a woman of a few thousand gestures and a hundred words, and they are going one by one into the ranks of the seraphim, and amid the mighty army of the church, and one by one they'll fly away into forgiveness, stock and shirt and breech, redeemed into the kingdom of heaven, and who am I that I should be damned forever and ever, Amen?

The first Dr. O'Connor is family doctor to the Ryder family, but he figures in the novel as the sympathetic masculine alternative to the spoiled and totally licentious Wendell Ryder whose sexual organ houses his mind, spirit and heart. And, of course, Dr. O'Connor of *Ryder* is only tenuously masculine; in desire and by nature he is a woman. The first Dr. O'Connor is an attendant good spirit to the women of Ryder. Masculinity has been besmirched by Ryder and is removed altogether in the alternative, O'Connor.

The second Barnes Dr. O'Connor is a far more assertive and domineering character. He has long philosophical monologues where the earlier and somewhat younger character had only short ones. He swoops into matters of myth and history, which are present in *Ryder* but are not put into the mouth of Matthew O'Connor. And yet the O'Connor of *Nightwood* speaks in a manner which is both far less poetically stylised and far more artistically powerful:

> —You are, he said, testing the wine between his lower lip and teeth, experiencing the inbreeding of pain. Most of us do not dare it. We wed

139

a stranger, and so we "solve" our problem. But when you inbreed with suffering (which is merely to say that you have caught every disease and so pardoned your flesh) you are destroyed back to your structure as an old master disappears beneath the knife of the scientist who would know how it is painted. Death I imagine will be pardoned by the same identification; we all carry about with us the house of death, the skeleton, but unlike the turtle our safety is inside, our danger out. Time is a great conference planning our end, and youth is only the past putting a leg forward.

The final O'Connor speaks in this way, out of Montaigne and Pascal in drag, and even his most bawdy turns and analogies are filled with high seriousness as in the passage in which he speaks to his penis in church:

—Kneeling in a dark corner, bending my head over and down, I spoke to Tiny O'Toole, because it was his turn, I had tried everything else. There was nothing for it this time but to make him face the mystery so it could see him clear as it saw me . . .

And there I was holding Tiny, bending over and crying, asking the question until I forgot, and went on crying, and I put Tiny away then, like a ruined bird, and went out of the place and walked looking at the stars that were twinkling, and I said,—Have I been simple like an animal, God, or have I been thinking?

The Matthew O'Connor of *Nightwood* is a great character, of Shakespearean stature and certainly one of the most memorable literary characters of our century. But, once again, he is essentially a minor character in the novel, who surges up to tower over the drama of the tragic love of Nora and Robin which is the main story. Given what we know about the way in which Barnes used the story of Felix Volkbein as a distraction from the too painful centre of her short tale, it may well be that the figure of Dr. O'Connor was strategically deployed to be a distraction as well.

There does remain, though, the question of the relationship between the literary O'Connor and the real Dan Mahoney, who, by the way, performed the abortion on Djuna. There is one further bit of slight evidence to consider, six brief letters to Djuna Barnes, written between 1935 and 1950, which have chanced to survive. They are not the true voice of the café and bar Mahoney who interests us, but they are all the same a real voice of Mahoney, Dan-the-letter-writer. He wrote to her in 1937 from his flat at 40 rue de Seine. (It had been a street full of bordellos in the not too distant past and still had more than a few in the late Thirties: Mahoney like O'Connor earned his living as an illegal abortionist.) Mahoney explained to Djuna about the old woman who is distributing the marked copies of *Nightwood* and concludes:

—Can you imagine such a slut? If she knew how much it worries me she would be surprised. I am going to try to infuriate her some more so she will go on buying books and sending them out, as she is very rich.

Love from
Minty Manure

We are prisoners of the texts we possess, always, and it may well be that Mahoney did indeed possess a manner closer to that of Dr. O'Connor than is evident in those little letters. But on the face of it the evidence suggests that it was McAlmon, not Barnes, who simply transcribed the speech of the real Mahoney, and that from an artistic point of view this was rather limited stuff.

There are strongly differing opinions about the eloquence of Dan Mahoney among surviving witnesses of the period. A close friend named O'Connor, who had come to Paris in 1923 to study piano, knew him over many years. Robert O'Connor told me that —*he had a brilliant, allusive mind; was very literate, and had an extremely witty manner of expressing his opinions about people and things.* Edouard Roditi in an interview in *Antaeus* remembers a Mahoney even larger than the O'Connor of *Nightwood:* —He was a remarkable man—it's a great pity that the tape-recorder was invented too late. Djuna Barnes did the best she could, and it's brilliant, what she did, but there was more gab, more blarney to him than even appears in *Nightwood.* But John Glassco told me matter-of-factly —*He was the sort of fellow who was very interesting to talk to for about five minutes, and then he was a bit of a bore.*

Mahoney was from San Francisco and belonged to a rather large Catholic family. His father was a rough Irish sort and had little patience for this particular son. Dan attended St. Ignatius School in San Francisco. One of the twelve surviving 1914 classmates of Mahoney, U.S. Vice-Admiral William M. Callaghan, told me that it was his impression because of Dan's much greater sophistication and his extremely dark afternoon beard shadow that Mahoney must have been several years older than all his classmates. He was born circa 1895 and was thus more or less a contemporary of Barnes.

Mahoney was an unusual character even at school. He had a feminine voice, no inclination whatsoever to engage in athletics, and he used a woman's compact to powder away the five o'clock beard growth that spread across his young but already pronounced jowls. There was a counter to these oddities in that his language was ex-

141

tremely earthy and ribald, not at all the way in which a "fairy" was supposed to speak. As a result of this, along with his ability to play the piano very well by ear, he was accepted by his classmates. But there had to be difficulties, too, even in comparatively sophisticated San Francisco at that time. Mahoney kept up an acquaintance with one classmate, Vincent Hallinan, who became a prominent Bay Area attorney. He was especially fond of Hallinan's wife, Vivian (years later he was their guide when the Hallinans visited Paris), who alludes to him in her 1952 memoirs *My Wild Irish Rogues* without mentioning him by name. Admiral Callaghan recalls that Mahoney in this youth never once indicated that his eccentricity extended to the practice of homosexuality. He always got along with women, with some women, anyway, and it would be his pattern to pass from a male friendship to a much closer friendship with the man's wife. A Paris friend named Gabriel Javsicas told me how Mahoney and Javsicas' wife, Erma, would have long discussions about how men in general, and he in particular, were no good. He would always say — *us girls.*

Jimmy Charters has Mahoney living for a time with an American couple named Woods and accompanying Mrs. Woods to the cafés when her husband went back to America. —*We are the Widows Woods,* he would introduce himself and her. Jimmy, however, swallowed one of the doctor's tallest tales—that he had been married and was in fact a widower. Another frequent woman companion was the abandoned wife of a *New York Times* correspondent. Roditi recalls that Mahoney was quite friendly with a weird old painter named Lilian Fisk, and that he sometimes would go on night expeditions in the streets of Paris with her. In private he much enjoyed participation in the bridge circles of elderly ladies, some of them titled and some of them lesbian. He is said to have played abysmally poorly.

When Mahoney was more or less forcibly repatriated in August 1941, according to Roditi, he was quite furious at having to be back in the United States. He returned to San Francisco where he frequented the Black Cat, a rough café with cheap and sometimes awful drinks. Its slogan was: We Reserve the Right to Serve Refuse to Anyone. Saroyan would hang around there and sometimes Steinbeck would drop in. It was the place on the West Coast which was thought to have something closest to the flavour of Paris, primarily because it was totally lacking in self-consciousness, except on Saturday nights when the social set from Nob Hill would go slumming there to watch the lewd scenes which regulars sometimes enacted especially to shock them. But it wasn't Paris. Mahoney returned to

Paris and died, of cancer, in a small home on the rue de Cels given to him for his use by one of his ladies.

In public he was rarely seen without a retinue of lesbian ladies with whom he was extremely popular. He had fluttering hands and was much given to light body contact.

Mahoney is said to have spoken French and German fluently and to have been extremely well-versed in literature. But he was not a writer and was in print only once, an essay titled *Perfumes* which appeared in *The Ignatian* (vol. 6, no. 3). It is a brief history and passionate defense of perfume. For the young and intensely individualistic Mahoney perfume represented the sole art wholly free of control by critical arbiters: —In art our taste is probably conventional; in music also. We like what we are told to like. Literary critics tell us just what we should approve, what not; but in our selection of perfumes it is very different. After St. Ignatius he is supposed to have entered Stanford University to study medicine. There is no record of him there, and so we must incline towards the Barnes version of O'Connor in *Nightwood*, that he was an unqualified practitioner in Paris.

We are on the slipperiest slide of reality when speaking of Daniel A. Mahoney. He is said both to have been always short of money and also to have had an independent income and to have performed his abortions without fee. I tend to believe the former story because Robert O'Connor said that during one period of his life Mahoney lived in a servant's room at the top of a Left Bank apartment house, and there is Dr. O'Connor surreptitiously filching money left on a dresser top while treating Robin Vote in *Nightwood*. No one ever questioned his story that he practised in a French hospital.

Here is a story Dan Mahoney told about himself. He had befriended a French farmer and his wife whose land was mortgaged to the chimney. The woman had complained to him about how cold she was during winters because she didn't even have a warm coat. On a visit back to his mother's house in San Francisco (the return trip to the United States is in McAlmon's *Miss Knight* but not in the Barnes versions) he noticed an old and ugly grey fur coat which he packed up and sent off to the farmer's wife. Sometime later his sister fell to wondering whatever had happened to their mother's chinchilla. He said nothing, but upon his return to France he got the coat back from the woman and took it to a furrier, who gave him a "vast fortune" for it with which he paid off the farmer's mortgage. In all of his accounts to people in Paris about his San Francisco past, he comes from a very wealthy family. Yet it is certain that Dan Mahoney was extremely generous in spirit, because compassion is the cardinal vir-

143

tue of Matthew O'Connor, and it is his enormous generosity of spirit that makes Matthew O'Connor a tragic figure rather than a bawdy turn in a Weimar music hall.

There are many stories about Dan Mahoney. He was interned in France during the Second World War at Chantilly, where he apparently lived very comfortably. One story has it that that was because of his friendship with a Nazi officer, while another has it that Mahoney spent all his time teaching English to a group of Chasidim who assured him that as a teacher he would find pardon in the eyes of the Lord even though he worshipped a wrong god in the wrong religion and had other problems as well. However that may have been, he was shipped back to America sputtering at the circumstances of his forced return. He stayed for just a short while in Los Angeles and San Francisco and visited his friend O'Connor on Nantucket before returning to Paris. While in California he wrote to Barnes about how he was being bothered by two Negro boys whom he had befriended and helped in the detention camp and who had followed him to California. —*They are angels, but I am sure they think I'm their father! God help us.*

Mahoney had himself decorated in the First World War. There is no record that he served in the armed services, but his finest story comes from his alleged war duty. He used to say that he was so profoundly shocked when he first discovered that he was homosexual that he enlisted in the army as a relatively subtle way of doing away with himself. He survived anyway, and to make matters worse, he claimed that as an army medic he was given the job of circumcising nearly five hundred soldiers. But we should remember that Dr. O'Connor tells Nora that he is the greatest liar this side of the moon in order to distract —people like you, to take the mortal agony out of their guts, and to stop them from rolling about, and drawing up their feet, and screaming, with their eyes staring over their knuckles with misery which they are trying to keep off, saying, Say something, doctor, for the love of God! And me talking away like mad. Well that, and nothing else, has made me the liar I am.

The best and fullest description of Dan Mahoney is by John Glassco from his old Paris notes made in 1929, and it is in exact concord with the drawing of Dr. O'Connor done by Djuna Barnes for *Ryder:*

> —Height about 5′6″; short legs, broad shoulders, heavy build. Square face, ace-of-clubs nose, thin and very mobile lips always darkly lipsticked, massive jowls. Wore a small toothbrush moustache about ¼″ long, and had stiff wiry hair cut *en brosse,* both obviously dyed jet black though iron-grey at the roots. Eyes large, grey and protruding,

144

heavy-lidded and artificially blued, eyelashes coated with mascara; his glance was always moving restlessly. His face was covered with dead-white face powder through which a strong black beard showed. He always wore a white shirt with starched collar and cuffs, black four-in-hand tie and black suit, without waistcoat, that seemed too large for him, its trousers too roomy in the seat and the jacket too long so that it gave the effect of a skirt. Small black pointed shoes; ugly, hairy hands. His gait was a kind of hip-swaying waddle; he always stood with his knees slightly bent and his arms held out in front of him, the wrists falling outward and down, like a dog walking on its hind legs (both Djuna Barnes and I made this comparison independently: the likeness was irresistibly suggested). He was a beautiful dancer, and very light on his feet. His voice was a light tenor, his accent a straight New York nasal twang, with "fairy" intonations and an artificial lisp. He was rumoured to have been a professional boxer, and was in fact a redoubtable bar-room fighter: I actually saw him break the wrist of a young American who had been gibing him in the Dingo bar on the rue Delambre. He was regarded as dangerous for his terrible temper.

It seems clear then that the figure of O'Connor is indeed Mahoney, but the *words* and *tone* and *substance* of what O'Connor says belong solely to Barnes: seeds of his discourse can be found in all the best early Barnes short stories and plays written long before she knew him. He was, in his own simple but eloquent favourite description of himself, —poor Minnie Mahoney, the girl whom God forgot.

xiii

The opinion of *Nightwood* that has had the greatest currency apart from Eliot's is Joseph Frank's, which appeared first in *The Sewanee Review* in 1945 and was subsequently included in his influential book *The Widening Gyre*. The thesis of *The Widening Gyre* centres on the concept of a spatial rather than simple and sequential narrative as something held in common by the great works of modernity. It is a considerable virtue of Frank's work that it so easily and naturally places Barnes beside the accepted masters of modernism, Eliot, Joyce and Proust. According to Frank, *Nightwood* has been constructed on the same structural principle as *Ulysses* and *À la recherche du temps perdu*. That juxtaposition and context are worth much even if many of the statements with which Frank buttresses his thesis are questionable. Frank writes of the novel that — the naturalistic principle is totally abandoned: no attempt is made to convince us that the characters are actual flesh-and-blood human

145

beings. Another critic, James Scott, to take the opposite view (and the one which is obviously closer to my views and evidence), stresses that in spite of her constant manipulations of form and style Miss Barnes has a —consistently naturalistic vision. Nor will it do for the cause of theory-mongering to proclaim that the kaleidoscopic style of *Ryder* is insubstantial and anomalous, and that the new spatial concept only crystallizes into a definitive and comprehensible pattern in *Nightwood*.

Djuna Barnes has consistently inclined towards the framed scene rather than the flowing story in her writing. There is also her own word, from a letter to Charles Henri Ford (April 10, 1934), that she always found it extremely difficult to think up plots. There is both as much and as little plot in *Nightwood* as in any other Barnes work from as far back as her 1919 *Passion Play*. The notions of the "spatial narrative" and the "archictectonic novel" (a phrase used by another Barnes critic) have a certain use but should not be carried too far.

The most important and key sentence in the Frank discussion presents us with an image rather than a theoretical proposition, and the image speaks very well indeed to the formal reality of *Nightwood:*

> —The eight chapters of Nightwood are like searchlights, probing the darkness each from a different direction, yet ultimately focusing on and illuminating the same entanglement of the human spirit.

That sentence is true beyond question, for, as Frank and others have indicated, the initial chapters introduce us one after another to the major characters: Felix Volkbein, the foolish Jew who extinguishes himself by bowing before all signs of purported nobility; Robin Vote, the animal-beauty who is outside language and is attended by every other character in the novel; Nora Flood, who is the heroine and the victim of the tale; Jenny Petherbridge, a spiritual capitalist who collects people and plaster madonnas; and Dr. O'Connor, who talks a lot. By the midway point of the novel Dr. O'Connor and Nora virtually take over the narrative, and her plaints and his long responses simply curl back over and over upon the one time that is the story. The plot does not move forward, it merely is, like the portraits of the individual characters, or a scene set in a paperweight.

It is, however, a fundamental error to claim as Joseph Frank does that *Nightwood* lacks a narrative structure in the ordinary sense and cannot be reduced to any sequence of action for purposes of explanation. Whatever "in the ordinary sense" may mean, there is a simple and main story in *Nightwood,* and it is, moreover, a story which re-

146

peats rather closely a series of events which really did occur. That story is the profound and impossible love of a woman who contemplates and understands for a woman who rages and destroys. This plot may, granted, be slightly difficult to specify at the very first encounter, primarily because of the narrative lines that are tossed out and then not followed through. There is, too, the very great problem of perspective because Dr. O'Connor is both of and not of the main story. Dr. O'Connor is an entire Greek chorus put into a single character, and that character, moreover, stands very near to the reader so that his apparent dimensions are much enlarged. Once that is seen, once the painterly trick of perspective is grasped, whereby the main story is moved upstage where it must appear somewhat reduced, then *Nightwood* has a plot. Its fire is no less intense because it has been set at a slight distance. The heat may be less, but the light which is shed on a whole range of matters beyond the particular lesbian love affair is considerably greater.

xiv

Thelma Wood claimed American Indian blood, which was a reasonably common affectation among the Midwestern expatriates. In fact, one of the Paris bars, The College Inn, actually employed a full-blooded Indian barman. In the generation before, Americans such as Whistler or Henry Harland, the editor of *The Yellow Book,* had tended to invent mysterious St. Petersburg births for themselves.

When Thelma Wood was dying of cancer in December 1970, Berenice Abbott visited her in Connecticut and was struck by what seemed to her a severe Indian visage and mien. Miss Wood was nearly seventy and had grown quite massive, things which, Djuna wrote to a friend, she had been quite convinced would never happen to her.

Thelma was born in St. Louis, Missouri, in 1901. Her mother's maiden name was Crawford. She was said to have a twenty-five-dollar-a-week living allowance in Paris, and so from that and the red Bugatti one may assume that the family was well off. She had a sister named Wilma. She said that she was a graduate of Washington University in St. Louis, but they have no record of her. Very likely she attended but dropped out before the first year was over to go to Paris.

She was six feet tall, tomboyish, and extremely striking. There is a problem with memoir descriptions of the American ladies—they are all just too beautiful, and in the end the phrase loses currency. But even within this context there seems little doubt that Thelma was indeed a beauty.

We are fortunate once again to have John Glassco's *Memoirs of Montparnasse* as a mirror to hold up against the realistic backdrop to *Nightwood*. He calls Thelma "Emily Pine" (which is a most curious coincidence) and describes her as —a tall, beautiful, dazed-looking girl . . . who had the largest pair of feet I had ever seen. I heard later that Emily Pine was a fatal woman, at least as far as Willa Torance was concerned, and was also a kind of female *bourreau de coeurs*. The twenty-two-year-old Glassco plays a trick and has her called away from her protective lady friends at a café for a false telephone call, but the young man is nearly put off his conquest when the splendid young woman comes out to him and laughs at what he has done in an alarmingly deep bray.

She downed her Pernod —in a single awesome gulp, and they set out together along the boulevard du Montparnasse. They went into a working-class bar. She said that she liked him because he had a gamin quality, and he saw immediately that she was merely repeating in childlike fashion something that was said of her. He, wondering precisely how he was going to go about getting her into bed, told her that she reminded him of a leopard:

> —Why? she asked, her eyes lighting up for the first time.
> —Because you are independent, luxurious, and quiet.
> Her response to this opening gambit was surprising. Her lids came down over her eyes, then all at once she gripped my hand and ground the knuckles viciously together; her strength was remarkable and I felt such pain that I impulsively raised my heel and drove it back against her shin. Showing her teeth, she dropped my hand and began to laugh. Did I hurt you?

They eventually went off to the Petite Chaumière, which was one of the more expensive camp bars cum dance hall. She drove him there in her usual manner in the dangerous-looking Bugatti. One of her friends told me that Thelma drove to racing standard but only when she was drunk. Glassco found her a very bad dancer. He concentrated on the magnificence of her body and avoiding her giant feet. He asked her bluntly to come to bed with him and added, —Sorry, I hope I'm not frightening you, to which she replied, —Frighten me? No one frightens Thelma Wood. She went off to speak with Madame Maillot, and in a few moments they were upstairs in a stifling little room of mirrors, red plush and tassels. Thelma was staggering with drunkenness and holding on to Glassco. He absented himself from the room decorously and then:

148

> —When I came to her a few minutes later she had taken off her clothes
> and was lying on the bed with her eyes tightly closed. I had never seen
> a more beautiful body; to find it was quite frigid was a great disap-
> pointment.

The mundane reality of the actual beautiful woman—and John
Glassco is far more reliable as a portraitist than Robert McAlmon
was—has only tenuous connection with the literary character
created by Barnes.

The Robin Vote of *Nightwood* is not presented to us in her sexuality. There are oblique references to lovemaking and passionate embraces between Robin and Nora. Yet there is no lovemaking scene in
the novel. Rather she is presented in her bestiality. *Nightwood* is, essentially, about the struggle between the forces of love and bestiality,
and the sexual evidences of that struggle among the main characters
are not that important. The promiscuity of Robin is something that
Nora knows all too well, but it is something that happens away from
her except on the chance occasions when she discovers Robin drunk
and allowing herself to be mauled over in a café. Nora often skulks
about on the outside or to the side of the cafés where Robin is cruis-
ing among the clientele.

Robin Vote's animality is both ferocious and domestic. She will not
be controlled in any way, but at the same time she feels an intense
need to be kept and sheltered like a wild pet. It's Nora who is closest
to the narrator's voice, and the narrator keeps Robin Vote at a slight
distance through emphasis upon pattern:

> —In the years that they lived together the departures of Robin became
> a slowly increasing rhythm. At first Nora went with Robin; but as time
> passed, realizing that a growing tension was in Robin, unable to endure
> the knowledge that she was in the way or forgotten; seeing Robin go
> from table to table, from drink to drink, from person to person, realiz-
> ing that if she herself were not there Robin might return to her as the
> one who, out of all the turbulent night, had not been lived through—
> Nora stayed at home, lying awake or sleeping. Robin's absence, as the
> night drew on, became a physical removal, insupportable and irrepara-
> ble. As an amputated hand cannot be disowned, because it is ex-
> periencing a futurity, of which the victim is its forbear, so Robin was
> an amputation that Nora could not renounce.

That is another way of saying that Robin Vote has meaning for Nora
beyond her person, and one of those meanings is as an aspect of
Nora's personality that both is and is no longer. In other words, the
"futurity" of Robin is also very much the past in disguise.

XV

In the novel Robin and Nora meet by chance at the circus. There is a striking foreshadowing of this meeting in *Nightwood* in one of Djuna Barnes' early pieces of journalism, her description of the New York Hippodrome Circus in *The New York Press* (February 14, 1915). At the end of the circus she hangs behind to confront the animals alone:

> —I went down afterward into the depths where the animals are kept and, slipping up to the cages of these animals at last privately—no longer before the public, no longer in the limelight or the footlight—I stepped up, paused without, looked around for any trainer that might be present, for any keeper, for any intruder, and, finding myself quite alone with nothing but my iniquitous past, I slowly and softly raised my hand—in salute!

The only difference in the episode in the novel is that it is an animal, a lion, who recognizes and silently salutes Robin.

In *Nightwood* the startling feature of Nora's home is the pair of circus roundabout horses in the bedroom, which Nora and Robin have fossicked up in the flea markets of Paris. They flank either side of the large bed. I found no carousel horses in the inventory for the flat which Barnes owned at 9 rue St.-Romain (fifth floor, stairway D—the building still stands, "next door to Proust"), though I felt and expected that they should have been there. It should be noted that Barnes spent a number of years with Thelma Wood in a flat at 173 boulevard St.-Germain before she purchased the lease to the rue St.-Romain place. Certain features of the St.-Germain home, particularly the garden, are also amalgamated into the *Nightwood* description.

Horses are important. Natalie Barney first became famous for her horseback riding in the Bois de Boulogne, which drew the attention of Remy de Gourmont and made her *l'Amazone;* and Barnes, who was an accomplished equestrienne from her Cornwall-on-Hudson and Long Island farm days, evokes the horse in her most powerful and famous short story, *A Night Among the Horses* (1923), in which a stableman is trampled by his own horses to which he has fled in drink and full evening dress to escape from the mistress of the house who has been toying with him.

It was Colette who so astutely saw the importance of the horses among these women:

150

—These mannish women I am calling to mind were, indeed, almost as fond of the horse, that warm, enigmatic, stubborn, and sensitive creature, as they were of their young protégées. With their strong slender hands they were able to break in and subjugate a horse, and when age and hard times deprived them of the whip and the hunting crop, they lost their final sceptre. . . . The exciting scent of horses, that so masculine odour, never quite left these women, but lingered on after the ride.

But if there are no horses, many of the other effects correspond very well to the domestic nest of *Nightwood*. The house, Nora comes to feel, is essential to their love and, if anything is so much as disarranged in it, Robin might become confused, lose scent like an animal, and not return.

Such things as the Venetian chandeliers, cherubim from Vienna, and ecclesiastical hangings from Rome in *Nightwood* are actually exceeded in the inventory of rue St.-Romain. The inventory is a veritable museum of a relationship, its exhibits clearly the result of countless forays through the old Les Halles market and its environs. There were many mirrors in the flat, which tended to be primarily red, yellow and gold in its decor owing to the large number of liturgical ornaments. The salon was scattered with ecclesiastical pillows. The curtains were silk and cotton, yellow with red blossoms. On the walls were two heart-shaped mirrors and a glass cross. There were two grape and pear glass chandeliers and four matching glass side lights on the walls. The dining-room chairs that went with the provincial oak table had tapestry seats. The large couch in the room had a yellow throwover cover. In the hallway leading to the salon there was another large mirror, a small brown wooden bookstand guarded by two red and gold chairs, and a red and yellow glass chandelier with one broken red lily. There were three gold-framed epinals: Saint Claude, Saint John, and Gargantua.

I imagine that the effect, warm and close, must have been something like that of a bohemian chapel. The bedroom's colours, on the large double bed which dominated the room and the two satin bedroom chairs, were pink and blue, but the churchly element was even stronger in this room where there were in excess of sixty pictures, largely liturgical in theme, and a church runner which was draped over an unused fireplace mantle. A Venetian mirror, the largest one in the flat, was hanging there, and further reflections were picked up by the three-panelled mirror on the dressing table as well as by another, smaller Venetian mirror. There was a picture painted on glass of St. Stephanos and a china Virgin. The bedroom, too, had its slightly chipped glass chandelier.

151

The inventory of the kitchen implements proves that cooking was a serious activity in the Barnes–Wood household. The cooking was predominantly American rather than Continental. There is one extant menu, thanks to a genially indignant letter reproaching Allen Ross MacDougall for his frightful impudence in forgetting an invitation to dinner which Djuna and Thelma made to him while they were at the funeral of the Baroness in 1928. The dinner he missed was a large flank of venison and cherry pie. They ground their own coffee. In a letter that she wrote to Djuna after they parted, Thelma tells her that she wishes she could cook them a chicken, sit in front of the fire with her, and then play cards as they used to do.

There was a cat of orange hue, and its name was Dilly. The name was taken from dilli-darling, a term of endearment for the youngest child in a family (and also, affectionately, for a wanton) that goes back to the sixteenth and early seventeenth centuries. Djuna likely learned the term from the Urquhart version of Rabelais, or it is the sort of word which she might have learned from her grandmother. Dilly's trick was to know when the lift was coming before anyone else did and go and wait in the hallway. Dilly was to be the last animal of Djuna Barnes. After the household was broken up and Djuna began to travel (to Munich, Vienna, Budapest, Tangiers and England), Dilly was left with Mina Loy, who lived on the second floor of that apartment building; when Djuna went to New York, Dilly passed to Thelma. After the death of Dilly, Barnes wrote to Loy, who was still in Paris, that she had at last passed over into being a completely savage, old-maidish sort of person who could not even endure having an animal stare at her.

The real child of the rue St.-Romain household was a doll. That, too, is in *Nightwood*. When Nora goes to see Robin's new lover, Jenny Petherbridge, she knows that she has found the right person and place because she sees a doll propped on a pillow. Robin had given her a similar doll. Nora tells Dr. O'Connor:

> —We give death to a child when we give it a doll—it's the effigy and the shroud; when a woman gives it to a woman, it is the life they cannot have, it is their child, sacred and profane; so when I saw that other doll—Nora could not go on. She began to cry. —What part of monstrosity am I that I am always crying at its side!

Nora tells the doctor about how Robin would sometimes sit at home all day playing with toys and animals and windup cars but actually keeping an Argus-watch on her to make sure that she got no mail, received no visitors, and was totally in her control. Robin's destruction of the doll accompanies the end of the romance:

> —Sometimes, if she got tight by evening, I would find her standing in the middle of the room, in boy's clothes, rocking from foot to foot, holding the doll she had given us—"our child"—high above her head, as if she would cast it down, a look of fury on her face. And one time, about three in the morning when she came in, she was angry because for once I had not been there all the time, waiting. She picked up the doll and hurled it to the floor and put her foot on it, crushing her heel into it: and then, as I came crying behind her, she kicked it, its china head all in dust, its skirt shivering and stiff, whirling over and over across the floor, its blue bow now over now under.

The time of all this is given funereally in *Nightwood* as the year of Our Lord nineteen hundred and twenty-seven, which is confirmed by the Barnes correspondence for the period. In August 1928, Barnes writes to McAlmon saying that she is pleased that things are going well for him because life is hell for her. In her correspondence with Emily Coleman, Djuna speaks of but does not elaborate on Thelma's desire to kill her.

Mina Loy was throughout these terrible years a very important friend for Djuna. She was easily accepted for her bright and warm personality and her total lack of felt judgment over the oddities of Barnes' or any of her other female friends' lives.

It was perhaps natural that Barnes, herself basically heterosexual (a judgment, by the way, made of Nora by Dr. O'Connor), should have been closer to Mina Loy than to any other of the expatriate women, certainly closer than to Natalie Barney, who it seems never even visited 9 rue St.-Romain. Although the role of comforter in *Nightwood* is given to Dr. O'Connor (he is also burdened with guilt because it was he who introduced Robin Vote to Jenny Petherbridge), it seems likely that that part in Djuna's life was played by her neighbour, Mina. For several years they saw each other virtually every day.

Loy, who had a fine-boned Jewish face and hated her Jewish blood, was an entrant in the expatriate beauty stakes together with both of her daughters. In *Shakespeare & Company*, Sylvia Beach writes:

> —We had three raving beauties in "the Crowd," all in one family, which was not fair. Mina Loy, the poetess, and her daughters Joella and Faby (but that is the wrong spelling of it, no doubt), were so lovely that

they were stared at wherever they went, and were used to it. But I believe if a vote had been taken, Mina would have been elected the most beautiful of the three.

Djuna took a warm interest in the children. There were nasty innuendos and expressions of mock-concern cast about in certain quarters for the safety of the girls, particularly Joella. It was absurd, and Mina Loy, whose only concern was that Joella not marry one of the homosexuals who seemed ubiquitous among the expatriate men, took no notice at all. A far nastier specific incident was the formation, deep in their cups, of a committee to protect young Gwen LeGallienne, who was a talented sculptor and Richard LeGallienne's stepdaughter, from the purported interest of Barnes. The "chairman" of this "committee" was Ford Madox Ford, a gifted artist but a weak and sloppy human being who ought to have known better, in several ways.

Mina Loy was a poet (her major book of poems was published by McAlmon with the misspelled title—McAlmon's fault, not Loy's—*Lunar Baedecker*), but mainly she happily pottered on the periphery of art and earned her living making wraparound-collage lampshades. They were quite fashionable for a time, and Peggy Guggenheim backed her in opening a little shop where they were sold. The Loy flat was full of lampshades and one had to thread one's way in past stacks of them. Both Barnes and Loy loved the building, though Miss Barnes felt oppressed by an old devil on the sixth floor who would cause a tremendous fuss whenever anyone spoke above a whisper.

From the fifth floor the Barnes flat looked down upon a pathetic drama: two old ladies occupied a little house in the courtyard where the new wing was to be built—the house had been purchased by the developer, but the tenants refused to budge. Workmen were sent to remove the roof of the little house "for repair," and of course they did not replace it, leaving the old women bravely trying to cope with the elements in an open doll's house. They were driven away. Decades later, Natalie Barney faced a similar strong eviction threat when the rue Jacob house in which she had lived and held her salons for over sixty years, but which she had never bothered to purchase, was acquired by a cabinet minister. Eviction papers were served on her in August, the one month of the year in which such matters are by tradition not to be initiated in Paris because everyone is away. The lovely house and garden that Djuna and Thelma had tended for Natalie during the summer of 1927 was lost. Natalie died in 1972, aged ninety-six.

When she was back in New York in the summer of 1930, Djuna

Barnes looked to rue St.-Romain with great affection and even greater pain at the thought of the mess she had made of her life. She saw, too, the probability that she would not be able to return. She remembered how a minor fire in the building had caused a general alarm but she had stayed put and declaimed her work to Mina while the fire was being brought under control. There had been many jolly times there, together with the torture. That was the past. Now, several loved antique pieces, including a fine old colour cabinet, were already being endangered by worm and rot. So reluctantly she gave the instruction to have the lease and the contents sold, though she knew well that in once-again-expensive New York the proceeds of the sale would scarcely sustain her for a year.

xvi

Between them Thelma, now child, now man, was Simon. Robin Vote has a pet name in *Nightwood,* but it is not given. Dr. O'Connor, however, knows it and tells Nora to think of —*Robin with nothing but a pet name—your pet name to sustain her; for pet names are a guard against loss, like primitive music.* It is easy enough to hear the confluence of the names Robin and Simon. It is an even more reasonable supposition to see the shadow of Ibsen and of Joyce's wife behind the name Nora. Djuna's secret name was Irene.

When her papers were being prepared for archival sale, Miss Barnes wrote to a friend telling her that she herself, reading over the correspondence, had forgotten quite how horrible the romance with Thelma was. She wondered what people would think of it all someday.

How many facts does a life story require? What is a fact, and what is a life story? There is an answer to this question given in *Nightwood* —The more facts we have about a person the less we know.

A letter from Simon, undated but obviously written very shortly after the first and major (but not the last) 1927 parting, still clutches at the hope that the relationship will continue, and she seems prepared to try to change somewhat the false fantasy terms of their previous life together. It was Colette who had wisely observed that two women may live together happily for a long time, provided only that one of them does not yield to the temptation to play the man. But there is no sign that the role would be abandoned by Thelma. Simon was not a peaceful lady of Llangollen. She wrote:

—I keep saying—Simon, you've got to be a man and take your medicine—but then always in my head goes—There is no Simon and no
Irine and I can't bear it and go crazy . . .

I feel so shy at saying any thing for fear it sounds like excusing which
God knows I don't—but I've thought over it all and I think if I didn't
drink maybe things wouldn't have happened—as that is usely when I
get involved—

Now Simon will not touch one drop till you come to America and I'll
have my exhibition done—and I'll try and be financially independent—and then maybe if you still care—and look him over—and he
again looks sweet to you. Perhaps we could try it a new way—perhaps
that too would make things better—and if you will I will never again as
long as you love me take one small drop of anything stronger than tea.

If this sounds like bunk to you precious—drop me a little note and
say no use. But if there is any slight chance for Simon if he bucks up let
him know that too—I tell you angel darling the only reason your Simon
doesn't drop off that boat is because I've made you sufficiently unhappy as it is—

. . . You must know I suffer doubly because it's my fault—so if you
think you could give Simon first chance it would be a great help—and
if thats possible then don't listen to things against him and try forget
the rest—I don't ask my sweet for you to commit yourself in the least or
make promises or anything—But on the other hand I'd like sort of definite—go to hell—

And if you . . .

That, surely, is all that we need to know about the love between
Barnes and Wood, except that it was a very intense and totally fore-
doomed love. In *Nightwood*, Nora calls it the greatest love of her life.
What is important is that we see the connection between the love
and the crystallized and highly stylized relationship of the novel. The
one came out of the other, but, like the portrayal of Dr. O'Connor,
the texts which we possess prove that the real and the fictional romance have a substantial distance in tone and character.

xvii

Djuna spent a great deal of energy trying to get Thelma to stop
drinking. In the end, drinking became a very serious problem for
Barnes herself. She did not drink to unwind but to take refuge. For
long stretches of time Thelma would come home merely to sleep off a
hangover. One good friend (it was "Jenny Petherbridge") told me
that there had been various sorts of difficulties in Thelma Wood's
immediate family. Though she was from the Midwest and clearly

shows herself to be only narrowly in control of language in her letters, it was said that she spoke with a refined American accent, a result perhaps of the fact that she tended to mix with the English crowd. Dazzle, warmth and generosity are the words which were used to describe her to me by various people who knew her, but in a conversation which I had with Janet Flanner not too long before her death, she described Thelma as —*the bitch of all time*. Another expatriate artist, Hilaire Hiler, was said to have fallen fatally in love with her. Barnes describes Robin Vote in *Nightwood* as though she were an ancient or primeval being. She is —the infected carrier of the past, newly ancient, and Nora's face, a lovely touch of secret irony like the title itself, is—that wood in the work, the tree coming forward in her, an undocumented record of time.

There was certainly something demonic and desperate in both Thelma's own wildness and her draconian control of her lover. We see her in the Guggenheim memoirs, *Out of This Century*, down on her knees making a public and immodest proposal to Peggy Guggenheim. Miss Barnes, on the other hand, complained to a friend how Thelma would go into jealous rages and withhold her affection if she so much as saw Peggy's then-husband Laurence Vail (they are Sally and Terrence Marr in the Glassco book). Vail and Barnes had been lovers a very long time ago but he had been to bed with almost everybody in their circle. Barnes vacationed with him in 1925 when she had migrated to Cagnes for the winter with a large group of American painters and writers. They were now simply friends, Peggy, Laurence and Djuna, but Thelma would not tolerate it. After the romance with Thelma was over, Barnes would see Vail again often in the 1930s. She saw him again for the last time in 1938, when she made a brief visit to Mégève, where Vail was living with Kay Boyle. In 1938, Barnes was exhausted by the decade that had produced *Nightwood*. The poet David Gascoyne who was in Mégève, too, remembers her reclining on a divan hard up against central heating pipes and murmuring —*Now whatever is it that makes people want to go climbing mountains? However do you manage if you want to relieve yourself while climbing a mountain?* She complained that she had the worst room in the house, over the kitchen and seven wailing puppies. During this period she developed a strong dislike for Kay Boyle who, she decided, had an affectionate nature just to get by but was really as hard as flint inside.

Laurence Vail is an important figure in the life of Djuna Barnes for only one reason: a French book. He was an enthusiast and translator of the French writer Charles-Louis Philippe (1874–1909). Philippe's reputation has held remarkably well over the years in France, but it has somehow never travelled abroad. Vail translated one of Philippe's best works, *Bubu de Montparnasse* (1901), a novel about a Paris streetwalker. By her own statement, Djuna Barnes could never manage more than two or three words in French, even though *Nightwood* is liberally salted with French. There can be no doubt whatsoever that Barnes read Philippe's novel in Vail's translation, which appeared in 1931. It was very well known among the literary expatriates. Eliot considered it a most important modern French novel and wrote an introduction to its English translation. There also can be no doubt that the manner of Philippe exercised a strong vectoral force on that of Barnes and, in combination with her own manificent antiquarian language, constitutes an essential stylistic component of *Nightwood:*

> —She was walking bare-headed with her hands in the pockets of her smock, which was taut against her belly, and she dragged her feet childishly. From the days of her childhood, when she used to filch 100 sous from her boss, there had come a day in a cheaply furnished hotel room when she had let her virginity go in the hands of a pimp, and then later the natural inclination of her body and her way of thinking brought her closer to the career which eventually she freely chose. She lived with a sense of assurance and a spontaneity, she was attractive and knew the right things to say—she became a streetwalker as M. de Musset became a poet, and at an equally young age. Syphilitic by vocation, without casting a glance backwards that might have given her some regret, her head was crawling with lice without any desire to be free of them, and her skirts wrapped her in a smell of vice and filth, which drew the men to her. She was living joyously and without any conscience . . . She was her own mistress, her own government . . .

Barnes had been depicting characters in somewhat this manner for fifteen years. It was a fortunate coincidence. Both writers have a tendency to use casual and yet strange metaphors and majestic turns of phrase. Certainly in no other modern writer will one find "Barnesian women" to the extent that one may meet them in the works of Charles-Louis Philippe. Barnes is the stronger writer of the two and puts the few borrowed strategies of Philippe to uses of greatness in *Nightwood.*

The main shared characteristic of the two writers is the ability to distance, so that subjects of deep pain and emotion are rendered with a hard-edged yet comic beauty that produces a very strange effect. It is like a fish shop or butcher's window arranged by a Huysmans or a Wilde.

There are, for all the enormous differences of time, sex and culture, certain similarities of personality between the two figures as well. Both chose solitude. And certainly Philippe's famous declaration, —I should have been quite unhappy if I had achieved happiness, might easily have been said by Djuna Barnes or any number of her characters.

xviii

One important part of Thelma Wood's life is left entirely out of the character of Robin Vote in *Nightwood*. Thelma Wood was an artist. She began as a sculptor, but the only piece of which we know is the fine kneeling woman with huge feet which appeared in *Gargoyle* in 1921. Feet figure as an occasional motif in *Nightwood*. In life, they were even rather fashionable in the Twenties because Greta Garbo had noticeably large feet, which was also widely noted about Thelma. She changed to silverpoint as a medium at the instigation, according to "Jenny Petherbridge," of Barnes, and she spent the rest of her artistic career in silverpoint. Her work was at a high professional level and did find buyers, though none of her shows was ever a major success, and she did not draw too much critical notice. Silverpoint is extremely demanding in that no line can be erased, and so every stroke must be placed exactly as it is wanted the first time. A single serious slip of the hand can destroy days of work. It is not the sort of thing wild Robin Vote could have done.

The theme of Thelma Wood's art was almost exclusively —very tortuous but exquisitely imaginative plant and animal themes (*The Arts*, 1930, Vol. 16, pp. 493–94). The pathology of her sexual nature is fully apparent in her plants and flowers, especially her vaginal orchids, often being caressed by human hands. Her essential narcissism shows clearly in the silverpoint of a tall leather boot surrounded by orchids which she presented to Berenice Abbott. The magnetic animal figures of Thelma Wood demonstrate what must have been the strongest shared disposition between the two women. Thelma Wood had a brief spell in Africa and did many drawings of elephants and tender, melancholy-eyed giraffes. The jagged fears of the subconscious are represented by quietly overwhelming insect figures and fearful, sinister fish of the sort that inhabit the farthest depths of the Pacific.

Thelma Wood was a minor artist, to be sure, but a real one. For that reason she had cause to feel particular terror as their love fell to the side, and she could see Djuna limning her forever. The advice is given by Nora in *Nightwood*: one should be careful into whose mind one gets. Nora tells O'Connor that once she wanted Robin to die; but by placing her in art, an eternally recurring murder is enacted. She tells the doctor:

> —Perhaps, Matthew, there are devils? Who knows if there are devils? Perhaps they have set foot in the uninhabited. Was I her devil trying to bring her comfort? I enter my dead and bring no comfort, not even in my dreams. There in my sleep was my grandmother, who I loved more than anyone, tangled in the grave grass, and flowers blowing about and between her; lying there in the grave, in the forest, in a coffin of glass, and flying low, my father who is still living; low going and into the grave beside her, his head thrown back and his curls lying out, struggling with her death terribly, and me, stepping about its edges, walking and wailing without a sound; round and round, seeing them struggling with that death as if they were struggling with the sea and my life; I was weeping and unable to do anything or take myself out of it. There they were, in the grave glass, and the grave water and the grave flowers and the grave time, one living and one dead and one asleep. It went on forever, though it had stopped, my father stopped beating and just lay there floating beside her, immovable, yet drifting in a tight place. And I woke up and still it was going on; it went down into the dark earth of my waking as if I were burying them with the earth of my lost sleep. This I have done to my father's mother, dreaming through my father, and have tormented them with my tears and with my dreams: for all of us die over again in somebody's sleep. And this, I have done to Robin: it is only through me that she will die over and over, and it is only through me, of all my family, that my grandfather dies, over and over.

Art is not immortality. It is execution without blood, and the artist is always the patriarch and the executioner. The terrible curse of the artist's eye which first sounds in *Nightwood* becomes, in *The Antiphon*, one of the great themes of Djuna Barnes. The beloved victim Robin knows and fears more than anything the fact that her fate is being made colossal. "Jenny Petherbridge" told me that Thelma found the portrayal of Robin Vote —*all too accurate* and was very bitter about it. Unlike Dan Mahoney, she evidently went to considerable lengths to dissuade her friends from reading the novel. She knew, after all, that even the name Robin was taken from one of Peggy's dogs.

160

xix

Jenny Petherbridge, the other woman who lures Robin away in *Nightwood,* is another of the characters who is drawn reasonably close to life. In a novel which seethes with the rhetoric of passion, the portrayal of this character is challenged for power only by that of Dr. O'Connor himself. The passion is not in the character but in the novelist's hatred of her. Like Matthew O'Connor and Felix Volkbein, Jenny Petherbridge is another minor character moved downstage, in part perhaps as another distraction from the main play of passion. She is a hermit crab of a human being, ready to steal any shell at hand, and a person who, we are told, could make any truth false. Jenny Petherbridge represents the triumph of human triviality and meanness. She is the powerful petty demon of anti-love, which corrupts so much and so many in life. Barnes said that she wrote *Nightwood* by converting poetic lines into prose, but that that one chapter about Jenny was written as prose. She described her as she was.

In the novel, Nora tells Matthew that she has to suffer the tortured lovers of Robin on her lap for solace and comfort. In life, the story was even more entangled, for Barnes evidently allowed herself the tentative revenge of exhibiting the ability to take control of "Jenny" from Thelma. Thelma recounted the whole trauma of the breakup from her point of view in a letter to Djuna, undated but probably written in June 1930:

> —I simply cannot understand what you mean by keeping ["Jenny"] in a state of such "bewildered hope." She seems to think so too—What in heavens name can I say more than I have—The morning you saw us, I had said such terrible things I hated myself—and because I would not go with you two you said I "shirked."
>
> How could I feeling as I did towards her—and in front of you? I have asked her not to come here but have gotten letter after letter saying it would be alright—and that I loved her—I became frantic—then hypnotized and resigned—like the measles . . .
>
> . . . I did not want such a thing to be known between us—something I did not care about—it seemed a shame for foolishness to spoil us—I wanted no acknowledged disloyalty and after you came back from N.Y. I loved you so terribly—and my one idea was to wipe out the fact I'd been stupid—I tryed desparately—with her I wheedled and raved, I was cruel and sweet—and no good—always if I did not see her or call she sent something or a note—and it made you unhappy—and I did see—till I thought I'd go mad. I spent one morning till six pleading and trying to keep her from doing anything foolish—yet insisting I wouldn't see her again—and then I got a note from Ros saying she was in a high

state of fever—and I was stupid enough to listen. I told her I was going to you with it all—I saw I was losing you—and I felt I could save it if I came to you—and again I listened to her—She swore it would be alright she would meet you and become friends as I had always begged her to.

Then she played tricks and sent a note—and you were going out and asked me to come with you and I wanted so to—and didn't dare—and you were so beautiful—and we got you a flower—then I went to her and cried and raved for two hours—and again she promised to be good and friends—But she's mad—she gets things out of the balmy blue— She tells me and writes me things I have never said or done—I have lied to you, my precious—but I swear—never to her . . .

As for the rest of our eight years you seemed to have had a pretty rotten time—with my brutishness and I'm sorry—sorry—you say you *know me now so terribly well.* Something is undoubtedly wrong with me—I lack perhaps a conscience or sensibility or memory or logic or all—when I left France I felt as you say just unfit for human dignity . . .

. . . I did not mean to reject your friendship—that I took for granted in the course of events—as we loved each other—But perhaps it's grown so collosal in your mind you would not want that either—for after all why an untrustworthy and unmannerly friend?

A kiss for Dilly,
Your Simon

Thelma waited in hope of forgiveness which never came. Barnes told Mina Loy that the problem was merely that Thelma did not yet realize that she did not need her, and that from her own point of view there was not even any special point in closing the door on the relationship since, although it was over, there was nothing else to take its place in her life. She simply preferred being alone, which she regarded as both something and nothing. In the end Thelma and she stayed in touch by telephone, which seemed the only ease that was left to them, personal and yet impersonal.

And "Jenny"? She was originally from the Midwest but took pride in the degree to which, she claimed, she was accepted in French society. She told me that the real French would always laugh at the Americans behind their backs, but then when she would protest that, after all, she was American herself, she would be told: —*Ah yes, but you have a French heart!* She worked for the Condé Nast organization in Paris, and one of her jobs, when Frank Crowninshield decided to drop someone on the European staff, was to take that person to lunch and break the news. She also claimed to have been the one first to introduce Negro entertainers in Paris. Now, in her eighties, she is passionately interested in animal welfare. "Jenny" was a widow with some means. Her husband had been a reasonably well-known artist in the first decades of the century. She took Thelma into her New England house where Thelma lived as a houseguest for nearly twenty years. After that, Thelma finally left "Jenny" and moved to a neighbouring town where she lived the last fifteen years of her life with another woman who will have pride of final comment on her, for I fear that this chronicle, and her own self-judgments most of all, have not always been kind to Thelma Wood:

—Thelma was born with love to give, she loved the arts, animals, flowers, and humanities with the freedom to make her own decisions which showed profoundly in her work. She gave of herself generously, shared whatever she had, and asked for nothing in return.

XX

There was a terrible vengeance, for Djuna Barnes now turned not only away from Thelma, but also away from the very terms of their love. It is in *Nightwood*, too. Nora gives herself to a sailor in despair. In life, she began a close association with Charles Henri Ford in the summer of 1931, when she returned to Paris from New York where she had been living with Thelma in Washington Square. Ford had dropped out of high school in Mississippi in 1929 and started to edit his little magazine, *Blues*. He was very pretty (Barnes thought that his huge eyes went around the sides of his head just like an animal's) and very tough. Nearly twenty years her junior, his peculiar deference before Barnes was well received. He met her in Greenwich Village in 1929. Ford reviewed *A Night Among the Horses* in an unsigned note in *Blues* (No. 7) that year and struck just the right tone:

—In these stories of abnormality Miss Barnes reveals an astuteness of manufacture and an intellectual tension verging at times on genius or insanity. Aside from the poetry, derivative in most cases, every piece in the book is almost too deeply disturbing.

Djuna Barnes remembered, surely, for four years later she endorsed the novel that Ford wrote in collaboration with Parker Tyler, *The Young and Evil*, by stating: —This novel could only have been written by a genius or Charles Henri Ford. Gertrude Stein boosted the novel much less equivocally, but it somehow failed to generate sufficient notice even though it was one of the boldest of the expatriate publications.

Once there was an encounter between Barnes, Stein and Ford.

Djuna and Charles had gone out with Margaret Anderson in her car, and she parked and went into a shop. While Barnes and Ford were waiting and chatting in the back seat, Stein came along walking her dog. She stopped, and they talked. Then she moved on. Ford felt that he had been gauche in not inviting her to sit down on the front seat. Barnes was delighted: —*Did you see the jealous look she gave me?* she asked him.

At my first meeting with Ford, he said that there was a *lot* about Djuna in *The Young and Evil,* but in subsequent years and discussions Charles would state that there was actually very little about her in the novel. Theodosia, the female character who would appear to have some relevance to Barnes, actually refers in the main, he says, to a minor poet, whom he also knew. Barnes is named in passing. There is a conversation early in the novel between two characters named Karel, who is largely Parker Tyler, and Julian, who is Charles Ford:

> —Julian said I think I like Djuna Barnes which is a good way to think.
> Karel crossed his legs and forearms with the glass in his left hand. Yes and if Miss Barnes were to come past my gate I'd say come into my yard Miss Barnes and sit upon my porch and I will serve you tea and if you will recite one of your poems I will be glad to learn it backwards.
> Julian said all things of course are going backwards past her ear.

The remark is most perceptive, particularly for the date at which it is made, although it is quite possible that it is simply a repetition of something that she had remarked about herself. Theodosia has a — disquieting beauty, sarcasm, violated eyes.

At one point in *The Young and Evil,* Theodosia says:

> . . . do you know where bottomless places are and their reality? did you ever have to go down to the blank wall of death (I have died so often life seems stiff and awkward she said) and when you were there find even reality a little forced?

This aspect of Theodosia at least is unquestionably Djuna Barnes.

The Young and Evil is set entirely in Greenwich Village. In the Parker Tyler biography of the émigré painter Pavel Tchelitchew, *The Divine Comedy of Pavel Tchelitchew* (1967), a quarrel between Tchelitchew and Ford is reported:

> —Demon! I don't say, like Djuna said, Parker is the angelic half of your team, but anyway, you are the devilish half; enough to be Lucifer himself, I should say!

—Djuna, Ford retorts quietly, *changed her mind in Paris. In New York she thought I was the angel.*
—I know! said the artist. *—She was wise to change her mind and now I change mine. SA-TAN!*

Charles came to live with Djuna when she returned from the American hospital in Paris in 1931 after an appendicitis operation. He visited her in hospital and offered to come and look after her for a while. She accepted, and he was installed in the upstairs servant's room that went with the flat.

According to Charles, Djuna Barnes was one of the most totally unbourgeois women he ever met. He claimed that she couldn't boil an egg, and so the venison and cherry pie must have been the handiwork of Thelma. Ford and Barnes got on very well for a considerable time, and so they should have, for they are both superb and rare mavericks. The most serious quarrel of their time together occurred when Miss Barnes came back to the flat one day to find Charles perched on the edge of her bed chatting with Tylia Perlmutter, an attractive blond Polish-Jewish woman with whom he was friendly. (Barnes used her in a short story.) It was all very innocent, but it was made abundantly clear in the storm that followed that Djuna's bed was strictly off-limits.

Djuna celebrated their arrangement in 1931 by giving a dinner party. The occasion was simply Charles' birthday, but it was jocularly put about the Quarter that this was their "engagement party." It was at this party that Ford met Tchelitchew, who had been living in a ménage à trois with Tyler and Serge Nabokov. Barnes had met Tchelitchew through Margaret Anderson and Jane Heap. Pavlik invited Ford to dinner shortly afterwards, and the romance between them became the most tempestuous relationship in the Russian painter's life.

Ford and Barnes went on one trip together in late 1931 through Vienna (it became her favourite city), Budapest and Munich, where the picture of her and Ford and Putzi Hanfstaengl was taken. Then, in early 1933, Charles, taken up by the enthusiasm of Paul Bowles, went down to Tangiers and wrote back to Djuna about it in glowing terms.

Barnes had gone to England at the invitation of Peggy Guggenheim. The Paris flat was being sublet to a friend of Natalie Barney's. She had been working ferociously on *Bow Down,* and the manuscript, though very rough, was already quite substantial. Ford did her typing for her. And so she decided to join him.

It was an ill-starred visit. It had been put to her as a terribly cheap place to live, but it turned out that the cost of decent accommodation was considerable. Moreover, she received word from Natalie that there was some difficulty with the flat because the concierge was pretending that he didn't have a key to let the tenant in.

The first eight days in Tangiers were spent in what she described in a letter to Mina Loy (to whom she gave the simple instruction: Never come to Tangiers!) as a hut, without water or light, and she had to sleep on straw on the floor with insufficient bedcovers. After this gruesome beginning, she and Ford made an arrangement to have the partial rental (for 1,000 francs a month) of a house owned by Bowles, which he used for working on his music. They were to vacate the house for certain hours every day while Bowles composed. But this house, on the Marshan, was virtually unfurnished except for a large number of jackal pelts and one giant python skin hanging on the walls. These Djuna had put away at once. She herself rolled up the snakeskin. The house came with an Arab cook, who, she found, could not cook. They did not stay there past the first month, after rats got into her suitcase and ate her stockings. In his memoirs, *Without Stopping* (1972), Bowles recalls how they used to sit at the Café Central in the Zoco Chico, and how Djuna's blue, purple and green makeup used to make her an object of fascination at the café. Bowles records that she did not mind in the least being stared at, and on one occasion she virtually turned the entire café into a theatre with an imitation of Sir Francis Rose.

The third Tangiers house promised to make up for the first two. It was a splendid house in the Casbah. The house, which overlooked the bay, was built on two levels and had a magnificent inner courtyard around a giant fig tree. It was owned by an Englishman who always asked three months' rent in advance. (Another well-known tenant of this house was Cecil Beaton.) But Djuna Barnes was to have only a short time there.

Shortly after they moved in, she realized that she was pregnant. She was then forty-one. Immediate arrangements for a return to the Continent and an abortion were made.

The pregnancy caused quite a flurry among the expatriate women in Paris. Those lesbian women who did not like Djuna took malevolent joy in the occurrence. Decades later one of them "let slip" some information about it in the most transparently contrived way and then made a big fuss about her unfortunate indiscretion. Her good friend Janet Flanner, on the other hand, was full of indignation with Ford whom she took, incorrectly, to be the responsible party. It was true, however, Charles told me, that he had proposed that they have a child together. The pregnancy was actually the result of a

166

brief romance she had had with the French painter Jean Oberle in the latter part of 1932. He was a well-known artist of the Dufy School whom she had met through Peggy Guggenheim. A reference which I take to be to him in a letter from Natalie Barney indicates that he had a rather violent nature, and Ford recalls how horribly jealous he was of Ford's presence at rue St.-Romain. Djuna Barnes herself evidently did not view the romance with any seriousness.

She returned to Devonshire and the large household being maintained there by Peggy Guggenheim. She would return to Paris, and it would be from Paris that she would finally depart for America in 1939. Essentially, her Paris days were over now. In retrospect, Ford feels that in some ways she was a bit too puritanical for his taste. He also told me that —*she did the honesty bit into the ground.* Barnes thought that Ford was extremely honest, too, but in a different way. When Dougie MacDougall complained to her that Ford had held a wild party in his flat which had caused much damage and then had categorically denied that there had been a party there, Djuna expressed astonishment at the denial because, she said, he did not ordinarily give enough of a damn to lie about anything. She said that she had never known another human being so careless of other people and their needs. —*Loose?* she said. —*Loose as a cut jockstrap.* For her, his name was Charles Impossible Ford. In the end anger seemed wholly insufficient to her; there was only departure. Yet she never denied how charming he could be when he wanted to be. The thing they had most in common was their mutual desire for independence and freedom. In a quatrain from one of his best poems, *Reptilia,* Ford wrote:

> Nothing, nothing is so valuable
> as freedom, Dante said,
> Nothing, nothing is less haveable:
> ask anyone. Dante's dead.

In a charmed manner, Charles Henri Ford was to obtain more of that freedom than is given to most. He could boast to me at age sixty-five that he had never held a job of any sort in his life, and yet he had started out in life with no family money. (Pavlik complained that Ford had come with his toothbrush and left with the Oldsmobile.) Djuna Barnes was never to enjoy this sort of freedom. But by 1934 she had a firm first claim staked on endurance, solitude, and a certain obscure greatness.

XXI

The few years with Charles and the dalliance with Jean Oberle are perhaps best looked upon as nothing but a dark solstice necessary to enable her to assuage her grief and to write the novel. The passion and the introspection, and the revenge, of *Nightwood* freed her surprisingly quickly from her love. Thelma Wood was nothing more than the ghost of a mistress past, and the mind of Djuna Barnes, no longer held in Paris, could now range back with its former intensity to the farms, Storm King and Long Island, and the story of her childhood and family. She would have nearly half a century left to her to brood upon it, the freedoms of her father and her grandmother. But she saved the broken doll and kept it with her until she died.

CHAPTER FOUR

—Never, never, have children. And God forgive me!
—Forgive . . . ?
—For making you mortal; if you live you will be a fool. It takes a strong
woman to die before she has been a fool. No one has the imagination; I
did not, you will not.

Thus speaks the wife of Wendell Ryder, Amelia, to their daughter, Julie. It is one of the most persistent of the Barnes themes, childlessness, and it is one, moreover, which she does not to my knowledge share with any other major contemporary writer. It was clearly a deeply held belief in both her art and her life.

the sole footnote of this story:

It was not an uncommon or unrespected notion in antiquity. The Encratites is the collective term used to describe those early Christian heretics who chose to abstain from flesh and marriage, among other things, in the belief that matter itself is essentially evil and must be resisted. There is an apocryphal tale about an encounter between Jesus and Salome which apparently enjoyed some importance among the Encratites in the centuries immediately following the death of Christ. In it, Salome asks Jesus how long death will continue to hold sway among men. And he replies *—As long as ye women bear children. For I have come to abolish the functions of woman.* To which she responds *—Then I have done well, for I have not borne children.*

As late as the fourth century A.D., a sect called the Abelites proposed spiritual unions to ordinary marriage and opposed all procreation. They took their name from Abel, who, they assumed, had had a wife but had never sought to have children by her. The Abelites adopted children in order to spread the teaching of their sect and taught them to abstain from sexual intercourse. They were a strong sect and eventually became extinct according to the tenets of their own doctrine during the reign of Theodosius the Younger (A.D. 408–450).

The best-known advocates of childlessness were the Saturninians, who followed the teachings of the Gnostic Saturninus at the end of the first century after Christ. Children were held to be the result of a muddled vision on the part of the archangels. God took pity upon their imperfect creations and added His own divine spark to man which re-

turns to Him after man's death. For the Saturninians, man's link to the animals is more strongly felt than in any other time in Western thinking prior to Darwin. Because of its emphasis upon human bestiality and the need for mankind not to take the world seriously and to abstain from procreation, the thought of Djuna Barnes, if we wish to label it in any systematic way, would have to be called Saturninian Christian in character. It gives her the air of some sort of mammoth creature thought extinct who has suddenly appeared sternly alive from another far-distant era. Sternly alive, and, with reserve, laughing and grieving. The connection of Miss Barnes with early post-Christian sectarianism is not a fanciful one. Her great-uncle, Thomas Cushman Buddington, one of several spiritualists in her family, published a book in 1886 dealing with Julian the Apostate and the relations between paganism and Christianity. The ideas were in the family. We are told in *Nightwood:*
—By temperament Nora was an early Christian . . .

The belief of Barnes is the bitter fruit of a windswept family tree.

ii

Djuna's grandmother, Zadel Barnes, was descended, like most members of that family name in America, from three brothers Barnes who came to America from England in the early seventeenth century. There is a witch in the early American history of the family whom I wish I could claim for this story, but unfortunately she belongs to the family of one of the two other original brothers. She was Mary, the first wife of Thomas Barnes of Hartford, and she was hanged; subsequently he married a fourteen-year-old. The family of Zadel Barnes settled originally in East Hampton and had moved to Connecticut by the beginning of the eighteenth century.

Zadel was born in Middletown, Connecticut, on March 9, 1841, the fourth of fourteen children that Duane Barnes had by two wives.

Once again we must consider the problem of naming. The most conventionally named of all Zadel's brothers and sisters were the sister born immediately after her in 1844, Lillian, who died the following year, and the firstborn son, who had a relatively simple name, Llewellyn. (Llewellyn Barnes was taken prisoner-of-war during the Civil War in 1864.) The other brothers and sisters borne by Duane's first wife, Cynthia Turner, were named as follows: Marilla, Hinda, Reon, Gaybert, Culmer, Kilmeny, Justa and Everet. The strangeness of given names increases still more in the children borne by Duane's second wife, Frances Tibbals. Their names are unusual enough—

Urlan, Niar and Unade—that one cannot even determine their sex from their names, though the discovery of Urlan's headstone at Middletown shows that name to be masculine.

It is not unknown for American given names to display this degree of oddity in the nineteenth century, and these Barnes names help indicate what sort of family this Barnes branch was. The New England families which tended to use strange names were ones which, while they might be old and could occasionally be wealthy, tended to be of marginal social status and to make up what they lacked in education with enthusiasm. Names were quite frequently meant to be one-off affairs in an age in which the spirit of the individual took precedence over staid tradition. The English origin of the names Barns and Barnes is from the Norse Bjorne. This American branch of the Barnes family was clearly aware of the Nordic provenance, since the family tree is intermittently hung with Scandinavian names, which are, however, scarcely ever quite right, though it is hard to know where that is willful and where ignorance. The name of Djuna's elder brother, Thurn, is one such semi-Scandinavian form, and their great-uncle Urlan would seem to be another. Only one member of the family, a son of Hinda named Odin, has a Scandinavian name in the accepted and correct form.

The most frequent form of appellation in Zadel's family appears to have been the bizarre combination of two given names. Thus Marilla could be a combination of, for example, Margaret and Priscilla; Hinda, of Helen and Linda; Reon, of Robert and Leon, and so forth. The historical literature on Christian names in America bears ample witness to this phenomenon. Because there does tend to be a class function involved in combined names, those who carry them are not so often encountered in history and literature. The children of more established American families, when they do not carry standard English names, tend to bear Biblical, Greek and Presidential names.

When given names become totally strange, as they do with Urlan, Niar and Unade, it usually points to the practice of spiritualism in the family. The account of the Zadel-figure's childhood in *Ryder* indicates that there was a spiritualistic disposition in the Barnes family. She tells her son in the novel that he was conceived by the figure of Beethoven passing mystically through her. When she was sixteen, Zadel Barnes, as we shall see, was to marry a professional (and far less frivolous) spiritualist in Henry Aaron Budington.

Zadel's father, Duane Barnes, would have been the ideal community service club member had there been such organizations in his time. *The Commemorative Biographical Record of Middlesex County, Connecticut* (1903) records that he donated and personally

171

planted many of Middletown's fine shade trees and was active in the establishment of the railway and the widening of the Narrows. He himself built a stone Gothic cottage on High Street, which was held the city's most "artistic" residence. Although he had not studied at university, Duane Barnes was a schoolteacher as a young man, and he practiced the trade of bookseller throughout his mature years. It is said that he would refuse to sell any book which he believed would exert a harmful influence. He was also a poet, so that Djuna Barnes is in fact a fourth-generation poet. Miss Barnes claimed that her great-grandmother went out of her mind for a period but gradually recovered.

During the youth of Zadel Barnes an important transition in style and subject was taking place in American letters. The early writers of America wrote in standard English about life in their new and provincial country. Emerson, Irving, Thoreau, Hawthorne and Melville had no doubts about where their linguistic and artistic roots were. Even Poe, who would seem an exception to the Greenwich Village bohemians of a subsequent generation, was merely adopting certain Byronic propositions to American terrain. But a division starts to show among Americans in literature within a decade of the end of the Civil War. Some sang America; others felt for the first time the cultural poverty of their situation and the unexpected pain of the assertive break from European culture that was America.

From this latter grouping came James Whistler, Henry James, and eventually T. S. Eliot and Djuna Barnes herself, who were all Americans at a certain remove. There began after the Civil War a debate about the viability of American culture that lasted until well into the 1920s. It was part of the tide that brought Djuna Barnes to Paris, and it was certainly within the terms of that debate that one should take Hemingway's famous remark: —*Something happens to our good writers at a certain age. We destroy them in many ways.* A strained but jaunty young journal that began in New Orleans in 1920, *The Double Dealer* (the title was from Congreve, and it had contributions from Djuna Barnes, who did not think much of it, and Edmund Wilson, Jr.), asked in 1921: —Is there anything distinctively American or "United States" in the work of Poe, Emerson, Hawthorne, Bierce? and obviously did not think so. A feeling was about that, as Calvin Tomkins remarks in *Living Well Is the Best Revenge,* America had not yet managed to catch up with the new century, and that the best which came out of America was not necessarily best classified as American.

Zadel Barnes Budington, who is one of the keys to the life of Djuna Barnes, came from that undergrowth of literary nationalism that flourished after the Civil War. This generation was conspicuous for the role of women in it. The elderly Harriet Beecher Stowe had pride of place. Zadel Barnes claimed acquaintanceship with her and with several leading feminists. She is mentioned in passing in the memoirs of Elizabeth Cady Stanton. Due to economic pressures, some social restraints upon women were relaxed after the war, and women had certain opportunities for economic self-sufficiency for the first time.

In this period one encounters both an intense nationalism and an equally intense reverence before European culture in a manner that was not quickly to be repeated in American cultural history. The famous line in Oscar Wilde's *A Woman of No Importance* (—*They say, Lady Hunstanton, that when good Americans die they go to Paris*) was in fact pinched from the American Oliver Wendell Holmes who used it in *The Autocrat at the Breakfast Table.* It was still an era of easy cultural intermingling, which contrasts considerably with the attitudes of the real and spiritual children of the generation which was to come. Something happened to the moist patriotism of the grandmother Barnes by the time it reached her granddaughter, even though Zadel Barnes lived with Djuna and was in large part responsible for her education until she left home. Wald Barnes demonstrated an unmistakable resentment of European culture all his life. Djuna Barnes aspired to connect herself with that culture and had few tolerant words for the country of her birth, even though it was to America that she returned.

During her twenty-year marriage to Henry Aaron Budington, Zadel Barnes was an active journalist with a leaning towards feminist problems and themes. She, like the grandmother of *Ryder,* wrote articles and leaders for *The Springfield Republican,* the newspaper of Springfield, Massachusetts, where they lived. The singer Genevieve Ward, in approving the dreadful biography that Zadel wrote about her, told her (in March 1880): —*I have perfect faith in you, womanarily and literarily* ... Evidence of lesbian disposition can, of course, only be inferred from nineteenth-century texts and letters. In the 1920 Barnes short story *Oscar,* which appeared in *The Little Review,* there is a widow who has been married twice —*Of her two husbands she seldom said anything. Once she made the remark: Only fancy, they never did catch on to me at all.* American women, excluded from so many masculine arenas of life and expression, did form very close friendships with one another in this period. We have few facts, but there are some: the poems of Sappho had high sales in America in the second half of the nineteenth century.

Exactly a year after her divorce in 1877, Zadel married Axel Gustafson, whom she had met after her return to Middletown. He was seven years younger than she, a renegade Swede. In *Ryder,* "Axel Axelson" was —initiated by a priest. They went to Europe together and collaborated on a quasi-spiritualistic work, *The Foundation of Death,* in 1888, which went through five editions. The tale would have it—as witnessed in *Ryder,* the unpublished play *The Biography of Julie von Bartmann,* and the factual note *About the Author* written by Miss Barnes herself for the Harper & Row reissue of *Ladies Almanack*—that grandmother Zadel had a literary salon in Grosvenor Square, and to this salon came Oscar Wilde. Oscar's mother, Speranza, also was a visitor to the salon. Zadel is supposed to have gone to Sweden and to have met the king of Sweden there. All of this may very well be, but there is a problem in connection with her English literary salon in that there is absolutely no record whatsoever of it to date in published letters and memoirs of the time. There is firm evidence, however, that she was friendly with Karl Marx's daughter Eleanor.

The passages in *Ryder* which tell about the days of the English salon are in Chapter Four, Wendell's youth:

> —He remembers his mother's soirees (she had just returned from a tour in the States with Elizabeth Stanton). Why should he forget? Was it not at one of these that he had been called, by no less a person than Lady Mary Glynn, "Prophet in the wilderness," and had not Archbishop Benson deigned to hold word with him, in regard to our Saviour, the same evening, as he tapped his varnished boot upon the rug? Had not Oscar Wilde himself, with his then not-to-be-denied right hand, lifted his, Wendell's auburn forelock, murmuring, "Beautiful, beautiful!" He had indeed.

There are numerous other such references in the novel to the elevated levels at which the Zadel-figure moves:—among the Pre-Raphaelites as accustomed as a glint of steel. I have substantiated one visit by Zadel to an Oscar Wilde salon at the Falstaff Club in June, 1882. It is quite possible that Zadel and Axel Gustafson moved to Shepherd's Bush (where Wald had met Elizabeth Chappell who lived with her sister in a next-door garden flat in Cromwell Grove off Shepherd's Bush Road) after royalties from *The Foundation of Death* ran out and they could no longer afford the grander residence with its "noble marble staircase."

The salon-without-record then could in fact have flourished, or it could have been a mere evening or two. (Zadel's London address was not Grosvenor Square [*Ryder*] but Brunswick Square.) In *Ryder,* wife and narrator confront the satyr-father, but it is Julie

174

(Djuna) who sees her grandmother as she really is. When one follows the life of Zadel Barnes there are everywhere legends which cannot be substantiated. She is supposed to have been one of the first students at Mount Holyoke College, but there is no record of her there. She is, in the novel at any rate, a schemer and a mendicant who takes tribute from former lovers whose rash letters she possesses, but all the same is heroic in her absurdity and worthy of love and forgiveness.

Zadel was practiced in the memorable and timely gesture. One of Djuna's earliest memories was of the death of a pet canary when she was five or six. Her grandmother gave it an elaborate funeral and buried it wrapped in her very best Liberty pink silk scarf. And later, when a half-sister named Shila died at nine months, Zadel buried her in a good fleece jacket because Djuna was worried that Shila would be cold in the ground.

The Harper & Row autobiographical note gives equal importance to Zadel and Wald in the education of Wald's children, who were kept away from the Cornwall-on-Hudson school system. But Mina Loy's daughter recalls that Djuna told her mother that she had really been educated by her grandmother Zadel, and that it was from her that she received all her talent and much encouragement. One specific moment of that domestic education that we have (a passing recollection in a letter) is that Zadel read Thackeray's *The Rose and the Ring* to her. Her father read her Kipling's tale about the beast that walked like a man. The way in which *Ryder* is peppered with real family names such as Elisha and Gaybert even for minor characters proves that an oral history of her family was certainly a part of her education. Djuna told Charles Ford that her grandmother had read Shakespeare and the Bible to her. (Hemingway said that the Old Testament was all any writer needs.) It takes some effort, but I think that the reader can manage to discern far across the ghastly, treacly prose of Zadel Barnes the etched but equally excessive diction of her granddaughter's writing. In a novel called *Can the Old Love?* (1871), for example, Zadel writes:

—The volume of life had come into his hands gilt-edged, gold-clasped, and richly bound. He had himself unclasped it, and looked, perhaps, upon the title page. Love, lightly fluttering its first chapters, dipping her glowing fingers in the rainbow tints of hope, had written promises. Now, Sorrow leaned upon him heavily, holding the book broad open, and writing where the vellum was colorless and gray, death, separation, desolation—heads of chapters, which, in the inappeasable hunger of the heart, Paul must read, and read alone, and read continually.

175

This florid style seems to have served as a templet for the writing of Djuna Barnes, both at its strongest and its weakest, but her prose, of course, doesn't suffer from the falsely warm tone which is never absent from her grandmother's writing.

Miss Barnes' paternal grandfather, Henry Aaron Budington, was also a writer, but of an entirely different sort, though there are thematic links with his writing, too, particularly as regards some of the motifs of *Ryder.* He called himself a Spiritualist in religion, though he was the son of Methodist parents "of the quiet sort" who practiced strict temperance. His father, Aaron Budington, was a fairly successful farmer, an Abolitionist Republican in politics, who owned four hundred acres on which he ran merino sheep. Henry left the farm at eighteen and went to Wesleyan University, which was one of the strongest church-affiliated universities in New England, after a short stay at a seminary in Rhode Island. He graduated from Wesleyan Phi Beta Kappa in 1857 (he married Zadel that same year) and took an M.A. in 1860. For a number of years he was a secondary school teacher in Washington, D.C., New Jersey and Connecticut. He passed the Civil War as an Internal Revenue assessor in Massachusetts. After 1869, he sold insurance, founded a newspaper in Greenfield, Massachusetts, and then settled in Springfield where he was both a reporter and advertising salesman for the same *Springfield Republican* for which Zadel wrote editorials.

His Spiritualist writings are morally very strict. They amount to an admixture of morality and Darwinism. The influence of Faraday is quite strong. In his 1899 work, *Man Makes His Body, or The Ascent of the Ego Through Matter,* Henry Budington declaims:

> —Right thinking builds good heads; bad thinking builds bad heads. The deposits of brain matter continue far into middle life, if the person thinks. Many people have larger heads and deeper brain fissures at fifty than at twenty, and especially if they think on rich lines of experience, and dwell much in the realm of intellectual and spiritual themes.
>
> If anyone indulges in abnormal physical habits: the use of tobacco, alcohol, chloral, opium, hasheesh, gluttony, sex excess—all these habits force the spirit to deposit in that part of the brain, protoplasm to enlarge the special organ which is needed to intensify that habit. The balance of the faculties is upset, the desire for the abnormal experience is increased, the brain organ for that special passion is enlarged, and the spirit, thrown out of nature's proper channel, rushes on, building up the structure which will gratify that desire, until the habit becomes so overpowering that the spirit can no longer supply the organ, and collapse of the special organ occurs, and the spirit leaves the body in an abnormal manner.

If, during the period of this abnormal life, a monad should unite with the ovum, that monad would be tainted with the excesses and defects of the man, and no gestation, however perfect, could eliminate those excesses and defects.

And so forth. The thoughts of Budington, which are a kind of internal phrenology characteristic of the period in which he lived, did not enjoy particular influence in his time (though he did count Harry Houdini among his followers). It is clear beyond question that the lives of both his former wife and their son were played out in precise reaction against everything that he was and stood for. Whereas Henry Budington championed the spirit of man ascending, Wald Barnes and then his daughter chose the theme of man bowing down to his animal nature. This portion of the family history is a common enough one among families of their type—a violent rebellion against the prohibitions of strict Methodism. Henry Budington died in 1921 at the age of ninety. After the separation of his son and daughter-in-law, Budington established relations with Elizabeth, who was named in his will (written on the back of hymn sheets), and was also in contact with Djuna herself before he died. The mother of Miss Barnes is named Elizabeth Chappell Budington in the will. For several years she lived in East Orange and Summit in New Jersey.

Henry Budington was the family genealogist, and it is thanks to his little booklet, *The Leyden Branch of the Budington Family,* that we have a full picture of the Budington family's position in American society. The Budingtons were originally a whaling family from Groton and New London. Henry's grandfather, who died in 1810, was a captain who sailed to the West Indies and China. His circumstances were much reduced by the Revolutionary War, for he held several thousands of dollars in the old Continental currency, which the new government repudiated. Henry Budington recalls having seen a Chinese tea chest nearly full of this money in his grandfather's house when he was a child. Afterwards his grandfather was a Jeffersonian Democrat and a local esquire who helped settle disputes and draw deeds. He ran a country store in the basement of the large house which he built for himself after living for many years in a log cabin. He had crossed over to Leyden in Massachusetts as the result of accepting land there in lieu of payment for a bad debt. Some subsequent members of the family did become prominent, chiefly in medicine, but the family in the main never really recovered from its initial economic setback during the course of the nineteenth century. There occurs the following curious passage in Henry Budington's account of his grandfather:

177

—He owned the best two-horse coach in town. It was very heavy and strong. My grandmother used to say, it was about all two horses could do to pull it up the hills to the old Methodist church (which was originally built by the Baptists) which stood on the sightly and breezy hill at the West Center, afterwards nicknamed "Sodom."

It is in this real chapel that the imaginary end of *Nightwood* is staged, for we are told that Robin circles closer and closer to Nora's part of the country in her wanderings and finally —At the top of the hill she could see, rising faintly against the sky, the weather-beaten white of the chapel ... In life, of course, Thelma Wood settled in Connecticut upon her return to the United States with "Jenny Petherbridge." Connecticut is very much "Djuna's part of the country" on both sides of the family.

Thus, this rather puzzling concluding scene of Robin Vote's act of apparent near-sodomy with a dog on the floor of a country chapel is given very specific historical reference by the final residence of Thelma Wood and the chapel called Sodom, which was well-known to Barnes. Thelma Wood never went to that church, any more than Dan Mahoney ever mingled with the Barnes family as he does in *Ryder,* but that does not alter the fact that all the components of that concluding scene in *Nightwood* have reference to various realities. Once again we are dealing with a documentable page in the Budington-Barnes family mythology, and indeed an actual act of sodomy would have been both vulgar and unnecessary for the purposes of Barnes, which are far more Proustian than that.

The genealogy of Henry Budington and the family tree of the Middletown Barnes family reveal patterns which are highly relevant to the life and art of Miss Barnes. The incidence of divorce and solitary life is rather high. The Barnes family even has a divorce in the seventeenth century, when such things almost never happened, though there was early legal provision for divorce in several of the New England colonies and New York. By the time Henry and Zadel separated, in 1875, there exist reliable statistics for divorce, which in that particular year, for example, occurred in only 0.3 percent of the populace. Elizabeth Cady Stanton did not yet have the backing of most feminists in her fight for women's right to divorce. Yet both of Henry's sons separated from their wives. Miss Barnes' cousin, William Budington, told me that the divorces of both their grandmothers, Zadel and Ida, were very bitter and all souvenirs of their married lives were burned. One has a picture of a family composed, on the one hand, of committed churchgoers, including a minister who was a —vigorous, shouting Methodist and another family member also re-

178

nowned for his joyous shouting in church, and, on the other, plain-spoken agnostics who did not hesitate to act on their feelings and beliefs. It would not be fair to say that either the Barnes or Budington families were consistently unstable, but both families did unquestionably house notable eccentricities of behaviour and belief. Djuna Barnes stands very much in a tradition.

The family in which Djuna Barnes grew up was a matriarchy over which "Mother" Zadel presided with benign but very considerable power behind her odd son. Miss Barnes' lover of her English period, S—, told me that Djuna very clearly and strongly saw her father as the spoiled American son of a powerful mother. His story is simply that of a desperate searching for individuality. In *Ryder*, Sophia ruminates both coldly and indulgently on her son Wendell after their return to America:

> —My son is weak, he has great gifts, but do we live forever? Life is strange for him. He is like the criminal in a famous murder case, that had been forgotten. So I, who gave him birth, have seen his sleeping at forty, the ageing symbol of a forgotten action. He plays, he writes, he can do many things; he has, only imagine! operas to his credit, with full orchestral directions planned, and executed amid the din of hungry children, on a deal table, littered with nothing more than the never-out-of-sight-of-the-hungry-and-the-distressed, bread and water.

The several sources of revenue which had been drawn from over the previous decade had all for one reason or another evaporated. Djuna was the proper progeny and prodigy to fulfill the literary and feminist aspirations of Zadel. Who could know that one of the costs of this achievement would be an epic history and judgment of the family, both comic and bitter, with no one excluded?

iii

There is nothing at all unusual in the circumstances, if one examines the clinical literature on the subject, which led Djuna Barnes on the path she followed. As regards all the recognized statistically significant factors, there are deep emotional potholes in her childhood: An eccentric family and a sense of social isolation and oddity. A negative attitude towards her father who appeared ever weaker as she grew into her teens. Strongly ambivalent feelings towards her mother for letting herself be a martyr in a ménage-à-trois situation.

179

And finally, as a result of all this, a compelling need to achieve radical independence in every way—with grandmother Zadel there to serve as a role model. I am persuaded by the medical literature which indicates that in such unstable family constellations there can frequently be observed a homospiritual arc or link between a such-minded grandmother and a granddaughter, who will have a very much increased statistical probability of developing homosexual inclinations. I fancy that something very like this is what happened to the young Djuna Barnes.

After her separation from Axel Gustafson, Zadel took Wald and her daughter-in-law to live on the country estate of her other son, Justin, who had attended Cornell and had become a successful eye surgeon in New York City, specializing in difficult cataract operations. The figure of the uncle in *The Antiphon,* who offers a vision of what a relatively normal life might have been like, is modelled on Justin. It was on the grounds of his beautiful house, constructed dramatically on the side of the mountain Storm King at Cornwall-on-Hudson, that Wald Barnes built with his own hands, just as his great-grandfather had done, his much more modest house. It was here that his second child, Djuna Chappell Barnes, was born on June 12, 1892. She lived there until she was sixteen.

Cornwall-on-Hudson was in the main a summering place. That stretch of the Hudson had become so popular with bohemians who had either grown affluent or simply settled down that it was jocularly known as Greenwich Village-Gone-Pregnant. Apart from the summer months Justin only used the Storm King house, with his mistress, intermittently, which put Wald in the position of caretaker for the property. For a brief period, under the influence of Zadel, Justin Budington and his two sons also used the name Barnes, but they reverted to Budington, which that branch of the family keeps to this day.

In his family history, Henry Budington waxed lyrical about his elder son:

> —He built a beautiful home on the side of the mountain, Storm King, up the Hudson River, where in the few hours of leisure, snatched from the crowded days of professional life, he gratified his intense love of forest, brooks, glen, birds, flowers, moonlit, starry skies and sunny days; a love inherited and intensified in boyhood, by life amid the mountain scenery of his ancestral home in old Massachusetts.

And glided over his younger son's idleness by saying:

> ... with a numerous family he finds labor, health, physical and intellectual development. A dealer in real estate, an artist in music and painting, an Agnostic in religion and politics.

The claim that Wald Barnes dealt in real estate has no corroboration in *Ryder,* where a great point is made of the fact that Wendell does nothing at all to earn a living. He fished, grew mushrooms in his cellar and kept poultry and a few animals. In good times, when Djuna was seven, Wald took his family to England and Jamaica.

Wald Barnes' most important mistress, or perhaps I should say his one well-known mistress, for we have no way of knowing if it was a dalliance or a serious relationship, was Marguerite Amelia d'Alvarez, who came to Cornwall-on-Hudson on the rebound from Oscar Hammerstein. She was one of the several outstanding opera singers whom Hammerstein brought to America. Her vague autobiography, *Forsaken Altars* (1954), is extremely coy about her relationship with Hammerstein. It claims that he was in love with her but that she, though bound and held by her contract, tried to flee from him. Hammerstein purportedly promised, threatened and reproached her, and even built a theatre especially for her in order to win her over.

She was a contralto, a mountain of a woman with a voice that was frequently compared to a mighty organ. She claimed to be Peruvian, the daughter of a nobleman of Incan and Spanish blood and a French mother. In the years before she fled Oscar Hammerstein, according to her autobiography, she had also left Belgium to escape the fancy of the king. Though an opera singer, Mlle. d'Alvarez had interests in jazz and ran with a fast crowd. In 1909, she told an interviewer:

> —A Frenchman or a Spaniard will fall in love with a neat wrist or a trim ankle. Americans . . . seem more sincere than most Continentals. A little crude, too, in their lovemaking.

She could have been thinking of Wald Barnes, who carried a damp sponge on his saddle to wipe himself after intercourse whenever the chance presented itself, as it evidently did at several stops in the region. This anecdote about her wild father is one that Miss Barnes told to several of her Paris and London friends.

Djuna hated her. There are several witnesses to that in addition to her fiction. D'Alvarez is first described in the 1933 short story *A Boy Asks a Question* as Carmen La Tosca, a "stupendous" singer who had played the Queen in *Aïda* (one of d'Alvarez's noted roles) and

181

who appears in a country village —snuggling among the foothills to rent a rather large house together with a manservant and a maid.

—Of course there was no end to the gossip, she did not court attention, she got attention. People said she was not exactly handsome, but neither was she ugly; her face held a perfect balance of the two—and then she was outrageously "chic."

In the story she sits in bed reading French and Spanish newspapers and journals. This incidental story is a classic early Barnes tale for its non-connective dialogue. The lady leaves as suddenly as she had appeared in the little town, and the story is over.

In 1923 Miss Barnes worked for nearly five months, first in Paris and then in Cagnes, on the three-act play *The Biography of Julie von Bartmann.* (The name was used in the published short story *Aller et Retour.*) The play, which was nearly finished, is quite good. It was never played or published, perhaps because of the narrative position she took and then thought better of. For the mistress in this play is in fact the Djuna-figure, that is, a combination of d'Alvarez and Djuna. There is also a daughter, but she thinks and talks rather like the mistress in the play. It is not so much that there is a strong Oedipal situation in the proud mistress confronting the father of several boys and a girl, a man who is unquestionably Wald Barnes because of the biographical incidents which are ascribed to him. It is rather that the mistress has too many good lines, too much spirit. When the mistress figure *next* appears in Barnes prose, in *Ryder,* the large opera singer is not given as generous and stylish a description. There she is an exceedingly foolish and slovenly cow named Kate Careless. The only time Djuna referred to d'Alvarez in print was in a little snippet in *The Playgoer's Almanac* in 1931:

—Marguerite d'Alvarez, Prima Donna, who has the most Gothic Roof in the signing architecture of the Mouth ever seen, is on her way to Berlin, where she will do a movie of Mary Magdalene. She selected Germany as the only country robust enough to support her in her attempt to be contemporary with the Fall of Woman at its initiation.

Wald Barnes was short (five foot seven, if we believe the play), red-headed, and he had a full and rather curly beard. Winter and summer he wore a red wool cap and appeared the proper woodsman, even if he didn't do the work itself. He farmed mainly aphorisms: That freedom consists in keeping the wood cut, the fire lit and the animals productive. That women are monstrous and beautiful; man, active. That knowledge is knowing that the horse founders, the ship sinks, and women take comfort in what has no evidence. That time is a slut with whom one mates, and life is best faced backwards. He aspired to create myths and allegories which would forge a new sort of person.

These etiolated but still powerful lessons were all that Miss Barnes needed for themes in the course of more than half a century. It was by most standards an unusual education. Wald Barnes literally, according to his daughter, burned his Credo. But she carried much of it on even while rejecting him for his weakness. If the diction and sentence structure of Djuna Barnes go back to her grandmother, the main structure of all her major works belongs equally to her father. Though many of Barnes' critics have commented on the sense of varying symphonic movements and the feeling of mixed genre in her work, it has not been realized how specific the form which Miss Barnes follows is. It is the form of ritual folk music-theatre in which characters give disconnected recitatifs (sometimes in mime, sometimes playing instruments, speaking, singing) and which is best known by the old folk opera *Bow Down*. It was the form of opera composed by her father, and he, in turn, had the idea of mixed genre from his mother.

The original title of *Nightwood*, then, both proves the direct link back to her father's and grandmother's failed art and also proclaims the organizing theory that underlies the whole novel and much of her other art as well. In an unimportant piece of journalism written for *The Sunday World Magazine* (February 22, 1931) she makes a remark in passing which is absolutely seminal for the novel: —Folk drama, perhaps more than any other type, requires a tough cord on which to thread its incidents. The original *Bow Down* tells the story of one man's courtship of two sisters at once. In the telling of the tale, short versions return to join the start of another similar version like a reprise, which is one way of understanding how all the lonely, eccentric characters of *Nightwood* stand and recite on their little narrative islands essentially the same song of despair. The mixed genre of *Bow Down* is present most strongly in *Ryder*, where parody of Chaucer and assorted poems are mixed with prose and drawings. *The Antiphon* is unmistakably set upon a deserted stage where a *Bow Down*-like spectacle has played. The discarded musical instruments are lying all about the stage. As a folk opera, *Bow Down* has a naive form, but its content is passion.

The phrase "bow down" is elevated to an incantation in Barnes and means not becoming humble, but man's descent back into the kingdom of the animal, which is something both preferable to his human captivity and yet obscene. The scene in which Robin Vote thrashes about with the dog at the end of *Nightwood* is foreshadowed in *The Biography of Julie von Bartmann* when the father, Basil, explains his life's purpose, which is to pass the mystery that everyone else has forgotten on to his children. Basil relates how it was his custom from the time of his own childhood to repeat incessantly certain staid maxims, but now he has turned to a different way, which is to be celebrated by his union with Julie von Bartmann. Basil grows intoxicated with his own joyous eloquence as he orates before Julie and the children, and then suddenly he slips and falls to the floor on all fours, where he remains with his head lowered and is silent for a long moment. When he speaks it is to acknowledge that he is The Beast. His daughter quietly tells Julie von Bartmann that she had better go, and she does, full of immense wonder at the strange man and his family, which, she senses, is all of a piece. The curtain falls.

There is no evidence for Wald Barnes' practice of sodomy with animals except for his daughter's testimony in her art, but it is a strongly reiterated theme for Miss Barnes. In the Chaucerian poem of *Ryder, The Occupations of Wendell,* Wendell's cows, Sweet Dolly Sodam and her twin Gamorra, are festooned with jewelry like his women, and the poem ends with a double entendre as Wendell's horse stares deeply into his eyes and . . .

So now I will make close
By saying, on mine honour he arose!

The only one of the "experiments" of Wald Barnes of which we have firm knowledge (because Barnes told Janet Flanner about it) was his attempt to have his children emulate the regimen of poultry by swallowing a small amount of finely pulverized gravel as hens do in order that their systems might be cleansed by it. There are several experiments in a very similar vein in *Ryder.* It is prudent, however, to point out that the testimony against Wald Barnes is the testimony of his daughter, and to remember that Edgar Allan Poe's account of his family turned out to be more fanciful than factual.

What Wald Barnes didn't or wouldn't do, his women and his children did for him. As a young girl Miss Barnes not only sewed and baked, but also planted and plowed fields both at Cornwall-on-Hudson and later on their 105-acre Long Island farm. The family ground its own flour and killed its own chickens. —*Who does any of that now?* Miss Barnes exclaimed in wonder about her past.

Her father, according to Djuna Barnes, could play half a dozen in-

184

struments (badly) but played the piano fairly well, while she herself could play the banjo, violin and French horn. The best musician in the family was one of her brothers on the trombone.

When Professor James B. Scott brought the manuscript of the critical study he had written on her for the Twayne series to Miss Barnes in 1971—it was the first book-length study of her art—she was not at all hesitant about admitting that both Ryder in the novel and Titus in *The Antiphon* were in fact her father:

> —Yes, Ryder and Titus, they are my father. Where did the basic story come from? From my life. Every writer writes out of his life. Ryder is my father. And Titus. Ryder is a foolish man who wants to get rid of all the whores—doesn't believe there should be any—and has this perfectly ridiculous notion. Ryder is one of those impossible people who are going to save the world—how can anyone save the world?

There was one important difference between reality and *Ryder,* Miss Barnes told Scott, and that was simply that the family left Cornwall-on-Hudson because they ran out of the minimal amount of money they needed rather than that the local Puritans were out to get her father for living in sin and refusing to send his children to school, though it was true that he was under attack for both these things. The critical event that dislodged the unruly family was the death of Wald's wealthy brother, Justin, in 1907, because they were, of course, living on his estate.

A confrontation with the school authorities at the little red schoolhouse did take place. It is related in *The Biography of Julie von Bartmann.* Wald Barnes received notice to show cause why he should not send his children to school, and triumphantly beat back a solemn principal who tried to convince him that he was raising his children as heathens who would grow up deflowering women and defaming God. Wald Barnes retorted that education and religion as the principal understood them only make a man a coward and a monolinguist in the presence of his God instead of a disciple. There was also an investigation into the marital status of Wald Barnes and the two women with whom he was living, but that, too, as in *Ryder,* was successfully fended off by him on the basis of sheer bravado. Elizabeth Chappell was not married to Wald Barnes when she came to America with him and his mother. They married in New York State, but the ceremony did not come to light for some time, because Wald Barnes elected to marry under one of his occasional names, Harold. For some time it appeared that his daughter's name at birth was, legally,

Chappell, which is what, an old English friend told me, she herself once said. But Djuna's parents would have been married, even if it had been without certificate, for during that period in New York cohabitation as man and wife constituted legal marriage. In 1955, Barnes made extensive searches to locate her birth certificate, but could not find it. Nor could I. It likely does not exist.

The family had no money and was now on the verge of splitting up, but before that happened they wended their way back to Long Island, the seat of the Barnes family two hundred years earlier.

iv

Djuna Barnes dedicated her first two books to her mother. The second, and simple, dedication, to *A Book* in 1923, is the one of the two dedications which is known, because it has been carried on in the regroupings and retitling of that collection over the years as *A Night Among the Horses* and *Spillway*. The interesting dedication is the first one, to *The Book of Repulsive Women* in 1915:

> TO MOTHER
> *who was more or less like All*
> *mothers, but she was mine, —and*
> *so— She excelled*

The dedication is ostensibly an acknowledgment by child to parent of what a difficult daughter she has been, but there is a strong undercurrent of ambivalence, too, which surfaces savagely in *Ryder* where, in the penultimate chapter, one of Julie's brothers says about himself and his father that he is only *—one of his plays with a kitchen slut in Shepherd's Bush.* Those words, even with the typical transference mechanism we have learned to recognize in Barnes and the distancing which must be allowed for in fiction, are not kind. The matter reaches a slow but persistent climax in *The Antiphon,* which is a quiet and deadly duel between mother and daughter in which at one point they change places in grotesque "play," and at the end fall down dead together.

A strong child from such a family constellation must sooner or later be estranged from all the other members of the family. In her "Cautionary Note" to the publication of *The Antiphon,* Barnes instructed her future readers and players that though the mother can be by turns both timid and imperious and the daughter can show impassioned fury:

... never between the two women is there any sluttish whining. Their familiarity is their estrangement. They do not scold or bicker. Their duel is in hiatus, and should be waged with style.

V

Rutland, located in the East Midlands, was historically the smallest county in England. In 1974, seven hundred and seventy years after its establishment, it was merged with Leicestershire. The inhabitants to this day evidence that special pride that comes from living in a small old place, and thus the name Rutland survives even if it is no longer on the maps. Oakham, where Elizabeth Chappell was born in November 1862, is simply a modest market town located a few miles along the Uppingham Road (once Hangman's Lane) from larger and better-known Uppingham. Uppingham is notable for its public school and its inn, which has an interior courtyard to receive coaches. The town of Oakham does not possess a castle, but the region does have Burley-on-the-Hill—a simple and dignified manor house which was built on the site of the older mansion that had been burned down by the Parliamentary forces. It occupies a commanding site on the brow of a hill at a distance from the town, and is one of the lordliest residences in the county. Burley-on-the-Hill for a long time fell into disuse and was uninhabited, but special bricks were cast, and it was restored in the late 1930s, only a few years after Djuna Barnes visited her mother's birthplace. That ruined house is the setting for *The Antiphon*. The ruins were quite real, as well as symbolizing the ruinous state of the family.

The seat of Burley-on-the-Hill was constructed by Sir George Villiers, later Duke of Buckingham, who was a favourite of James I. He built the house with an earthen bank and broad ditch around it. Ben Jonson performed his *Gypsies* at Burley-on-the-Hill, and Sir Jeffery Hudson, the famous English court dwarf, was born in Oakham. The important Oakham personage for our story is Titus Oates, for it is from him that the name of the father who looms behind all the action in *The Antiphon* is taken. This is one of Miss Barnes' most pointed transference-namings, for Titus Oates is usually, and justly, identified in history books as one of the vilest characters in all of English history. He was the seventeenth-century imposter and fabricator of the story that there was a popish plot to burn London, assassinate the king, and massacre Protestants, and was responsible for many deaths. In choosing Titus as the name for the father (there would also have been the added flavour of the Paris bookseller Titus, whom she personally disliked), Barnes provided as clear a sign as we have of the extent of her antipathy towards her father.

The family of the play has come from America (Titus, who is the main subject of conversation but who is dead when the play begins, was from Salem, Massachusetts) for a reunion in England at the old family seat of Burley Hall in the township of Beewick. But the family of Miss Barnes' mother never lived on the hill. They lived in the heart of the village below in the oldest house in Oakham—a smallish stone house with a tight staircase and grotto-rooms. It is called Flore's House. Flore was the controller of works for the original manor house, and Sheriff of Rutland. Though the little house was much altered over the centuries, it has retained its modest main hall on the ground level and its typically medieval pointed entrance with molded orders on the jambshafts. It also kept its essential class position, for Elizabeth Chappell's father, Henry Chappell, was, like the original inhabitant Flore, a successful tradesman. Flore's House finally made its own contribution to art, however, for it was there that the future Sir Malcolm Sargent had his first piano lessons.

Djuna Barnes, undoubtedly relying upon the account she had from her mother, told James Scott that her maternal grandfather, Henry Chappell, was an artisan who made fine furniture. Doubtless he did—a manuscript variant of *The Antiphon* refers to a piece of his cabinetry—but the 1861 census returns for Oakham list him as a Master Slater and Plasterer. His father, Thomas, was also a plasterer. Henry's wife, Anne, came from nearby Hambleton. They had at least six children of whom Elizabeth would have been either the youngest or next youngest, and so the family, with one maidservant, would have fairly filled Flore's house. It was a successful working-class family. Henry Chappell was proud of Flore's House and affixed his name to an outside wall on a cement plaque. Though the Chappells were Anglican, Oakham was a town in which Methodism was a very strong influence. It would appear that the American Budington-Barnes families and the English Chappells had very similar positions in their respective societies.

There are numerous passages that can be culled from *The Antiphon* and together they comprise a family history which closely parallels the one found in *Ryder*. Where details are exactly repeated it is reasonable to assume that one is dealing with reality as well as art. There are, of course, also differences—in her fictional version the mother is married at seventeen and pregnant at nineteen,

188

whereas in fact Elizabeth was twenty-eight when her son Thurn was born.

The family dispersed after the death of Henry Chappell. Of the three brothers, one emigrated to Southern California where he became a colourful skipper who is mentioned in the local literature. In *Ryder*, Miss Barnes tells us that another brother lived in London and suffered from venereal disease. The third (in life) went to Australia. The older sister who accompanied Elizabeth to London was Susannah. She remained unmarried and worked as a dressmaker. In *Ryder* she is the one who continues to correspond with her sister after she has gone to America with Wendell Ryder. She falls on hard times and is reduced to becoming an ill-treated maid-servant. Djuna met her in the English years, and for a long time sent her a pound a week, though that was from the money that she in turn received from Peggy. The other sister, Sarah, is presumably the one who was made pregnant by the local squire and given a large sum of money and married off to a young guard who loved her and suspected nothing. This affair was the secret scandal of the Chappell family and their only connection with Burley-on-the-Hill.

The early drafts of *The Antiphon* underscore even more heavily than the printed version the fear that the entire family has of the writer-daughter, Miranda. Miranda may herself be doomed, but it is she who passes judgment. The name Miranda is another important and clear transference—Miranda is the daughter of Prospero, of course, but there may be a Miranda closer to hand. The only death certificate that could be located for the period in which Djuna's friend Mary Pyne died belongs to Miranda Pyne. It could be a close relative and another Barnes name transference. However that may be, as one critic observed, Miranda is Djuna, as were Julie of *Ryder* and Nora of *Nightwood* before. The hostility towards the father by Djuna-Julie-Miranda is a simple continuation of a well-articulated basic Barnes theme, but it is only in the discarded drafts of *The Antiphon* that there is shown at last the precise basis of the hostility between mother and daughter.

Miranda's accusation is that there was virtual collusion between her father and her mother in the welter of mistresses and in the way that she, the only daughter in the sprawling family, was treated. She calls herself the scapegoat, the recipient of all her mother's frustrated fury. In the discarded variants of the play the mother has admitted to weeping when she saw that she had given birth to a daughter. Miranda senses that she is the unloved one and is fated to spend her entire life wondering what her crime is. The mother Augusta (adapted from Joyce's middle name—Barnes wrote about it in an unpublished fragment) in the play is self-pitying. She tells her children that in her day it simply was not done to leave your husband, that she has done her duty by bearing them, and that, anyway,

>—*You all seem to know much more than I do.*
> *I, like the poor man-handled mendicant*
> *Sit down alone, to banquet in a dream;*
> *Say I mothered children in a vision.*

But Miranda will not be fended off by pity and simpering. Her weapons are obdurate memory of what happened and bluntness. For her the entire saga was:

>—*All to amuse a frightened man, his generation;*
> *And astound one woman of great folly.*

Miranda wishes that she had not been born—certainly her mother's primal offense—and rails against any resurrection scheme that will include her terrible past. Her father is Titus Adam, a crusading madman and a cheat, who has filled his foolish Carrion Eve with —*a belly full of thumbs.*

There are several more specific grudges between the two women, who have reached that vague equivalency that old age can give to people even of significantly different years. The mother's reproach is that her daughter, in leaving the family, also drew her youngest son away. Miranda rounds upon her mother in one of the fiercest exchanges of the play for suggesting that she might have been a party to subjecting her baby brother to a continuation of the family fate. In the play that son is Jeremy, who has come back to the family seat disguised as Jack Blow. He closes the play by walking away after the death of his mother and his sister.

Shangar (Charles) died in December 1966. Saxon is still alive as this is being written. Another brother, Thurn, also discarded the name Barnes. He reverted to Budington. He and Wald were particularly antagonistic towards one another.

The brothers in *The Antiphon* are portrayed as sinister and dangerous figures, enemies of both the mother and her daughter. In draft versions of the play there were three brothers, in addition to the disguised "Jack Blow," making four in all just as in the Barnes family, but in the printed version the number is reduced to two plus the disguised brother. The brothers of the play, after the collapse of their father's wild kingdom, conform passionately to the laws of the marketplace and go on to become successful businessmen and bankers.

They worship money and are highly wary of their writer-sister for two reasons: they think she could become a financial drain on them; and they wish to prevent her from making their family origins famous.

The brothers of the play have conspired against both mother and daughter on separate occasions, something once again which is made far more clear in discarded variants of *The Antiphon*. They would have had their mother committed to a poorhouse except for their sister's intercession:

> —Why mother, they'd have had you by the scruff
> Still in appetite, in sense, and quaking cold,
> And thrown you to the gammers of the pit—
> Except I put my foot against that door.

The bitterness which Miranda feels towards her two brothers is all glare and knows no soft shadowing:

> —You have such sons
> Would mate the pennies on a dead man's eyes
> To breed the sexton's fee.

The attack upon Miranda is made with the full complicity of their mother. In the draft even Jeremy, who means well but sometimes does not understand sufficiently, concurs that Miranda should be committed to an asylum. Her most aggressive brother (the one who does not appear in the printed text) goes through her papers with their mother, and they burn the manuscript of a book which she has begun to write. The incident is referred to as the week of the war. That war took place in 1940, and there probably was the beginning of a manuscript that was burnt. At least, in a letter to Emily Coleman (March 25, 1940), Barnes says that she now intends to write about them all in a biography, since she has no reason to feel anything for them but hatred.

Mother and daughter share an admixture of love and resentment for each other. Augusta says that she loved her children no less than did the Virgin, and Miranda acknowledges a clenched love for her, too. But the mother wants the daughter to be a partner in suffering. As the claim is made in *Ryder* that Julie is essentially like Wendell, so the claim is made in *The Antiphon* that Miranda is like her mother, who wants her to be famous, but not too famous (—*I'd have you smaller—though cast up for glory*), and yet reproaches her for falling short of true fame and for not having made better use of her contacts. Whereas Wendell Ryder and Titus wish to have easy im-

191

mortality through their children, Miranda's mother, like Robin Vote in *Nightwood,* is afraid of fame and longs for safe anonymity. The childish cry of Wald Barnes was —*forget me—I am great.* Augusta is weak, too. She has something of the pitiful voyeur in her, and she wants to pry into her daughter's past in much the same way that she stood as mute audience to her husband's sexual careering. Pressed about the number of her lovers, Miranda retorts with contemptuous wit that that is just a bridge of asses that leads nowhere.

A bitter childhood is at the vortex of *The Antiphon,* and around it orbit money, poverty and art in perpetual conflict. In life, Elizabeth Barnes went to live with her sons, but they re-housed her in two small rooms on East Fifty-fourth Street. Djuna, who had nothing, also went there to live, but they often found each other's company unbearable, and her mother finally turned her out. Elizabeth Chappell became a Christian Scientist in her old age and wanted to do nothing but lecture Djuna on her bad habits and read her selections from Mrs. Eddy. Their beds were ten feet apart. Djuna said that her mother was the world's strongest weak woman.

Wald Barnes remarried, continued to depend upon the two children left with him, Duane and Muriel (half-brother and half-sister to Djuna), and died prematurely senile. Barnes herself stood sternly to the side, continued to write, and exchanged her Paris cloak for a coat of poverty and proud isolation. The years of silence began in earnest after *The Antiphon.*

vi

Barnes travelled to Oakham with her friend Peter Hoare (later Sir Samuel) in 1936. Miss Barnes was very interested in Dante in these years, and it is clear from her papers that the pair of Miranda and Jack Blow are meant to be like Dante and Virgil visiting Hell. Even Miranda's game leg in the play has a factual referent—in a letter to Charles Henri Ford written in the summer of 1934, Barnes recalls how she had had to limp the length of Victoria Station with a sore toe the pain of which reached deep into her hip. *The Antiphon* is totally English in its high language and in its setting. The metre is Shakespearean iambic pentameter. In an article which she wrote in 1930 called *Hamlet's Custard Pie,* Barnes advocates a return by modern drama to Shakespearean eloquence, and we know from letters of this period that she was frequently thought of as being an Elizabethan herself and evidently enjoyed the part. But the heart of the play really remains wholly on the American side, what happened down on the farm at Cornwall-on-Hudson.

There is in the draft versions of *The Antiphon* yet another version of how a girl lost her virginity, and it is essentially the same as the deleted incident from the draft version of *Nightwood*, except that the later scene is now put simply and without any of the stylistic obfuscation that the earlier one had, though there are even here several versions tried in successive variants, so historical certainty makes its escape, probably forever. It must be all the same, I think, what actually happened, whatever the specific true details of the incident which we have to choose from in various manuscripts may have been.

Wald Barnes' Code was evidently in the main sexual, like the Code of Titus in *The Antiphon*. It was a latter-day extension of early Mormonism with himself as the godhead. It was a limited cult, but Titus in the play is said to have had as many as four mistresses under his roof at one time, several of them in various stages of pregnancy and lamentation, and he enjoyed a certain following among local farmers and farmhands for his views.

In an undated initial draft of *The Antiphon* (probably written in the early 1950s), Titus himself tries to rape the sixteen-year-old Miranda in open view in the farmyard. She succeeds in fending him off with teeth and feet in a battle of perfect silence fought at the gate of the farm. Unable to have his way with her himself, Titus binds her up like a side of beef and hoists her up to hang from a rafter in the barn while he goes off to barter her virginity for a goat among the local men. A deal is struck with a farmhand named Jacobsen who is nearly sixty, and the dazed young girl is led off to an upstairs room with the farmhand and one of her brothers to stand as witness to the rape. She is to be the first virginal sacrifice of his new religion, he tells her. The young Miranda is terrorized but submits because she feels that her mother is acquiescing in what is happening, and so she is finally willing to do what both her parents want. It may somehow atone for the guilt she has been made to feel in the family for her very existence. The only thing that her mother does is sprinkle salt in the hallway and on the stairway so that she can know that her husband has not gone to take part in the molestation. That salt or flour is a constant in every one of the variants of this rape tale Barnes has ever told. She and her husband remain downstairs while the rape takes place, she with her apron pulled up to cover her face, he rubbing his hands together gleefully. When the experiment is done the girl crawls from the bedroom on her hands and knees bleeding and moaning for her mother. Her young brother has been transfixed with terror at what he has been made to watch.

Wald Barnes, Henry Budington, Basil, Titus, Wendell, which is, by the way, a traditional Barnes family name. It does not take much to understand why this tale of cold and stupid horror has always remained the story behind the story in Barnes' writing, either removed or disguised or only obliquely told. In spite of the obvious anguish of the event, Miss Barnes does not have a taste for overly heavy melodrama in her writing. She prefers the protection of high stylization. Such a life. Dostoevsky and Faulkner even working together probably couldn't have invented it.

Djuna Barnes and
Natalie Barney, Nice,
c. 1928–30; photo from
The Amazon of Letters
by George Wickes
(courtesy of the author)

"April," drawing from
Ladies Almanack,
Paris, 1928

Djuna Barnes, photo by Berenice Abbott
(reproduced by permission of Berenice Abbott)

Thelma Wood, Paris, 1920s; photo by Berenice Abbott
(reproduced by permission of Berenice Abbott)

Mina Loy with Barnes, photo by Man Ray, 1920s (copyright Juliet Man Ray)

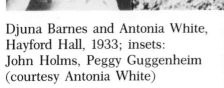

Djuna Barnes and Antonia White,
Hayford Hall, 1933; insets:
John Holms, Peggy Guggenheim
(courtesy Antonia White)

Djuna Barnes c. 1929

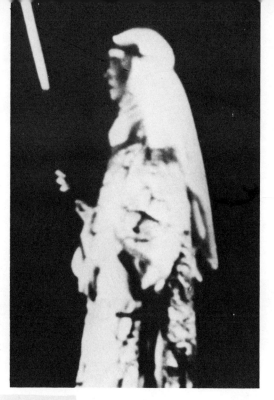

Barnes as a nun
in Claudel's play
The Tidings Brought to Mary,
Theatre Guild, December 1922
(photo courtesy Beinecke
Library, Yale University)

Portrait of Alice (courtesy
McKeldin Library,
University of Maryland)
with photo inset of
the subject, Alice Rohrer

Madame Majeska (courtesy
McKeldin Library,
University of Maryland)
with photo inset of
the subject, Emily Coleman

Georgette Leblanc, 1941,
drawing by Djuna Barnes

Djuna Barnes with Margaret Anderson and Carl Van Vechten,
Gotham Book Mart

Djuna Barnes, 1971 (credit: Jack Manning, *The New York Times*)

CHAPTER FIVE

—My roots, my affinities are with England, she said many years later.

Life in Paris was extremely unsatisfactory from both an emotional and a financial point of view for Miss Barnes by 1932, and so she had no reason not to accept Peggy's invitation to come to South Devon that summer. Peggy Guggenheim, then living with John Holms, had rented a large manor house with a baronial hall at the edge of the moor. Barnes arrived with the Guggenheim party (cook, maid, nanny, children, two cars, John and frenetic Emily) at Hayford Hall on a late afternoon in mid-August 1932 in a state of total exhaustion, but it happened that tea was waiting for them in the Grand Hall, and life suddenly seemed more plausible.

Hayford Hall was a simply built greystone building. The Grand Hall with its fireplace and a cathedral window at one end was well-proportioned, though the wall panelling, furniture and the ancestral portraits of shipbuilders from Clyde weren't particularly attractive. There were eleven bedrooms, and what with children, servants and guests they could sometimes all be occupied. Life centred on the Hall. Djuna did not have much clothing suited to an English summer, but she did have several elegant Paris dresses which she wore in the evenings.

At one point there were five children resident in Hayford Hall, and there was a steady stream of artists and writers from London passing through. Antonia White was a frequent visitor. Meals could assume a resort dining-room air. Two old Village friends of both Barnes and Guggenheim, Louis and Marion Bouché, were spending the year in England and living nearby. Peggy's rented manor removed temporarily the financial worry and provided a place that was both secluded enough and noisily congenial. Thelma Wood's irresponsible ways had always been a heavy financial as well as emotional burden for Djuna. Life had been possible before, but became less and less so as the American Depression dragged on and money from publishing and journalism was difficult to obtain. William Carlos Williams recorded a typical incident in his *Autobiography* of the way in which Thelma would take money from Djuna and lose it.

By the time she came to Hayford Hall, Barnes had several thousand dollars in various debts to worry about. Her personal life was a mess with Thelma, and Charles, Tangiers and the abortion all close behind her. She was in a nervous state, she was drinking and smoking heavily, and her health was generally bad (she was beginning to suffer seriously from asthma attacks).

It was her pattern once again to assume the role of ferocious but loving martyr. She had just before leaving Paris taken the manuscript of the Ford-Tyler *The Young and Evil* to William Bradley, and had hopes that she could arrange the publication through him to produce some money for Charles. They corresponded fairly regularly and extremely warmly between Devon, and later New York and Morocco. If she suddenly became rich, she told him, she would hire him as her literary secretary again. Barnes was also in correspondence with Thelma, who had gone to Florence. When she arrived at Hayford Hall, Barnes was hoping that Thelma would join her in Devon, but Thelma said she didn't have the money to come. It is difficult to imagine the writing of the novel that became *Nightwood* under the same roof with the prototype for Robin Vote, but if one understands such a possibility even occurring to her, then one understands something important about Djuna Barnes.

Djuna did have a terrible confrontation with Thelma over *Nightwood*. When she went to Paris with the nearly finished manuscript, she saw Thelma and began to read the novel to her aloud. The reading was quickly broken off. Thelma threw her teacup at Djuna and attacked her, punching her twice in the mouth. But later Djuna took Thelma in when she came to her in Italy, starving and without a cent. The exact favour, as it happens, was returned to Djuna in New York when Djuna had nowhere to sleep and no money.

Certainly it was just as well that Wood did not come to Devon, for Barnes was in a state of some tension. She began to work on *Bow Down,* but then ripped up the pages that she had written. She couldn't write. She didn't want to write anymore. Whenever anyone said anything kind to her she would be liable to burst into tears. And then, fortunately rather quickly, she began to work again, in a frenzy. This sort of rise and fall, forced grace and sudden despair, would continue as she returned to Paris at the end of the summer, then went to New York to try (unsuccessfully) to secure some writing that would provide immediate payment, until finally she returned to Devon for the summer of 1933. There she completed the novel—though there was still much editing to do—and was off again to New York to try to find a publisher for it.

She had not been able to get passage on the *Savvia,* and the *Rex* was sailing too late, so she had departed for New York on the *Augustus* in September of 1933. It was a bit of a shock because the first port of call for the *Augustus* was Tangier, which she had dearly hoped never to set eyes on again.

Her letters from New York are checkered. She remembers Venice and the beautiful ruins of Padua and is convinced that she cannot last long in New York unless she keeps her door shut and stays off the streets. She lived with her mother and her brother Saxon on Waverly Place. She found that she even had to hold back from seeing her mother in the morning lest the concentration of the morning be broken. There was a speakeasy next door. In her eyes there was little thought or feeling in New York—everything seemed to be just money and appearance. She saw little love, work or happiness. She thought the American people had become safe and smug and queer. And yet. She felt pleased at having reached forty, wise, alone, and contented with her lot in a way, particularly when she remembered how much less she had had in Morocco, and the torture that was Paris with Thelma. It doesn't matter if her New York friends think she has gone a little mad and has lost her ambition. She has *Bow Down,* after all, even if the manuscript does need more work, and knows—a moving letter—that other people do not have as much in their houses. But in other letters she confesses how terribly she misses Europe, and how sometimes now her life is so dreadful that she is forced to shut her eyes for fully ten minutes at a time thinking of what she has lost.

Carl Van Vechten took some photographs of her, and they struck Barnes as making her look like a peasant dug up after the chalk age, the beginning of the end of her beauty. But her nails were still bright red, and she worked at home in elegant black and white and green lounging pyjamas which had been given to her by her family. She continued to write and destroy in a state of high tension. The rumours of New York—that all but three publishing houses would have to close their doors within six months—did not improve her state of mind. She was equally depressed by a public taste which she saw would accept nothing less sentimental than Faulkner, Steinbeck and *The Postman Always Rings Twice.* Barnes was horrified that the dialogue in *The Postman* was being praised in the popular press as superior to Hemingway's. When a culture goes *that* far, she felt, all is over.

Barnes was advised by friends that the best way to make quick money was to do a popular play, preferably a comedy. She determined to set *Bow Down* aside and try to do something simple like *Ah, Wilderness* (she was given free tickets to that and had gone with Thelma), but she herself recognized that her hope for a popular suc-

197

cess was lost by the time she had written her third line of dialogue. She tried to get a job (at the Gotham Book Mart) and couldn't. She had once had some work with the WPA and wanted to get in that again, but couldn't. She was able to line up one workaday article, on Moroccan marriage, for Hearst's *Cosmopolitan,* but even her *Theatre Guild* perch as "Lydia Steptoe," which Langner had obtained for her, was lost. Her only real hope was the oblivion of working on her book, so that she could sometimes forget her present situation "beyond the end" of her story.

When summer came she returned to England and Hayford Hall. Steerage was only sixty to seventy dollars in those years, and that was more than offset by the possibility of another summer devoted to the book in sympathetic company with the business of living attended to by Peggy.

Once again Barnes arrived at Hayford Hall in a fairly weak state and in general bad health, and once again she grew stronger, though she did not feel up to doing any horse-riding that second summer. She did go wading and played a few desultory games of tennis. She would stay in her rococo bedroom working every morning until lunchtime at one. In subsequent years Peggy Guggenheim claimed that that bedroom was given to her because it perfectly suited her, whereas Barnes claimed that she got it because no one else wanted it. She would frequently eat far too much at lunch and afterwards do some reading and, if it was a nice day, perhaps go for a very short walk on the moor or simply wander around the extensive grounds. Djuna was in the main not a lover of greenery, and both Peggy Guggenheim and Antonia White recalled that on many days she would not be outside for more than ten minutes. Occasionally she would go motoring with Peggy, John and Emily. Sometimes she would take an afternoon nap. Tea was always served at five, and dinner was an early and light affair. The brutal ritual would begin after dinner.

ii

Everyone drank far too much, except for Emily (who was naturally overspirited and didn't have to), and, when the drinking was well along in the middle of the evening, games were played. There were the usual charades and imitations of friends and writers. Barnes was best in the company at that. And then, eventually, they would have to come to Emily's beloved game, which was a kind of Devil's biography called Truth. The rules of the game were really quite simple: The party took pen and paper, and everyone wrote a single paragraph on a nominated feature of someone present. It might be sex appeal, appearance, taste, mannerisms. Composition and the task of reading them aloud passed in rounds from person to person. The opinions were anonymous. After shuffling they were recited to the company by the elected reader, who was, of course, never the subject of that particular round.

When Truth was played the previous deadly earnestness of literary opinion edged with only slight personal insult would change gear to direct and deadly savagery. Emily played most ruthlessly. Djuna was the best reader because of her voice which was deep and sombre and suddenly would burst into an explosive laugh like shrapnel and then immediately continue on in its calm and grave way. Once, when Peggy grew exasperated and said: —*Emily, you've gone too far,* Djuna cut in before she could answer and said: —*That's one of her destinations.* Emily tended to aim at Peggy, while Djuna had most of her best epigrams at Emily's expense. They were very close friends, vicious friends, who were all the same important to one another. Djuna's epigrams were all founded upon the extremity which was the core of Emily Coleman's personality. Emily was —*a prima vera with blood on her lips;* and —*a girl hitchhiker with a primus in the realms of the infinite* and —*someone rowing across a fjord: not romance, just a getaway.*

The evening would usually break up at about midnight. Once Barnes chanced to come back downstairs after something she had left there and found Emily sitting crosslegged on the floor surrounded by crumpled pieces of paper and a wastebasket lying on its side. She was identifying handwritings from that night's Truth in order to know who had said what.

Emily Coleman was a Californian who graduated from Wellesley in 1920, married, came to Europe with her husband in 1926, and two years after separated from him. She threw herself into slightly more than a decade of various countries and passionate loves, beginning with a wild affair with an Italian and progressing to several poets, chief among them Dylan Thomas, and then a lover who regularly beat her up. Emily was always falling in love. She had a long and inconclusive tie with Peter Hoare whom she had met in Oakley Street in London because he had a flat in the same building she did. One source told me that there were affairs with two women as well. When Miss Barnes made a brief trip to London, her last, in the early 1950s, she automatically wended her way back to old regions and took a bed-sit in Oakley Street. The same street had seen much of Zadel Barnes nearly a century before because quiet Oakley Street with its wide roadway sweeping to the Thames and comfortable old-fashioned buildings had once been the location of salons in Lady Wilde's son Willie's house.

Emily Coleman had golden hair, which she kept in a boyish cut, usually wearing a beret that covered most of it. Her bright turquoise eyes were her strongest feature, but her face had overall the effect of a small hat-tree holding up her beret, because both her nose and her mouth were very long and straight—the mouth could have been turned upside down with no effect on her expression whatsoever— and her face gave the impression of an inverted-T. She wore one soiled sweater day and night, and that plus her slight build made her sometimes seem like an older brother beside her ten-year-old son. When she died at the age of seventy-five in 1974 she, like Thelma Wood, had grown fat and had an old Indian squaw air about her broad, immobile face.

When she first went to Europe, Emily Coleman worked on the European edition of *The Chicago Tribune*. Then for a while she was the society editor of the Paris *Tribune*. Her poetry appeared in *transition*. When Peggy met her in 1928 she was installed at St. Tropez as the literary secretary to Emma Goldman (the same job held by Hippolyte Havel in the Village in the previous decade) who was then being supported by Peggy in order that she might complete her anarchist memoirs. Emily introduced Peggy to John Holms. Emily was at the time having an affair with him. The circle was closed six years later because it was Emily who arranged the fatal operation for John after he broke his wrist falling off a horse at Hayford Hall. At first, in St. Tropez, Emily was very upset when Guggenheim became involved with Holms, but she made her peace with it and became a member of the Guggenheim entourage, which also, after an initial period of hostility, included Holms' estranged wife, Dorothy (an astrologist), who inexplicably transferred all her hostility against Peggy to Emily. Emily was aggressive, and she could be quite hateable. She had and showed a deep aversion to ugly people, and to many others as well.

In one early serious rift with Peggy, Emily gave her a black eye and had to be pulled off her by Holms. John and Peggy came to regard her as their unmanageable child who had to be humoured and suffered, though that was probably more his opinion than hers. Emily would offend both Peggy and Djuna with her bad manners. She could eat like a pig and always tried to commandeer both the one fine horse, Katie, which was John's, and John himself. She would talk to him for hours on end, sometimes until dawn. By the end of the second summer Peggy's patience with her was in tatters, and so,

200

when Emily told her what a wonderful summer it had been, Peggy snapped back that Emily was the only one who thought so. Coleman stamped upstairs to pack and depart immediately, and Guggenheim obdurately allowed her to proceed. She even drove her to the railway station in spite of the efforts of Holms to soften her. The quarrel was eventually smoothed over and forgotten. After all, what could one say? Emily. Djuna once told her —*You would be marvellous company slightly stunned.*

Coleman seemed capable of anything. Guggenheim judged her more severely than Barnes and was probably wrong. But there were reasons to fear Emily. The real reason that Miss Barnes did not often go outside during the second Hayford summer was that she was in terror of Emily, who had threatened to burn the manuscript of her novel if she revealed a secret that she regretted having confided to Djuna.

In the end it was Emily Coleman's experience in asylums that made her a genuine writer, for her 1930 novel *The Shutter of Snow* is one of the most convincing fictional examinations of the world of the asylum in the modern tradition which begins with Chekhov's *Ward Number Seven.* In addition to that book, she wrote another novel, *The Tygon,* which was not published but which Barnes thought was perhaps the best novel she knew on jealousy written from the woman's point of view. Her poetry was far less interesting. She also painted, in the sort of primitive style that would later come to be termed "Grandma Moses." Jesus figured prominently in her paintings. He always had Emily's face. Some years later, when her son became literary secretary to the Catholic writer Jacques Maritain, Coleman converted. Her demand that Peter Hoare convert with her effected the final break between them. Her friends, though all in some degree were of high church disposition, were exceedingly annoyed by Emily's religiosity, for she would do things like wish for the death of friends on the grounds that it would be good for their souls.

Though jealousy and rage were very much a part of Emily's character, generosity was, too, and she was, happily, convinced of her own genius as well as Djuna's. —*Make it marvellous!!!* she exhorted Djuna as she was finishing writing the novel, which was temporarily without title because she had dropped *Bow Down* and did not yet have a replacement. Difficult Emily Coleman is one of the heroines of this story, because, when Barnes returned from America with her much-rejected manuscript in 1934, Emily turned all of her considerable energy to getting it published in England and—after Edwin Muir had pressed the manuscript on Eliot—literally bearded the poet-editor in his office and made it clear to him that Faber would

201

publish the novel, or else. Barnes would subsequently say that Emily had to be given seventy percent of the credit for the novel's making it into print. That debt was repaid with the dedication of Barnes' last work, *Creatures in an Alphabet,* to Coleman.

iii

John and Peggy had a difficult time cadging the spare manuscript of *Nightwood* away from Emily to read it. Holms took a strong interest in Barnes' writing; he was particularly anxious to promote *Ryder,* which some years after its appearance in America had still not found an English publisher.

Holms produced a strong impression on almost everyone who met him for the breadth and depth of his knowledge, his physical strength, and especially his otherwordly character which combined strains of sadness and a great capacity for joy. By all accounts Holms had no aggression in him. He suffered terrible nightmares every night. Peggy Guggenheim was certainly not a writer, but in the few pages of her memoirs *Out of This Century* which are devoted to Holms, the man and her love for him manage to come alive on the page. She maintained that merely to be in his company was equivalent to being in an undreamt-of fifth dimension. Hugh Kingsmill, who was a good writer and a close friend of Holms, put the matter in a single sentence:

—In spite of the weaknesses in which his wonderful gifts of mind and spirit were entangled, there was something divine in him which I have never felt in any other man, and which seemed to make clear what is meant in Buddhism by an "older pilgrim," a soul which has learnt magnanimity and gentleness in many lives.

An even stronger affirmation, in part because of who was making it, came from Edwin Muir, who had known the fellow Scot since 1919. In a preface to a collection of Holms' letters, which his friends tried without success to have published after his death, Muir wrote:

—Holms gave me a greater feeling of genius than any other man I have met, and I think that he must have been one of the most remarkable men of his time, or indeed of any time.... His mind had a majestic clarity and order, and when turned on anything was like a spell which made objects assume their true shape and appear as they were, in their original relation to one another, as on the day of creation.

Muir was very conscious of the fact that the problem with Holms was that he had never been able to give lasting expression to his talents, and so they had to be a matter either of direct experience or faith.

There was no disliking John Holms, but, as it happens, Djuna Barnes was more resistant to him than anyone else. She found his manner offputting. It was a little, she told Antonia White, —*like God come down for the weekend.*

Holms was over six feet tall and was yet another person in the life of Barnes with flaming red hair. Holms had gone into service in World War I when he was underage (at the time he had just come up to Sandhurst from Rugby) and had been decorated for bravery. Peggy Guggenheim has the story ludicrously wrong in her memoirs where he is presented as having bashed in the heads of four Germans with a hammer from behind while they were sitting having their breakfast, but it is likely that that caricature came from Holms himself who took no pride in his war experiences. What actually did happen is recounted by a fellow soldier in the unpublished memorial volume. A German raiding party was advancing on the post being manned by Holms:

> —He opened fire on them, and when they retired, Holms leaped out of the trench alone throwing bombs at them. You can see that if you throw a bomb with a five-second fuse at a man thirty yards away, and at the same time run towards him as he runs away, the chances of your being hit are about the same as his. Well, he wasn't hit, and he got the M.C.

Holms loved to scrabble up trees at high speed, leap lengthways across long tables, and once he sailed directly into a fen on Katie, and he and the horse were just rescued in time as they slowly sank. He had developed the skill of moving at great speed on all fours without bending his knees, because walking bored him. Muir thought that Holms was like a powerful cat and saw in him not only a cat's sprung energy, but also its ability to slide into total immobility for a long time. Peggy Guggenheim has provided testimony to his sexual prowess. Holms was extremely indolent and thus good only at sports which rely largely upon native energy and bad at specialized sports which demand sophisticated technique. It was the same when it came to turning brilliant conversation into hard words. Peggy claimed that he was a Socrates, but if so he was a Socrates without either text or recording scribe.

Peggy Guggenheim relates in *Out of This Century* how one evening she fell asleep while listening to Emily's droning and then awoke suddenly to see John gently fingering Djuna's freshly washed soft red hair. She looked at them sternly and said to John —*If you rise, the dollar will fall.* Djuna continued talking affectionately but not amorously to Holms as though Peggy weren't there: —*You smug little red melon of a Shakespeare. Busy old fool, unruly son.*

The hagiography with which his friends surrounded Holms makes it hard to approach the little poetry, prose and criticism that he did produce without natural scepticism, but there is at least fragmentary evidence to give some support to the bold assertions about his powers. In an unpublished note called "True Art and Counterfeit," Holms defines art in a way that seems to justify his own lack of achievement:

> —For a great many people action is the main and proper business of their lives (their "essential") and art or religion are substitutes, or "escapes." One can always tell when this is so, however, because the art or the religion, in such cases, betrays itself by a great many signs, as being a substitute for the true desires of those concerned; isn't pure in fact. What such people really want, what would really give them happiness, their "essential," is something else.

Like such criticism, the poetry of Holms also has a quasi-philosophical cast. He wanted to be the new Blake, and there was the air of the Old Testament about him. One of his better works is a fragmentary drama about Noah on the Ark with his sons. The sensibility is modern, as when Japeth reproaches his brothers and his father:

> —I shouldn't be surprised if you'd each smuggled a woman or two aboard. I hope so, I don't want you squabbling over my wife. Father's perfectly capable of joining in, too. You can accommodate him and each other with pleasure. I prefer to keep my wife to myself. . . . It takes a man who believes in God to be really happily vicious. Father's a genius in his own way.

Barnes and Holms shared many artistic themes and attitudes years before they knew each other. Of particular importance among these shared themes are a passionate longing for death and man's links with all the other members of the animal kingdom. The great poem which Holms never wrote was to have been a description of the evolution of the species showing images of all forms of life as they developed from a single archetype with an enormous foreshortening of time. Though Barnes and Holms came independently to the theme of the primeval roots of the human personality, the concept of the high-speed telescoping of time originated with Holms, and after his death this device of time rushing backwards furnished one of the major devices both in *The Antiphon* and in the later Barnes poetry.

Barnes was the first of the four to leave Hayford Hall that second summer. The book was finished, and she agreed to take Peggy's son Sinbad to his father, Laurence Vail, in Paris before she sailed for New York. Djuna regularly did such little things for her patroness, particularly acting as the laconic go-between in the stormy patches between Peggy and her lovers. Of these, Barnes' least favourite was Max Ernst who exploited Guggenheim and whom Djuna regarded as barely human. She had a far easier time with her former lover, Vail. Once she dressed him down in a restaurant for the way he was treating Peggy.

Barnes was shocked by the news of the death of John Holms in January 1934 far more than she would be by the news of her own father's death four months later. It's curious, the way in which John Holms seems merely to have extended the failed aspirations of two important figures in Miss Barnes' life. Holms was another red-headed Adam, but he was much stronger than Wald Barnes and was not so much hostage to his own ego. He was a critic passionately interested in the deepest meanings behind the exercise of the critical function, but unlike Courtenay Lemon, he had at least begun to articulate his thoughts on the subject. All the same he was, like them, also creatively impotent. Peggy used to nag him terribly for the way in which he would let months go by without writing a line.

Barnes did not let death make her forget that his manner had been most unsympathetic as far as she was concerned, but looking back on him at his death it seemed clear to her that Holms really did know and feel more than other people. Djuna suddenly understood, she wrote to a friend, that she had lost her best critic. She refused when Peter Hoare asked her to write a memorial essay on Holms, saying that she had already given John all that she could, the dedication to *Nightwood*.

Djuna's primary feeling at the death was sympathy for Peggy. She understood that nothing could comfort her. There was a tremendous row between Peggy and Holms' widow over the project to publish his letters. John Holms was the one great love of Peggy Guggenheim's rather sad life. She was the poor little rich girl, even though in her relations with most people there were such strong waftings of the will to dominate that the misfortune of her situation could easily be overlooked. She knew better than anyone that her charm was involved with money. She was attractive in a slightly wispy way, but

205

not a beauty; sharp and quick, but not a wit. She made an important contribution to the arts, and often in a way that was both wise and disinterested. But she was very harsh with Barnes. They had a strange relationship, which might be compared with the situation of two sisters, one with gifts and one with control, who are to appearance extremely tetchy with one another and yet all the same possess real bonds of affection as well as hostility. They did not like each other very much, but stopped short of ever saying it, though Peggy did stop the support payments she had been giving her for several months at a time, while making a point of continuing to send the weekly pound to Barnes' Aunt Sue. Djuna was painting Peggy, but Peggy wouldn't pose. It was to have been oil on mahogany and titled "The Unhappy Vixen."

When Barnes finally returned to New York to live, Guggenheim arranged a regular monthly allowance for her. Emily Coleman, in a letter to Antonia White, claimed that it was she who had pushed Peggy into it. It started at fifty dollars and later was raised to one hundred. Her support of Barnes was by far the most protracted patronage into which she ever entered. There were many years when Miss Barnes had no income at all except for the monthly Guggenheim stipend and the continuing sale of *Nightwood*, which was steady but never more than two thousand copies a year. The rising cost of living finally made it almost impossible to subsist on that amount. Djuna wrote to her friend apologizing that she had too rarely spoken thanks for the support that she had been getting but that now, even by devoting much of her time to shopping for the cheapest possible food, there just wasn't enough. She asked for a bit more, was given it, and expressed deep thanks; but it was only a little bit more, in fact, that she was given. Two years later, in 1952, her stipend (sinecure is somehow not the appropriate word) was increased by twenty-five dollars a month. When the two friends next met it was necessary to raise the subject once again.

—*It's not enough to live on, you know.*

—*I know,* said her friend and smiled in a way that said the subject was closed.

Peggy gave both compulsively and grudgingly. She became very suspicious when she learned that Barnes had sold her literary papers, for Djuna had said nothing about it to her. Once Guggenheim was interviewed in *Time* (June 16, 1961) and reminisced about the various artists she had supported over the years. —*I kill myself for artists,* she said. —*The hell of it is I hate them.* Barnes carefully clipped and saved the passage.

iv

When she returned to New York with *Bow Down*, Barnes began to submit her novel to the publishers. It did not even suffer the usual agonizing delays but shot in and out of the publishers' offices as though it were being ejected from a greased revolving door in an old silent movie. Peter Neagoe, who had edited an anthology of expatriate writing, warned her that it couldn't be published in America without cuts. By March it was already on its third publisher. Apart from what was required in making these submissions she saw almost no one, the same cloistered pattern that she had followed during the last stages of her life with Thelma in Paris. Thelma had gone to live in Boston. She would occasionally drop by when she was in the city. Sometimes Djuna saw Marion Bouché or one or two of the other women in New York with whom she had longstanding friendships. An organ grinder outside her window made her ache to be back in Italy again.

After her intense work on the novel, Barnes did not write at all when she came to New York. She painted. Until this time her artwork had been pen and ink. But at Hayford Hall she had painted the portrait of an ambisexual art dealer. Now she set to work on another oil painting, a five-foot-tall portrait of her friend Alice Rohrer. Because she did not have an easel, Barnes had to work on the lower portion of the picture on her knees. She began the portrait at Alice's apartment, but Rohrer decided that she didn't like the painting, even though she had at first expressed pleasure with it, and they quarreled. Barnes took the picture away in anger and finished it for herself, copiously laying on the paint for days. It was never framed but leaned against her mantle for years like a graceful female stalagmite. When *Portrait of Alice* was finished, Barnes went straight on to another picture, of "Madame Majeska," painted in insistently harsh gold and yellow in the grotesque manner of the drawings she had done years ago in *A Book*. Barnes herself thought it looked like a divine monkey (the picture is of Emily; the reference is to the famous actress Madame Modjeska whom Zadel Barnes had met in London). The picture, though small, is so powerful in its radiant ugliness that it is difficult to stay with it in the same room for long.

Miss Barnes painted in a black lace dressing gown, rouged to the hilt and heavily perfumed. She had just had her first permanent, and it looked, she thought, like a sheep's rump. She was subject to fits of deep depression during these months and lost twenty pounds in a

207

very short time, so that she weighed only 126 pounds with her clothes on and wore a size twelve dress. She had one nervous breakdown in Ruth Ford's apartment and had to be taken directly to hospital by ambulance. Her face and shoulders acquired a birdlike frailty that made her look momentarily a little like her own *Portrait of Alice.* She knew perfectly well that it was silly to be painting. She should be writing. But as she felt that public taste had totally passed over the line into the realm of low-level insanity, it really didn't seem to matter much.

In addition to the problems of her own state of mind and situation in life, her mother was ill, and Miss Barnes was worried about her half-brother Duane and half-sister Muriel after their father's death, though she feared that it might already be too late for them. It was certain, she felt, that, whatever happened now, neither of them had had a chance while he was still alive. Her father's death was simply an added melancholia. The prosaic need to obtain some money was at the forefront of her worries.

Miss Barnes made up her mind. If fame would not come (a slender but lasting fame was only two years away, of course) she would twist her genius ever so little as Faulkner had done and write a scenario or two. Life was dreadful enough without lacking means of adequate subsistence. She consulted a play broker, and her worst fears were confirmed. The choice was between writing as one wanted and then turning on the gas or becoming commercial and sob-sister. She had nightmares about it in which her bed was full of little dead horses. Barnes felt that for a writer to have gone abroad for even six months meant that one risked being commercially cut adrift in America. She saw herself as fighting with her back to the wall as she waited for word from publishers, but that was, she knew, a natural position for a Chappell-Barnes.

American men appeared quite mad to her. She wrote to Ford that, while she did not delude herself into thinking that she was the handsomest woman in New York, she was considering carrying some means of protection from the old gentlemen, weak-chinned lads and middle-aged husbands who seemed to be seeking her out. She had carried a chain in Paris, but there it was a fashionable thing to do. She was a self-confessed savage creature, and she was going to have her solitude and her misery if it pleased her. As summer approached she began to write again and had several short stories and projects underway all at once. She tanned and read Henry James, whom she liked for his old-fashioned flavour, Pascal, about whom she had reservations, and she reread the *Religio Medici* and *The Anatomy of Melancholy,* two of her pet passions. Though she was still depressed and felt oppressed by the life that surrounded her, she had stopped drinking, and she was cutting down on her smoking. America seemed to her to be waiting for trouble and drinking like crazy.

V

By the mid-Thirties Paris was no longer the central locus of the expatriation. Peggy Guggenheim had opened her art gallery in London. She also had a new house in the country, Yew Tree Cottage, where Djuna spent some time and where in 1938 she met and grew friendly with Peggy's new lover, Samuel Beckett. It was Barnes who gave Peggy Ivan Goncharov's novel to read and first applied the nickname "Oblomov" to Beckett. There was a regular back and forth between England and France among many in Peggy's circle. Barnes by now adored Paris, but there was misery enough associated with her flat, and there were obvious financial and publishing reasons to be based in England. Her first reaction, however, was to think of living well in Paris until the last bit of money ran out and then to turn on the gas.

There was another reason, too. A new love affair had begun in England. Antonia White had become a great admirer of Barnes. Barnes invited her to come and visit her but then barked at her when she did come —*What the hell are you doing here?* On another occasion Djuna upbraided Antonia in a moment of crisis: —*Are you a writer or a wailing woman?!* Antonia did get her own back. Once she asked her: —*What do you really want, Djuna?* and was told: —*To die.* Antonia replied: —*Then die!* But Antonia remained steadfast in her admiration, and it was through her that Barnes met S—, with whom there began a romance in Paris in 1937.

Antonia had invited Djuna and S— to dinner with Emily. That night Emily was bored and sulky for some reason. White remembered that Emily spent the entire evening in a narcissus clutch with two letters that she herself had written. Djuna and S— were in complete accord from the very beginning. —*Walk away. I want to see you leaving,* she told him. —*Yes, you've got that gorgon look behind. The infinity that's in the Gothic. Take care you don't develop flying buttresses.* S—'s love letters to Djuna are full of what amounts to veneration of her gaiety, kindness, truth, and also her solitary nature and her air of inviolability. The trouble was that S— quickly passed from being her lover to professing to love her like a sister. Djuna was a very passionate woman. She saw that they made a pathetic couple because she was in love while he was in cool abstraction. She at first thought he was sweet and considerate, but then he did things like having an affair with Dolly Wilde, which he casually wanted to discuss with her. He thought that she didn't fit in well enough with the English manner. She was thinking vaguely of marriage, but he dumped her. More or less the same thing happened to Emily with Peter Hoare. Djuna contrasted S— with Thelma, to the disadvantage of Thelma. She couldn't forgive Thelma for the glib way she had spoken of "the beauty of our relationship" while deceiving her. But there were similar problems with S— that Djuna either could not or would not see. Though the affair ended fairly quickly, S— remained a great admirer.

Barnes decided to sell the Paris flat even though she knew she would not get much for it. She spent three days there with a maid cleaning up and putting things in order, and then several tense hours with drunken movers, who, it was clear after a few things had been smashed, had to be carefully helped in their packing. Barnes lived for a month on Oakley Street and then took a cheaper flat on Old Church Street in November of 1937. The flat was fitted out with some of the old chasubles and liturgical cloths. The oversize flat was more a storeroom than a bedroom, with four large bookcases and a library stepchair, two screens which partitioned off the bed, three largeish tables, and many chairs, two of them gilt lyre-back, and one of these broken. It is likely that a fair bit of this furniture may have belonged to the antique store downstairs. The two roundabout horses were there, so they were after all probably in Paris as well.

S— and Peter Hoare became quite good friends. Djuna thought their friendship was, in fact, too close. Both were promising careerists with very strong artistic interests. (Hoare occupied an important position in the Home Office, was after some years knighted as Sir Samuel, and eventually became a member of the English delegation to the United Nations.) Each faced certain problems with his lady for which they tended to lend each other moral support. It was hardest for Hoare because he lived in the same building as Emily. It was not uncommon for Emily to be screaming that witches were after her or that she was dying, and then a few minutes later be happily eating all Hoare's toffee in his rooms. The problem with Djuna was quite the opposite. She would drop out of sight for days on end, and there would be no response to frequent knocks on her door. On one occasion when the two men were particularly worried about her safety, they climbed onto the roof at 60 Old Church Street and peered down through the skylight. Barnes was there. All made up

210

and wearing a negligee, she was climbing into bed. There was a bottle of gin and a glass on her night table. She was dressed for a tryst and was in fact only preparing to write in bed.

Through Antonia White Djuna had not only a lover, but also a psychiatrist. His name was Alexis Carrell, and she saw him in 1938. He had also been treating Antonia. But the analysis was short-lived, perhaps because Djuna knew her Freud too well. She explained that her father's bastard children and mistresses had put her off marriage and babies. He raised a forefinger. —*Frigid?* —*Yes,* she replied casually.

She went to lunch with Edward James and made a hit by being nasty. Lady Ottoline Morrell sought her company.

Though it was her intention to remain in England, Miss Barnes by now had enough close English friends (in addition to Hoare, White, and S——, she was reasonably friendly with a woman who worked in advertising and with an English friend of Beckett's) and many more casual ones, so that she could see that she herself did not by nature fit much more into the English scheme of things than she had into the American. Her ideal state of affairs in the English-speaking world, she said in one letter written in this period, would be if all Englishmen were taken to America at birth and then shipped back to England at age five.

She was drinking heavily again. She had a char named Mrs. Bailey who came twice a week and to whom she would talk for hours on end. She fancied finding a husband who was as warm and sympathetic as Mrs. Bailey. Barnes would frequently enthrall perfect strangers with the sweeping saga of her life in the pubs along King's Road, and scattered recountings of these cathartic evenings became well known in literary London after the publication of *Nightwood* in October 1936. The legend of Djuna Barnes was entering a new stage.

About herself she now felt that no one cared whether she lived or died. She began to suffer from standard D.T.'s. She would awake at dawn to see strange things crawling on her walls. In addition to frequent fainting spells, she suffered from heavy sweats, heart palpitations, and occasional loss of her voice. She spent one night in a nursing home in London but was thrown out the next morning because the staff thought her insane.

211

vi

The novel had won many of its crucial admirers before it reached
print. Emily had shown a copy of the manuscript to Edwin Muir in
June 1935, and he was ecstatic about it. She had, in addition,
pressed it upon Dylan Thomas who evidently (it has been questioned) insisted on sitting up late into the night with a friend in bed
reading the novel aloud, and who praised the novel grandly and years
later read excerpts from it on his American reading tour. Peter Neagoe in New York had been mad about it, and a literary friend named
Lloyd Morris had begged her to read the novel aloud to him and then
wanted her to do it again. T. S. Eliot was not enthusiastic at first. He
did become so, though it must be kept in mind that this enthusiasm
would have had to be tempered by his acquired English reserve, and
also his knowledge of the considerable boardroom fight he would
have before him on the grounds of both the novel's subject and its
commercial prospects. A junior editor at Faber had, in fact, already
rejected the novel.

Barnes had written 190,000 words. By the time the manuscript
reached Faber it had been cut down to 65,000 by her own hand, and
after the novel was accepted Eliot indicated that he would like it to
be cut still slightly more. Barnes, who had begun to have grave fears
that the novel might never be published and who was, anyway, re-
sponsive to the fame of the émigré poet from Harvard and most perfect of all Englishmen, gave Eliot carte blanche in the matter of further editing. Eliot concentrated mainly on paring down the part of
the doctor who he was anxious should not be allowed to steal the
main attention in the novel. His single greatest contribution was the
title itself, which Barnes accepted with alacrity. One can easily imagine the Barnesian glee at his suggestion with its unwitting secret
watermark of Thelma's name in it, and with her knowledge of the
language Miss Barnes would not have missed the suggestion of
the Old English *wod,* or madness, either. The novel originally had
the subtitle *anatomy of night,* and that was very likely the spring-
board which suggested the title to Eliot.

Eliot's ally in obtaining the decision to publish at Faber & Faber
was Frank Morley. Years later Morley described how Eliot func-
tioned in the firm:

> —He had an unerring gift for spotting talent, but he would never fight
> for people. I used to watch and know him so well that if he quietly

suggested publishing [someone] I would take up the cudgels and be the loud hailer.

Another important reader for the firm, John Hayward, was Eliot's close friend and at that time his roommate. Thus, the manuscript came to the decision with very strong recommendations on its behalf. But the board was sure that it would not recover the cost of publication for a long time, and there were fears voiced that the novel might be banned and thus produce a considerable loss. Emily Coleman fraudulently cleared away that hurdle by telling Faber that she was a close personal friend of the censor.

There was a heavy price to pay for the acceptance. In the first place, Eliot had to agree to lend his imprimatur with a foreword. That was not a problem because Eliot had read the novel numerous times by then and thought more of it every time he read it. But Eliot also had to agree to pay the author no advance and to claim the full American rights for Faber, so that the sale of rights would offset the expected loss from English publication. Because her first priority was to see the book in print, Miss Barnes could struggle only half-heartedly against the proposal, but Eliot himself was not interested in pressing the firm's case. In the end they settled on twenty-five percent to go to Faber.

Nightwood received dream reviews in England, though equally striking is the absence of any comment whatsoever by the quality dailies and Sunday papers. Muir reviewed for *The Listener* (October 28, 1936) and Dylan Thomas for *Light and Dark* (March 1937). There wasn't a serious negative review, though some reviewers quibbled with Eliot's Introduction (which he subsequently reprinted in *The Criterion*). *The Spectator* (November 27, 1936) compared *Nightwood* with Virginia Woolf's work and said: ... it is clear that a writer of genuine importance has made herself known to us. Reviewing in *The New English Weekly* (April 29, 1937), Desmond Hawkins wrote: —It conveys a more intensive concentration than any woman in this century has achieved. Peter Quennell, who was the most reserved of the reviewers, wrote in *The New Statesman* (October 17, 1936) that the novel is ... in many respects, a very remarkable production. Graham Greene wrote in *The Tablet* (November 14, 1936):

—A sick spiritual condition may have gone into this book, but it is rare in contemporary fiction to be able to trace any spiritual experience whatever, and the accent, I think, is sometimes of a major poet.

213

The anonymous reviewer for the *TLS* had never heard of Barnes and was literally staggered by the novel:

> —It is quite impossible to convey in unemotional prose any impression of this extraordinary first novel by Miss Djuna Barnes.

And a windowcleaner told her that he'd read *Nightwood* and thought Rabelais was better.

Immediately after *Nightwood,* Barnes began to write poetry. Eliot told her that he wished he could write prose as well as she and gently threatened to give her a black eye if she persisted in writing poetry.

Nightwood ought to have been one of the artistic keystones of its time. While its story and its spiritual crisis are both highly personal and particular, the portrait of a world in intensely still crisis and on the verge of disintegration corresponds remarkably well to the social and political age in which it was written. If one understands the spirit of the Thirties at all, it is quite clear that, in spite of its arch language and manner (which can also be seen to a lesser extent in many other works of art of the period), *Nightwood* does not speak only to the question of lesbianism or the private life of Djuna Barnes but also to its time. The Elizabethan passion is there, and so is the mood of a time when Bakelite radios first said terrible things to the world. The sudden appeal of Catholicism to many writers and intellectuals of the period is also there. This contextual atmosphere of *Nightwood* has not been sufficiently noticed. There is much in *Nightwood* which shows itself contemporaneous with the school of "Realismes," as it has recently been labelled, in painting. To state the matter in another way, the novel can easily be viewed as a kind of verbal Art Deco construct with tragic purpose, or a kind of "realism in flight" which takes the shape of a strange, grotesque neo-Classicism that is both heavy and light in different ways at the same time.

Nightwood ought to have been one of the artistic keystones of its time, but it wasn't. To some extent certainly the organizational reluctance of Faber & Faber must have put brakes on its potentiality for broader success, but it isn't fair to blame the publisher entirely. The novel was published by Harcourt, Brace in America in 1937 and did receive broad review coverage there, most of it negative. There was a widespread reaction against Eliot's Introduction in America, and the novel was frequently seen as being incomprehensible. In *The New York Herald Tribune* (March 20, 1937), Lewis Gannett wrote:

> —Call it poetry, call it caviare—it is the poetry of death; there is no life in those eggs. It is a book of Gothic horror, not of Elizabethan tragedy.

This time it was the serious journals of America, with the single exception of *The New Republic*, which either ignored it or slighted it. Its only real champion was Clifton Fadiman in *The New Yorker*. Philip Rahv in *New Masses* (May 4, 1937) was one of those who lashed out at Eliot's judgment and tendentiously proclaimed that the novel contained nothing but

> . . . those minute shudders of decadence developed in certain small ingrown cliques of intellectuals and their patrons, cliques in which the reciprocal workings of social decay and sexual perversion have destroyed all response to genuine values and actual things.

There was enough interest to merit a second printing of the tiny first edition, but the publisher thought it prudent to drop the Eliot Introduction. In spite of the first indications in England that the book might be acknowledged as a classic, the first half-yearly royalty statement to Miss Barnes from England was for £43-0-8; from America, $350.23.

Eliot did his best to make some more money for Barnes by lining up a quick next book for her, a volume by and about her dead friend the Baroness, but Barnes resisted the idea. Eliot continually had to both apologize to her and scold her affectionately. He spent several months trying to get her to accept a dinner invitation to meet John Hayward. Barnes accepted and then changed her mind. Eliot made efforts to get André Gide, whom Barnes knew slightly from the Barney salon, to write a special introduction for a French translation, but he refused. Eliot told Barnes that eventually Gide would step forward to let the world know that he had been the first person to recognize the novel's merit. He also must have made certain representations on the novel's behalf in America, because he told Barnes that the "intense intelligentsia" of Harvard was currently still engaged in the delicate task of deciding what it ought to think.

When Barnes went back to Paris, it was to a little hotel on St.-Sulpice (she had done some of the work on *Nightwood* there). It was at this hotel, with S— but in separate rooms, that a porter tried to rape her at five in the morning. Djuna, who was extremely weak and sobbing, chased him out into the hall and woke everyone up. He coolly claimed that she had been drinking and imagined it. She was still in Paris when the Occupation began. There are only oblique allusions

215

in several letters from Hoare in England in 1939 to certain traumatic events in the life of Barnes at this time. In *Out of This Century,* Peggy describes Djuna perched at the foot of her bed wrapped in Peggy's marabou cover and telling her —*We'll be bombed in feathers.* Miss Guggenheim later recalled that Barnes had a fixed, vacant smile on her face while she diligently gnawed away at her fingernails. Peggy had been planning to go to Ireland with Djuna and the children. Djuna was having one of her breakdowns and was in a nursing home, and Peggy chose this moment to tell her that she must learn to stand on her own feet and to remove all financial support. As the German Occupation began, Emily was able to search Djuna out and remove her from the home in time. Peggy relented and provided the fare, and Djuna was put on the boat to America in a terrible state. Her only known comment on the entire war was quite oblique. She sent Hoare a book about her favourite composer, Mozart, in complete bewilderment at what German culture had come to. Just before she left France she received a stirring letter from Hoare in which he told her

—Don't forget, even if you are ill and things are as black as they seem to be, that you are Djuna Barnes and worth fifty healthy non-entities.

vii

From 1940 her health was not good. The years of heavy drinking and smoking hadn't helped. The asthma attacks were becoming quite crippling. The family legacy of robust good health and longevity, particularly on the Budington side where it was not at all uncommon for her forebears to live into their nineties in good health, had been badly strained.

The decade 1940–50 stands, by all available evidence and several comments from her own hand in various letters, as a particularly bleak time in her life. Before she moved in with her mother on East Fifty-fourth Street, she had a cold-water flat that was constantly full of furnace smoke. She would wake up at night to find mice nestling in the crook of her neck.

She had a very brief affair with the editor Peter Neagoe, who had compiled the well-known 1932 anthology *Americans Abroad,* but Neagoe himself told her that she was only interested in him because there was a little bit of the dust of Europe they had lost on him.

Shortly after she returned to America she did follow Emily out to

Arizona. She had nowhere else she was welcome. The endlessly surprising Emily had married a cowboy named Jake. Djuna wrote to
Emily that she was astonished by his name, and that it might be a
good idea to change it. Once there, Barnes did not fancy the situation
or Arizona. She thought it a derelict backyard equipped with blind
horses. Jake, it developed, didn't know what a lesbian was. On the
people she encountered: —*They are not in the least like anything one
knows.* She sat gloomily on their dusty veranda for several days
wrapped tightly in her cloak watching the marriage of Emily and
Jake disintegrate.

The three-day train trip to Arizona had been extremely stuffy, and
Barnes, according to Emily, had arrived at the station in Holbrook
slightly hungover. Jake took a dislike to Djuna at first sight. Emily
was in one of her berserk phases. She tried to play Peggy's part of so-
licitous hostess, but she did not have the backup staff that Peggy
had, and it was not a natural role for her. As the tension between
Jake and Djuna mounted at Concho, Emily became more and more
disagreeable and finally violent, until Jake and Djuna were unable to
tolerate her anymore. Jake left. Emily went absolutely wild. Then
Djuna left, and Jake returned. Emily viewed the misadventure in
Arizona as the source of the rupture between her and Djuna. She felt
that the fact that Djuna had refused to drink had meant that her wit
was dampened, and this had thus cast a pall on the visit. Emily felt
that Barnes had been an oppressively heavy presence in the ranch-
house, which Djuna called "the shithouse-on-a-distant-hill."

Djuna Barnes would not be anyone's ideal houseguest, but Emily
was at least co-author of the disaster. She had rounded on Barnes in
an angry moment and shouted: —*One can't LIVE with Nightwood!*,
and then she further compounded the affront by comparing Barnes'
work with Henry Miller's, something which she had done before and
knew was certain to infuriate. Djuna never really forgave Emily for
Arizona. She wrote to Bob McAlmon that nothing in her life compared with the horror of her visit there, and that she grew positively
lyrical when she contemplated the horror of it.

When Djuna was back in New York, Emily sent an article she had
written on *Nightwood* to Charles Ford for his journal *Blues*. Emily
regarded the article as one of the most important things she had ever
written. The article laid strong emphasis on the religious aspect of
the novel. Charles showed the article to Djuna, who didn't like it and
made many cuts without consulting Emily, who went into another
frenzy when she learned what was happening. It was suggested that
the article might be given to Edmund Wilson as an objective arbiter,
but Emily rejected him on the grounds that he was an atheist and a

217

Marxist, with the result that the article did not appear. Emily did not forgive Djuna.

In New York, Djuna, by a fluke, obtained an inexpensive room-and-a-half apartment on Patchin Place in September 1940. It was near the Jefferson Market Courthouse and the Women's Prison, and was to be her home for forty-one years.

There was the brief flurry of the exhibition of her paintings in 1944 at the gallery Peggy Guggenheim had opened in New York, but none of the Barnes pictures sold, and she did not continue painting. Djuna again became peripherally involved in the complicated life of Peggy, who was then at war with a new lover in a sprawling two-floor apartment. Barnes went out even less than she had in Paris and London, which often was rarely enough, though she did have one regular drinking partner in the Village at the White Horse and elsewhere, an English journalist named Peter Jack.

Her family now appeared abominable to Barnes. In March, 1940, she told Emily Coleman, she had been bruised head to foot being taken to a sanitorium by force. She didn't stay long but claimed that the family threatened to return her there if she didn't toe the line. The one warm patch in this entire decade for her is her correspondence and occasional meetings with Eliot. The friendship, though distant, was important for both of them. Eliot, in apologizing for one of his many unintended slights, explained that they were both intensely nervous and diffident people, as a result of which each was constantly falsely imagining that the other was in a state of violent annoyance and irritation. Willa Muir was struck by the difference that came over Eliot when he was with Barnes. She thought that the way Barnes had of treating him with an easy affectionate camaraderie caused him to respond with an equally easy gaiety that she had never seen in Eliot before: —In her company Eliot seemed to have shed some English drilling and become more American. The two handsomely framed photographs with pride of place in Eliot's Russell Square office in the 1960s were those of Groucho Marx and Djuna Barnes.

Eliot was openly worried about her future in America. Without Emily Coleman or himself at hand he could not see who would make her work or edit her or sell her writing. He considered the possibility of getting her a job in London in O.W.1, but saw himself the unsuitability of that idea. Barnes continually toyed with the idea of a return to England, but lack of money and the dampness of the English climate kept putting her off. Eliot, who was then living in a furnished room in Kensington, described to her the many difficulties of life in post-war England, which, deprived of being picturesque because of danger, was now grey and fretful with insufficient warmth, not enough to eat, and a bureaucracy that involved itself in absolutely everything. And he warned her that, although things seemed on the surface slightly better over there, she had best put aside ideas of a return to France for the moment.

Eliot came to regret his descriptions of English conditions, because the result of it was that Barnes set about organizing food parcels from Gristedes for him, and he correctly guessed that she was having a difficult time in satisfying the minimum requirements of her own everyday life. He tried very sternly to get her to stop, but she wouldn't. In reciprocation he attended to the storage fees for those of her belongings which were still left in England and kept up her English subscriptions for her for many years, though he told her that it was painful for him to service her subscription to *The New Statesman,* since he himself had assiduously avoided that journal for twenty-five years. He insisted on subscribing to one of his own favourites, *Time and Tide,* for her, but she thought it very odd and was relieved later, when the subject came up, to be able to ask him to change it to *Encounter.*

Most of his letters began "Dearest Djuna," and many of them concluded with emotional gestures such as "yours humbly" or "my love, whether you take it or not." In one letter (July 23, 1945) he acknowledged her as the greatest living genius, and she, most uncharacteristically, signed one letter "with love and a hug around the neck." Though she still told friends that Eliot's *Nightwood* Introduction was acceptable only because it had been written by Eliot. She wrote to Eliot in May 1949, that he, her novel, and his foreword to it were the only three things that had pleased her in twelve years.

Djuna felt that Emily had been hinting that she had had something to do with the writing of *Nightwood.* Eliot tried to soothe Djuna by reminding her that Emily had practically forced the novel down his throat and was full of respect for Djuna's genius. She had certainly never claimed to him, he said, that she had had anything more to do with the novel than her advocacy in its behalf.

Djuna felt under stress, and belittled, by her mother, who also wrote poetry and had told Marion Bouché that she could write better than Djuna. It seemed to Djuna that her mother considered herself a wonder and blameless in all respects.

Though she was announced to give a talk on James Joyce at the Poetry Centre in 1945, she did not give it. Miss Barnes did not really do anything to aid her literary career in New York. She told Mina Loy that she was in the grip of laziness and inertia. Eliot continued to try to do what he could to generate some money for her, but he wasn't forceful and it wasn't easy, particularly at his own firm. At first she had resisted the idea of reissuing *Ryder* and *Ladies Almanack,* whereas Eliot took the view that they were early skirmishes in her literary career, and why shouldn't they be published? Later, when she wanted her short stories to be published by Faber, they decided that this would not be likely to enhance her reputation in England, which infuriated her. When Barnes was told in 1947 that there would be a French translation of *Nightwood* provided that she was willing to delete the last two pages of the novel, because the French reading public would be offended at the mere idea of a girl and a dog behaving in that manner in a church, Eliot counseled that it was worth considering as long as the translation was a good one and they paid well. Eliot had to bear a portion of her displeasure when Barnes grew savagely displeased with her new American publisher, New Directions, because it was he who had advised her to make the shift from Harcourt, Brace. Eliot's literary star seemed to have no limits to its heights in these years; *Nightwood* seemed to be setting forever as a cult book.

The most important thing that happened to Djuna Barnes between 1940–50 was the death of her mother in 1945. Now that story could be faced and told. Elizabeth Chappell had declared that it was like a coil of snakes around her neck having her children still alive. Her daughter saw her as a Mrs. King Lear who took breaks to read passages from Mary Baker Eddy to her. Djuna thought she had the capabilities of a devil. Elizabeth had said that Djuna was full of self-pity and the rotten Barnes ego.

It had been simmering as an idea for years. It would be told as a poetic drama, at least in part because Barnes was now looking over her shoulder at Eliot as she once had at Joyce. She began to work on the play in 1947–48 and confessed to Eliot (September 16, 1948) that she had no idea how to put action into a play. That was always the fundamental problem for Barnes in whatever she wrote. *The Antiphon*'s basic situation (which is a better way to think of it rather than action or plot) derived from Eliot's 1939 play *The Family Reunion,* which Barnes became acquainted with before she left England.

viii

Miss Barnes listened to a radio program in 1950 and abruptly gave up drinking forever. But during this decade her asthma slid into emphysema, so that it was sometimes almost impossible to breathe, and it was necessary to keep oxygen cylinders in her room. At night she slept with her window open throughout the year, which once saved her life, because her gas refrigerator malfunctioned and would otherwise have asphyxiated her. From 1949 until 1954 her studio room was literally carpeted with scraps of paper and pieces of the play in progress. Eliot, who knew her working habits from a visit paid to her room in 1952, wrote to her as she was compiling the final text for typing that he could picture her searching for odd pages under the bed, the carpet, behind pictures, and then wondering where it was that they were supposed to fit in.

In October 1949 she tumbled over a large French dictionary on the floor with all her papers. She severely wrenched her back and broke some ribs. Her knees, her ankles, and her balance were all extremely weak, and on at least four occasions she nearly fell under traffic. Ear trouble was suspected. When Peggy Guggenheim offered to pay her way for a tour of Europe (London, Paris and Venice) in 1950 on the *Queen Mary*, it was necessary for her to get clearance to travel from a doctor. In June 1951, after her return, she had a fall so serious that she fractured her spine in two places. A little over a year later, in September 1952, she fell yet again and broke her arm. It was really medical bills which placed such a strain on her finances in those years, for she did not now eat very much at the best of times, scarcely ever bought any new clothing, and did all her reading at the public library. She had dental problems as well and had to ask Bob McAlmon if he could give her something to help pay these bills. Shortly before leaving Paris, she had been in a taxi that had an accident and she had cracked some teeth. She had always dreaded having to need a dental plate, and the cost, $375, was simply unimaginable.

Barnes had planned to have *The Antiphon* finished in 1951, but the first final version wasn't completed until mid-July, 1954. It was typed for sixty-two dollars and sent to Eliot. An awkward silence of several weeks followed. At the end of August he finally wrote to say that he had been waiting until he read the play before he wrote to her, that now he had read it, and that he still did not have very much that he could say because he found the play so difficult and obscure. He turned the play over to other readers and nearly four more months went by. In all the play had seven readers, a very high number, and the reactions ranged from enthusiasm to complete stupefaction. Eliot himself was still having difficulty in deciding how to respond. At last he took the tack of not reacting to the first two acts at all and concentrating on the final act where he said a kind of verbal nuclear fission takes place resulting in violent energy. It was cautious and ambiguous, and though Eliot's opinion gradually improved as it had with *Nightwood,* he never went beyond praising the third act highly. Two sentences that Eliot wrote for the book's jacket copy are quite out of character for him, but probably reflect his feeling in the matter:

—From the point of view of the conventionally minded *The Antiphon* will be still more shocking—or would be if they could understand it—and still more tedious—because they will not understand it—than *Nightwood.* It might be said of Miss Barnes, who is incontestably one of the most original writers of our time, that never has so much genius been combined with so little talent.

Miss Barnes protested about this lapse on Eliot's part that it was a shroud for the play and said that she thought these things were meant to promote a book.

One of the play's seven readers was Edwin Muir, who would prove himself to be the most steadfast of all her champions. He had been praising her work for nearly twenty years but only came to know her, apart from one brief meeting in London in 1936 or 1937, when he acted as Eliot's emissary in connection with the editing that needed to be done on *The Antiphon.* In all, Muir and Barnes met three or four times. He was at this time a visiting professor of poetry at Harvard. Muir and his wife were in New York in February 1956, and Muir went to spend the afternoon consulting with Miss Barnes on the copious notes that he had made on the manuscript. Miss Barnes' asthma was so bad at this particular time that she literally could not leave her room. Muir, as he showed in a ringing affirmation of its value when it was published, loved the play.

In the editing process he was well enough satisfied with acts two and three as they stood and concentrated on cutting down act one slightly. He felt that that act was too busily static, a comment which Barnes later reported to Eliot that she had enjoyed immensely. Barnes and Muir worked together easily, and she took many of his generalized comments, both those received before their meeting and at the working session, and used them as the basis for substantial reordering of the drama. She ignored nothing that he said, and, where she did not actually remove sections which he indicated might be deleted, she always at the very least removed lines in those sections and rearranged and corrected. Muir's editing did help, but it was not enough to overcome hesitancy on the part of Eliot and Faber & Faber. Because he was by now "Nobel-Prizewinner T. S. Eliot," *The Antiphon* would be published no matter what, but it was clear that the publication would be for Djuna Barnes rather than for the play itself. Eliot gently reproached Barnes for not attending to absolutely all the cuts suggested by Muir. She reminded him of his original opinion of *Nightwood*.

Muir thought he saw a good chance to win Eliot over, and he took it. The stratagem proved to be a disaster, though the publication went ahead anyway.

Muir knew that Eliot would be visiting the United States in a few months, and so he arranged for *The Antiphon* to be given a single "concert reading performance" by the Poets' Theatre Company. It took place on May 21, 1956, in Phillips House at Harvard. Eliot and Barnes met to work on the manuscript on April 17. She had a manuscript ready to be mailed to the Poets' Theatre at the beginning of the month so that reading scripts could be typed for the actors. Barnes and Eliot travelled to Boston together. An actress who was going to play Miranda was presented to her, and Miss Barnes screamed. Another actress was then put forward, and she produced almost as strong a reaction because she was heavy, and a rather portly actress was also going to read the part of Augusta. For Miss Barnes thinness was everything, and the actresses had at the very least in her mind to resemble Edith Sitwell perched sideways on a seahorse. (Barnes was friendly with Sitwell through Tchelitchew and had made one of her rare outings to dine with her in New York several years before.)

As it happened, it didn't matter much who read what because the reading took place without a rehearsal, and it was evident that none of the readers even knew what was happening in the play. Where Barnes had wanted quiet taut conflict, they thumped, scolded and bickered. Often they weren't able to read their lines intelligibly. They would even stop and ask questions of Miss Barnes as they read. Whereas Eliot, Muir and Barnes had entered Phillips Brooks House in an easygoing, convivial mood, an air of fatality settled over them as the reading progressed. With each explanation that was requested of her Miss Barnes grew more and more savage, whispering to Eliot through clenched teeth while Muir and his wife squirmed uncomfortably on the other side of her. Behind them sat I. A. Richards. Barnes had on a white sash hat which sat at an angle and lent the appearance of a loose combat bandage to the whole grim affair.

The reading did at least have the positive effect of making Barnes feel the need for simplification. She had, after all, written short plays when she was young and appreciated the vital difference between spoken and written lines. So she smoothed out many difficult lines and reduced the length still more, by about twenty pages.

The Antiphon was published in England in January 1958, and the

American edition, published by Farrar, Straus & Cudahy, appeared later the same year (also as a result of a push by the little clique of Barnes' influential English friends).

The two best reviews of the play in England were those of Kathleen Raine in *The New Statesman* (February 8, 1958) and the anonymous review by James Burns Singer in the *TLS* (April 4, 1958). Raine wrote as an admirer of Barnes who could not, however, bring herself to like the play, but she gave a most astute overall historical placement of Barnes as a writer:

> —One may say that Djuna Barnes is to early Eliot what Samuel Beckett is to Joyce. The emergence of two such remarkable writers, whose flowering is so late as to bloom in another world, ought at least to remind us of the astonishing transformation of language that was undertaken and achieved in the Twenties; and Djuna Barnes not only possesses the style of her period, she helped to form it.

As regards *The Antiphon* itself, Raine had to point to a lack of felt immediacy in any of the characters and to declare about the oversufficiency of the play's language: —Only in America is a tone at once so macabre and aristocratic still possible. The Singer review (which Miss Barnes was convinced for some time must have been written by Muir) notes that *The Antiphon* is an artificial concoction of several modes and styles—Greek tragedy, Jacobean, modern pantomime, play and poem. Singer praises her language above all and ends with the whimsically qualified claim that Djuna Barnes may have first place among women who have written verse in the English language. In the eyes of some eccentrics. Apart from these two major reviews the play was either ignored or mentioned in passing in group reviews in England.

All of the best American critics also fixed upon the play's linguistic texture. In *The New York Times Book Review* (April 20, 1958) the grand old man of American classical studies, Dudley Fitts, saw in it a work with —moments of poetry and true excitement, though he had serious reservations. Richard Eberhart in *Virginia Quarterly Review* (Autumn, 1958) called her poetic language extraordinary, and Howard Nemerov in *Northwest Review* (Summer, 1958) saw the play as a highly serious parody which was involved in —a breaking up of surfaces. Another good review, by the poet Marie Ponsot, was the first to spot the continuity of character in Julie of *Ryder,* Nora of *Nightwood,* and Miranda of *The Antiphon,* all of whom Ponsot saw as a portrait of a single woman growing older, and spoke of the effort made by Barnes to make her personal comfortless vision a universal statement.

224

The problem of the play is best articulated in several of its most intelligent negative reviews. Lionel Abel in *Partisan Review* (Summer, 1958) saw the play as an enigma upon which it would be very difficult to throw any light. Austin Clarke granted Barnes a gift for very powerful imagery but saw a weakness in her very strength because —by loading her lines with irrelevant imagery, she makes the same mistake as Beddoes, Darley, Wells, and other "neo-Elizabethan" playwrights of the early Nineteenth Century. The mistake to which he refers is encrustation. Most plaintively of all the critics, an anonymous reviewer in *The Listener* confided his confusion:

> —Miss Barnes' latest work reads like *The Family Reunion* rewritten by Christopher Fry after studying Ivy Compton-Burnett. That is not intended to be facetious: it is genuinely difficult to come much closer than that to this very obscure play.

The play as printed *is* very obscure, and, in spite of the high compliment that its author received in the *TLS*, *The Antiphon* had no impact whatsoever except on a small handful of poets. Its sales in both England and America were pathetic.

Miss Barnes herself let slip the degree to which she was a very calculating culprit in her play's obscurity, because she wrote to Muir about the *TLS* review expressing surprise that the reviewer had managed to figure out certain things *which she thought she had concealed.* Eliot and Muir, who were trying to play Pound to her *Wasteland,* cannot then really be blamed (Barnes did blame Eliot for not attending to the punctuation as he had promised he would do before the play was printed), since neither of them could have had any more idea than the play's most sympathetic reviewers did as to what precisely was happening. What is sad is that the material which would give sense and clarity to the drama is there, in the discarded lines. If Muir had known the story and been inclined to press for its fuller presence, the reception of *The Antiphon* might have been quite different.

As it stands *The Antiphon* is like an unfamiliar opera sung in a strange language. One may admire its passion, but only distantly. If, however, the reader or spectator is fully at ease with the story all the family in the play are obliquely recalling, which is basically the story of *Ryder* looked back on long after the demise of the father, then there is little obscurity, and the power of the play increases manyfold. If, and only if, that story is thoroughly familiar, then *The Antiphon*'s loosely Shakespearean verse rings out most clearly indeed:

Gone, gone! cast out and waning
Like a circle running from a stone
Pitched upon a frightful deed; forgotten.
I leave the whole catch to the resurrection!

MIRANDA

Do you?
Do you think there'll be no tussle in that trench?
And would you set this vile doll up again?
You who would un-breath my dying breath
From off the tell-tale mirror plate
To blow into the furnace of his mouth,
Haggling in a market place.
Why, at the first trump of impending Doom
You'll come roaring up the galleys of the dead,
The oar-arms banked and trussed upon the bone,
Crying "J'accuse!" and hale me by the browse
And in alarm bark out "Not this arouse!"
Guilt has her, let guilt haul her house!
Beating your belly's cage where I took stroke;
Running, halt, distracted, and about;
Counting which of my hairs be summoned at the root.

AUGUSTA

Mother of God!

MIRANDA

Precisely not.

There is a case—it is the opinion that Miss Barnes herself held—for taking *The Antiphon* as in many respects her finest work, in spite of its obscurity. The text and its discarded lines exist, and it remains only for some gifted poet-editor of the future to fashion a new main text capable of speaking directly instead of covertly, which could be fairly easily done using nothing but lines written by Barnes herself.

The Antiphon with its duel between mother and daughter represents the innermost whorl of Miss Barnes' feeling. There was in draft a simple and powerful epigraph to the play: —This my story, its crying of a woman and a Dog. (She had once inscribed a copy of *Nightwood* as *Memories of Dog Boy*.)

The play caused many of her friends to run for cover. One pleaded poor sight, another faulty vision plus hearing too poor to have it read. There was severe flu, a death in the family. Three knew the trick of immediately acknowledging receipt and saying they were going to read it, after which the subject was never mentioned again. Peggy was straightforward and said that she didn't understand it. Emily was the worst—she disliked the play because she said it was without love or truth and was an empty work. More, she insinuated that Barnes had somehow curried favour with both the Muirs in order to win his praise of it. Barnes felt that her little room grew smaller around her. Some friends did applaud the work: Sir Samuel Hoare was extremely enthusiastic, and Sir Herbert Read also liked it very much.

One critic said that *The Antiphon* was in an analogous position as a work of art to *Finnegans Wake,* and there was something in that. What *The Antiphon* lacked was a band of critics passionately devoted to the author and ready to engage in battle in its defense as had happened when Wyndham Lewis had ridiculed *Finnegans Wake.* Barnes had Edwin Muir. After the debacle of the play reading the Muirs invited Djuna to have a cup of tea with them that night in their chambers. But she had to excuse herself not too long after she came, because she spilled her cup of tea over herself. Later Muir came down to her room with the cigarette lighter that she had forgotten, and, as she took it from him through the partially opened door, he rose up on tip-toe and kissed her on the forehead. —*I wish I wrote poetry like that,* he told her.

ix

Muir's enthusiasm for *The Antiphon* was not in the least dampened by its lack of public success. His own background as a poet was rooted in a mythical Orkney farm childhood—he was just five years older than Barnes—and he shared many attitudes with her. He was an ideally receptive reader of a play which was both as obscure (Muir had an instinctive dislike of "ideas") and as forceful in a mythic way as *The Antiphon.* Muir was a fine critic and an exquisitely generous man. In a reprinting of the play after Muir's death, Miss Barnes dedicated it to his memory.

When Edwin Muir and the recently reelected U.N. Secretary-General Dag Hammarskjöld were both being awarded honorary degrees by Cambridge University, they chatted as they walked together side by side in the long procession, and Edwin Muir was full of nothing but Djuna Barnes and *The Antiphon.* The intensity of his enthusiasm sent Hammarskjöld, who had not until then even read *Night-*

wood, to read Barnes. He loved *Nightwood,* and, though he, too, had difficulties with the play, he found it most congenial and also became its champion and its co-translator. Hammarskjöld's Swedish translation was done in conjunction with Karl Ragnow Gierow, who was then Director of the Royal Dramaten Theatre in Stockholm. When *The Antiphon* opened in Stockholm in February 1961, Hammarskjöld had roses sent to Miss Barnes in Patchin Place. The Dramaten production flouted all predictions that *The Antiphon* would not play. The leading Swedish critic Ebbe Linde reviewed it and wittily referred to the play as—*an Imagist caviar party.* The drama critic Ivar Harrie's review appeared in the Stockholm *Expressen* (February 18, 1961) under the heading "The Victorious Antiphon":

> —Yes, the audience really caught on, gradually. After the first act people were very awed and a little afraid of showing how lost they felt. The second act had a bewildering but inescapably exciting effect. The third act, which contains the real antiphon, the antiphon between a mother and daughter, broke down all resistance: there was no alternative but to surrender to the dramatic poem. It was one of Dramaten's great performances.

In later years it was a source of some pride to Miss Barnes when she learned that Hammarskjöld, like Eliot, had told an interviewer that his work on behalf of Djuna Barnes was one of the things that he was proudest of in his entire career. The Swedish production had no resonance at all in the English-speaking theatre world.

Hammarskjöld possessed the characteristics which one almost invariably finds among the important contemporaries who admired Barnes: intense artistic sensitivity, great reserve, a highly developed feeling of separateness. In *Markings,* Hammarskjöld wrote: —Alone. But loneliness can be a communion, and also: —Because it never found a mate/ Men called the Unicorn abnormal. Between 1958 and 1960 Miss Barnes had dinner with Hammarskjöld at his home on East Seventy-third Street at least four times, once with Auden. She called Hammarskjöld "Your Excellency" and was always worried that she might be expected to wear evening dress, which she did not have, but all the same she saw him with an artist's eye, as a person who combined tremendous shyness and pride and who could even with company sit at a window and look out at the nighttime river like a quiet little boy lost in reverie. She employed an old formula that she had used about friends in the Thirties: People of the air and people of the earth. Hammarskjöld was decidedly aerial in this scheme of things; she was of the earth.

When the plane went down at Ndola in Northern Rhodesia while Hammarskjöld was on a peacemaking mission to see Tshombe in early 1961, she said she felt at first almost as though she had been blinded by the death. By chance, Charles Ford happened to telephone her after a break in communication between them of nearly twenty years while she was watching the funeral on television. She wouldn't talk.

It had been only a little more than a year since the death of Edwin Muir. Both her great new friends of old age were gone. She had loved them both, because they had loved her, of course, but also because of their graceful strength and simplicity. Hammarskjöld's attachment to Miss Barnes was well known at the United Nations. She was picked up and driven there for the memorial service, and as people throughout the building wept openly she was scarcely noticed in her stillness except as a craggy-faced woman who was for some reason being fussed over by attendants. Miss Barnes was given a place on the board of the new Hammarskjöld Foundation but said that she felt in a funny position accepting it because she did not have belief in the goodness of man as her friend had. Now she was old.

At about the same time Barnes watched, in his periodic visits to New York, the approaching death of T. S. Eliot. She had fallen asleep with the radio on and awoke the next morning to a broadcast announcing that the poet had been removed ill from the *Queen Elizabeth*. Barnes saw him for the last time slightly less than two years before he died. He still behaved in a very courtly manner towards her. When she complained that she had wasted too much time in her life, he replied: —*Yes, but think what you did when you were not wasting it!* Another guest that evening told her how much he had enjoyed reading *Under Nightwood*.

The last letters between Eliot and Barnes are full of mutual misunderstanding. Other friends were dying at close intervals. When Carl Van Vechten and Dame Edith Sitwell died, Miss Barnes wrote to her old friend Natalie Barney that suddenly she felt as if all the leaves of the forest were down. She wondered if two old ladies, themselves under death's whittle, should send letters to one another about the matter.

Miss Barnes herself had written *The Antiphon* with the impetus provided by a doctor's death sentence which was given to her in the early 1950s. He told her that she had cancer and would have to enter hospital immediately, otherwise she would not live more than six months. She told him not to be ridiculous, that she had no intention of doing any such thing until she had completed the play on which she was working. There were two more such medical death sentences, and she ignored them, too, having correctly guessed that her appearance made her seem an invitation to prophesy. She worked on the play for five years from her first death sentence. When it was done she felt that she would not now care at all if she were run over on the street. Miss Barnes went to hospital twice for minor operations, in 1963 and 1968, each time fearing cancer and that one way or another she would not get out alive. After the double hernia operation of 1968 she vehemently refused the doctor's order that she go to a nursing home for recuperation and returned home three weeks early. An intern had come up to her and said: —*Miss Barnes, do you have anyone who can get you out of here?* She said: —*Why?* and he replied: —*Because they are killing you here. Get out, if you have to go in a stretcher, a blanket, a wheelchair. But get out!* She called her brother, who came and signed her out, drove her back to Patchin Place and left her on the bed, alone again. To emphysema was added arthritis, which was sometimes so severe that she could do little more than sit up in bed for weeks on end. Her health could now be said to be a clinical shambles, and yet at the same time there was no longer any doubt that Djuna Barnes, willing, not willing, would go the long distance. When I met her she was waiting for a cataract operation and still working on her major new project, a long poem which she knew perfectly well the world did not need or want.

X

Djuna Barnes knew Patchin Place long before she went to live there. The courtyard of ten little houses in a double row was divided up into more than fifty apartments. Some of them were real apartments, but a large number were crannies like Miss Barnes' was to be. Patchin Place had been built in 1848 by Aaron Patchin to house the Basque waiters of the old Brevoort Hotel around the corner, and it passed from that to being a mixed residence of writers and actors and plumbers and sign painters. It gave the laundry lines an engagingly diverse character. The brick houses had Georgian cornices, and the courtyard was full of ailanthus trees whose budding branches would poke in through the open windows of the upper floors in summer. There used to be a Patchin Place postcard for sale in the local shops featuring the vast and powerful concierge, a Mrs. Wiedersweiler, filling a whole front stoop with her billowing self. In the Village days prior to World War I there was grass in the courtyard and a lovely gas lamppost. Later that was replaced by cement and electricity, and the brickwork was rendered. It was where Theodore Dreiser and John Reed lived, and a little later Cummings came to live there for over forty years. Jane Bowles also lived there briefly.

The great memory of Patchin Place for Djuna Barnes was a single perfect summer night when the theatrical contingent of the Patchinites had organized a war-benefit play in the courtyard. It was a Yeats play, *The King's Threshold*. The courtyard was filled with spectators whose limousines lined the alley outside. The Patchinites leaned out of their windows. Mrs. Wiedersweiler occupied a fire escape alone, not as guest of honour but simply because no one ventured to go out upon it with her. The play's director had requested the Interborough Train Company to run its elevated trains as slowly as possible during the hour of the play's performance in order not to drown out the speeches. The company responded with a grand gesture by stopping the trains on that line entirely during that hour. Barnes was in the audience, while beautiful Mary Pyne played the princess, dressed all in blue with her long red and gold hair hanging down her back.

Patchin Place was well established as a place of perfectly blended privacy and eccentricity long before Miss Barnes came to live there. One woman who lived there was an unsuccessful writer known as Dark Note, because she dressed only in black and would sit in the sun by the hour making scathing remarks about the life going in and out of the cul-de-sac. Another old lady, ninety-two when she died there, was renowned among the residents for the terse, bawdy comments she would make.

Barnes was, like Cummings, one of the least sociable of the Patchinites. Services were at an absolute minimum in the Patchin Place apartments, which were rent-controlled (Miss Barnes' rent was $49.50). The only occasions when the other residents would see her were when she was coming in and out with groceries occasionally or making the little walk to the footpath space near the exit to the alley where the garbage cans stand. That corner has always been the traditional place for Patchinites to meet and learn of the progress of each other's work. There one could find Padraic Colum holding forth on Irish folklore with a loaf of bread under one arm. Miss Barnes always passed by such encounters.

However limited the fame of *Nightwood* was in the 1940s and 1950s, it was sufficient to cause Barnes difficulty with people who wanted to press themselves on her. Her telephone was unlisted. One person who made it through, though only because of the strange behaviour of Alan Tate, whom Barnes knew casually from Paris, was a young woman from North Carolina. Tate had been involved in trying to arrange a French translation of *Nightwood*. Barnes recognized that he meant well but felt him to be ineffectual and too "dashing" in that matter. The woman had written to Peggy Guggenheim as the dedicatee of *Nightwood* to ask that she be put in touch with Barnes. She knew of Barnes' painting from the *Time* article, and she wished to commission a portrait of herself painted with violin and horses.

Miss Barnes received occasional letters of this sort, which she never answered, but this one succeeded in astonishing her. She asked Alan Tate, in his capacity as a member of the Southern gentry, whether either the woman's name or the town from which she came were known to him. He told her that he didn't know the family name, but the town was a milltown. Barnes felt that that being the case there were no prospects for real profit other than the collection of another lunatic in her life, and anyway, she joked to Tate, she could not possibly stable the necessary horses in her room-and-a-half and was unaccustomed to painting violins, with or without young ladies. Tate told her not to worry, he would paint the instrument and his wife would do the horse. As they parted he cautioned her not to write personally to her. He would handle the matter as her literary secretary.

Barnes was taken completely unawares when she received a carbon copy from Tate of his letter to the woman, which he had signed "Pamela Pickle." In it he said that Miss Barnes would be willing to consider painting the portrait under certain conditions, the foremost of which was that she would undertake to do only the portrait itself, and the background features were to be added by Mr. E. E. Cummings, the poet, and Miss Caroline Gordon, the novelist (and Tate's wife), both of whom were, Pamela Pickle assured her, themselves gifted painters. Tate's mischievous letter embarrassed Barnes frightfully and made her feel that she now had no choice except to write to her herself. The error was compounded.

Miss Barnes could not make up her mind whether the woman from North Carolina who promptly arrived at Patchin Place was under the influence of drugs or drink, or simply was living in a state of illusion. Barnes thought she had a mistakenly dramatic notion of herself as a Hedda Gabler or Marie Bashkirtseff figure, and Barnes correctly saw danger in her eyes in spite of her apparently lethargic nature. She was not the type of face that Barnes found interesting to paint except for what she saw as a Siennese length of the back of her head, but Barnes made up her mind that she would all the same try to paint her if there was even enough money in it to get her back to London for ten minutes. It soon became clear that the lady had not come to have her picture painted.

The unstable lady from North Carolina declared that Djuna Barnes was the woman she had imagined to herself when she was a little girl. She could not understand why she was being condemned for something which Barnes had described so beautifully in her novel. Barnes drove her away, but she kept receiving lachrymose love letters, which gradually turned furious. The last one contained a threat of rape. Fame is rarely what one expects it to be, but even so much of the fame that came to Djuna Barnes was to be for many years a weird and bitter parody consisting of the attentions of pathologically fixated and unbalanced people.

The strength of character that shows in all her writing and the very concealment that is her nature sometimes lashed her admirers on to obsessive lengths. The two most significant people who were obsessed with Djuna Barnes were the writers Anaïs Nin and Carson McCullers. Nin had admired Barnes from a distance in the cafés of Paris in the late Thirties without ever daring to approach her. *Nightwood,* she felt, had been pivotal in her own artistic development. At the time she wrote a long letter to Barnes which went unanswered. There began a compulsive usage in Nin's fiction of a character named Djuna, which irritated Barnes considerably because of the intimation that they were friends. Barnes had contempt for her and considered her to be an obvious case of a little girl lost and a sticky writer. Nin had described Barnes as a writer: —She sees too much, she knows too much, it is intolerable. According to Miss Barnes, she and Nin never met.

Carson McCullers did not admire Barnes from a distance or in print. She attempted to storm her apartment, but Miss Barnes was practised in privacy and quite capable of simply ignoring insistent pressing of the entrance bell when there was no one she was expecting. Stories are told of McCullers crying and moaning on the stoop to be let in. (McCullers had done the same thing to Katherine Ann Porter whom Barnes, by the way, knew casually and thought very vulgar.) There was silence, except for one occasion when Miss Barnes called down to her: —Whoever is ringing this bell, please go the hell away. She did go away, though eventually the two had a perfectly uneventful meeting years later, when Barnes was inducted into the American Academy of Arts and Letters in 1959 and was seated at the lunch afterwards with McCullers and Thornton Wilder.

By the late 1950s and 1960s nearly all of the handful of people with whom she was friendly on Patchin Place had died. The Village grew wilder and sootier. Miss Barnes and her friend Marianne Moore (they had known each other since the early 1940s, when Barnes came to help Miss Moore during an illness) admired each other as

233

writers and worried about one another in the city. They kept in touch largely through a mutual friend in Brooklyn. Once this friend engineered an unexpected visit by Barnes to Moore in Brooklyn. They discussed the two frightful operations that Miss Moore had had, and Barnes made a dramatically abrupt sideways turn of her head in sympathy and understanding. Occasionally they met and chatted while shopping in the streets of the Village. They had one such meeting in the mid-Sixties, when Miss Moore, loaded down with a cargo of green bananas and rolling grapefruit and in search of Dr. Brown's Celery Tonic, told her how she had been recently set upon by a band of small boys armed with knives. Barnes thought she was as determined as she was delicate, a poet with the bright eyes of a wood creature. But later she grew resentful of the way she felt everyone fussed over Moore when she was sick, while she was often left to the attentions of the janitor. She thought her old friend had marketed herself successfully.

In the mid-Seventies Miss Barnes, she told me, was herself accosted by a gigantic Negro as she entered the otherwise cold and deserted courtyard of Patchin Place with a bag of groceries. He wanted her purse and the groceries. She wasn't going to give them. They circled around and around in the courtyard, and he finally drew away in sheer surprise at the jagged ferocity of the old woman's voice, the savagery in her eyes.

Young admirers regularly loitered in the courtyard for a glimpse of the legendary lady, for the most part content to look at her from a distance. Her main danger, when she ventured out, she felt, was the possibility of being knocked over by the hordes of teenagers who coursed about the Village. Often they wore strange costumes and ancient military uniforms. Barnes was quick to spot that they were the grandfathers, who, when they rolled over in the gutters, turned out to be no older than twelve. She didn't mind The Beatles. It was their audience she couldn't tolerate.

As her contemporaries died Miss Barnes felt like old George Sand, ready to pull down the curtain and shut the door on a life that had passed in a time that appalled her. Harrison Dowd was found dead in his bed. She chanced to visit a Frenchwoman she had known in the courtyard for many years and found her struggling to hang on to life in her little room, watched by a cold-eyed niece who was waiting to receive her inheritance. When the woman and her husband used to quarrel, she remembered, he would always say to her: —*Go out, dear, if you must, but come back nice.* Miss Barnes' half-sister was operated on for cancer, while another friend died a furious death of it. The Bouchés, both in bad health, moved to Sixtieth Street. Margaret Anderson committed suicide.

234

But every so often—the space was in years not months—some piece of the past would return in benign form as she discussed ancient times with other survivors. In 1958 Edmund Wilson had gone to see *Ulysses in Nighttown* with friends and met Miss Barnes there in the company of Harrison Dowd. Afterwards the group went to a spaghetti joint in the Village together. Wilson and Barnes had not seen each other for many years. He was not an admirer of *Nightwood* and had not even bothered to read *The Antiphon,* but soon he and Barnes and Dowd were immersed in the old days, chiefly talking about Edna Millay, but also Margaret Anderson, Jane Heap and Thelma. He recalled how Barnes had attacked him for his insistence as the great expatriation began that American writers should stay in America, and he recalled how his proposal to her in Paris had foundered over the question of Edith Wharton. Wilson was surprised and impressed at the style and dignity with which she seemed to be coping with old age. When he complimented her, she replied sweetly that she was doing her best to be a kind old lady.

Four years later, in the summer of 1961, Peggy Guggenheim was in New York. She, Barnes and Hoare had a long and friendly Chinese dinner together in which they discussed their old times in England and spoke affectionately and at length about Emily. Djuna wrote to Emily about the dinner but received no reply. A few years later Marcel Duchamp and his wife, Mary Reynolds, who sometimes used to do the rounds with Thelma in Paris, took her to a swish restaurant where by chance they were amazed as they dined by the elaborate vulgarity of Salvador Dali dining at a distance from them. And a few years after that she dined at the River Club with Valerie Eliot after his death and learned from her some of the secrets of Eliot's life and the unfortunate circumstances of his illness and death. Of Eliot's high church manner and sexual propriety Barnes said: —*He kept his Auden in the Church.*

In 1965 Frances Steloff of The Gotham Book Mart received a $1,000 Academy of Arts and Letters Award and made the gesture of sending $250 to Miss Barnes whom she knew slightly and admired greatly. Barnes was seen so rarely by anyone now, and there had been rumours about her being in a state of destitution. Barnes proudly and with some embarrassment returned the money. Worry about money was always a problem, but it wasn't the main problem. In poignant letters exchanged with Natalie Barney in the Sixties, Barnes yearns for a Europe that she sees has been lost to her forever, not only for want of money, but also because of her solitary position in old age. Barnes notices with alarm about herself that sometimes strange voices suddenly speak through her mouth. It wasn't as much fun as one might assume to be an Anchorite, she told Natalie, and she did regret now that she did not have a companion in life. Barney, in sharp contrast with Barnes, still lived comfortably with admirers and visitors in the same house where she had begun half a century before, in quite another world. Natalie sensed her old friend's vulnerability and was very concerned for her.

As it happened, Barnes, like Barney, had to endure at about the same time an attempt to evict her from the place which had been her home for decades. In 1963 a developer purchased Patchin Place for $630,000 and said that, if the tenants would not permit him a reasonable return on his investment, then he would be forced to rip down the old buildings and erect a multi-storey on the site. There was a tenants' protest meeting (reported in *The New York Times,* September 30, 1963: "Patchin and Milligan Tenants Unite to Preserve Quiet Corner"). Miss Barnes spoke at the meeting and said that she would die if she was forced to move uptown. More than that, the neighbourhood needed to be preserved as it was so that the young people had a suitable place to practice their mugging. The landlord backed away, and life continued on for her as before in small, difficult days.

She sometimes would work three or four eight-hour days to produce two or three lines of verse. A doorbell or a telephone sounding could destroy her concentration for hours, even if they were ignored, which, in fact, is what frequently did happen. Depending on her health and how she had slept, Miss Barnes might get up as early as 5:00 A.M., make breakfast, and then go directly to the typewriter where she would work in spells, taking time to lie down to ease the pains in her back; or, when it happened that she awoke later in the morning, she would work off and on in the same way steadily from nine to four. Little by little she succeeded in giving up smoking her Kools and smoked her last one in 1962. At the end of a day she might write some letters, though she complained that she was often too exhausted to write letters and had lost the skill of it. Her daily fare was always simple: oatmeal or bread with tea for breakfast, perhaps some Lederkrans or Philadelphia Cream Cheese on bread or biscuits with drinks of Vegemato during the day, calf's liver or veal cutlet or suchlike and a plain salad for dinner.

Whenever you play upon the concertina of time, it is all too possible that its primitive and plaintive tune will draw attention away from the manner in which incidents must be squeezed together in the retelling to make the melody. A silent song hides where the tale must draw its breath. The Patchin Place days for Miss Barnes number more than fifteen thousand, and thousands of those days went by wordless, for mostly it was

xi

silence and the sound of her typewriter—only imagine: forty years of
maculate silence.

Ages ago in Paris her friend Dolly Wilde
said that people who spend too much
time alone, in the end, turn into enormous ears.

xii

So she worked at her past as though it were a fulltime job, seven days a week. Peggy became more generous with her allowance to Djuna, $300 a month, but she continued very often to be tardy in sending it, so that Djuna would be forced to write and ask for it.

To an extent quarrels with publishers had become her main social intercourse in old age. The first quarrel had been with James Laughlin when New Directions took over *Nightwood*. They offered her an advance of $150, and she let the offer lie on her desk for several weeks while she sought a better one, until finally she said that she would accept $300, which arrived, as far as she was concerned, too promptly, because, as so often happens in these matters, there was a belated offer of $1,000 after she had already committed herself to New Directions. Their first edition of the novel appeared under the series imprint New Classics in 1946. It was an edition of 5,000 and was printed in the same job-lot with Nathanael West's *Miss Lonelyhearts*.

Barnes had not yet even met Laughlin, but they had quarreled already. She objected to their edition because she thought it was silly to put her name in lower-case type, and she thought the design of the jacket was deplorable. She objected to other details as well: the book's trim, the fact that there was no contents page, nor any chapter headings. She thought the typeface was "torrid," and she found typesetting errors in the text. She finally encountered Laughlin as a strange tall man who somehow acted as though he knew her while she was dining with T. S. Eliot in a restaurant in 1948, and after that she kept a sharp eye out for him on the streets of the Village with always those same questions: —*How are your mother's knees, Mr. Laughlin?* (waving her cane at him) *What rubbish have you been publishing lately?* Barnes objected to a fair number of her fellow authors on the New Directions list, chief among them Henry Miller.

Laughlin was long-suffering and did his best to be kind, but to no avail. Not knowing that she knew no French, he proposed that she become Genet's translator, and, that failing, he proposed that she do a critical introduction which she also refused. When she came out of the hospital in 1962 he sent her $100 above royalty payments, and in March of the following year he offered her a still-functioning York air conditioner that was being replaced in the New Directions offices to help relieve her asthma. Barnes accepted both the money and the air conditioner, though she suspected that both were being used as a

238

ploy to get her to agree to a lower royalty rate for a proposed deluxe edition of *Nightwood,* and she complained bitterly about the hideous trouble and cost involved in getting the air conditioner installed in her window. He sent her another extra $100. She thanked him for the occasional strange movements of his soul.

Miss Barnes began to avoid the word publisher altogether. She said printer instead, and much worse. She had to contend with a pirate edition of *The Book of Repulsive Women* issued by a Yonkers bookseller. She noted with considerable fury the rise of the reprint industry which could reprint the whole of *The Little Review* without paying anything to any of the surviving contributors. She prevented Kenneth Burke, who had once lived in Clemenceau Cottage, from using passages from *Nightwood* when an article he had written about the novel was being reprinted by the University of California Press, because she felt that the article implied there was an aura of Nazi decadence about the novel.

Barnes scarcely ever went to see her publishers but would have prolonged telephone discussions with them. New Directions allowed Farrar, Straus & Giroux to reprint *Nightwood* in its proposed *Selected Works of Djuna Barnes,* and in the years leading up to and following its publication, 1961–62, that publishing house, and particularly Robert Giroux, would go on red alert battle stations whenever Barnes rang. It got so bad that Giroux would sometimes have a serious headache even as the telephone was being handed to him. On being told that Farrar had remaindered *Selected Works,* she immediately called for reversion of her authorial rights, but she was then told that as eleven hundred copies of the book had been retained it was still in print. What sort of mischief, she wanted to know, was this!?

Else Albrecht-Carrie, who dealt with Miss Barnes for New Directions, fared much better, though in all the years of long business conversations she never actually met Barnes. Another New Directions editor, Managing Director Robert MacGregor (he died in 1976), took to calling her Madame Legree after he chanced to observe her brandishing her cane and reticule in the West Side Savings Bank. MacGregor thought she was a terribly lonely person full of aggressiveness and hatred who could not believe that the world wasn't trying to cheat her, all of which, of course, Miss Barnes in more winning fashion freely allowed about herself. The Faber editor who dealt with her when he was in New York was Peter du Sautoy. He always took his wife when he went to see her and never had any difficulty. She received Victor Lange of Princeton on behalf of her German publisher, and she met with her bibliographer Messerli. Sometimes children of old friends would telephone or stop by.

Miss Barnes quarreled badly with Sir Samuel Hoare when he took her out to dinner and attempted to cut her meat for her and tell her what she thought about various things. She almost quarreled as badly with S— in England by letter, but he apologized in abject horror at whatever offense he might have caused her. There was conflict with her brothers who, she felt, trying to compensate hypocritically for their mutual terror at the thought of spending any money, fussed about to install the air conditioner for her. One, most likely Saxon, proposed that they all contribute $25 per month apiece so that Djuna could be moved out of her slum into a clean modern apartment, but that was scrapped because Djuna told them that she would far prefer her "slum" to thin walls through which one could hear conversation and tooth brushing with dreadful clarity. Saxon then invited her to come and stay with him and his wife on his Pennsylvania estate, and she went for one short visit, but she couldn't see any point in being hauled by the hair (a favourite figure of speech) around seventy acres when she scarcely had enough strength to put one foot in front of the other except to get to the typewriter and back. She went once more, shortly before she died. Visiting Pennsylvania meant getting dressed up, gathering together all her medicines and the oxygen tanks, and then spending several hours on the roads. She far preferred to remain in what she called her own little prison courtyard. Barnes' definition of her nation had been given years before when she returned from Europe in 1940: —*A fierce sadistic race crouching behind radiators.*

The American ladies from Paris were all scattered about in reverse exile in New York City, except for a few who maintained cottages at quiet Orgeval on the outskirts of Paris, where once upon a time (in the Twenties) Djuna used to sunbathe nude, and where now those who had the money, such as Janet Flanner and Solita Solano, could return when they went to France. Janet Flanner, through her work on *The New Yorker,* was the best known of the female expatriates. She still lived with Solita Solano, who had been the one to bring Djuna to and from the American hospital when she had her appendicitis operation in Paris. Janet Flanner was devoted to Djuna. In 1959 she literally forced money on her to buy herself a new typewriter. Though Djuna liked Janet well enough, for some reason she could never feel really close to her. Her friend Natalie had long ago passed judgment on Janet: —*Bright as a button. But who wants a button?* Janet would visit Djuna every year or two, rarely more often than that, and bring news of her to the others.

Barnes was in effective exile within the returned expatriation. In 1957 she had gone out to lunch with them—Martie (Margaret Anderson), Janet and Solita, and other friends, Katie, Alice, Elizabeth, and afterwards she sent back a note saying that it was nice to have seen if not exactly communicated with them all. It was the sole occasion on which she joined in the social meetings of the former expatriates. Solita had gone stamping off in a huff at something Djuna said to her. But the solitary nature of Barnes was well known to them all, and most understood.

When Louis Bouché died in 1969, Barnes wrote a short poem, *Quarry,* which was enthusiastically published by *The New Yorker* (December 27, 1969). Apart from one poem which she had revised for a book to honour T. S. Eliot on his seventieth birthday, *Quarry* was the first short poem she had published in thirty-one years. It and a second poem which *The New Yorker* published eighteen months later (May 15, 1971), *The Walking-mort,* caused consternation among the expatriate ladies. When the first poem appeared, Solita Solano had just had what she considered an important poem rejected by *The New Yorker,* and the obscurity of the two Barnes poems caused a vague resentment or estrangement to focus on the one among them who would never be easy or at ease. But she had never been any different.

Miss Barnes said that *The Walking-mort* was to stand as her epitaph. The poem is, like *The Antiphon,* about time run backwards to its source, and it is as simple and powerful as the play, provided that one knows the two key images—the gate, the wall—and the meaning they have in the life and art of Djuna Barnes. The poem speaks in two voices, but as always they both belong to a single woman:

Call her walking-mort; say where she goes
She squalls her bush with blood. I slam a gate.
Report her axis bone it gigs the rose.
What say of mine? It turns a grinning grate.
Impugn her that she baits time with an awl.
What do my sessions then? They task a grave.
So, shall we stand, or shall we tread and wait
The mantled lumber of the buzzard's fall
(That maiden resurrection and the freight),
Or shall we freeze and wrangle by the wall?

The "mantled lumber of the buzzard's fall" is the paternal beast slouching backwards, away from Bethlehem. Her days (I paraphrase) are devoted to bringing a past to account. The most important of the death-edged mobile of images is quite autobiographical: Miss Barnes was told by one of her surgeons that for a brief moment on the operating table she had been clinically dead. —*Now you know what death is like. You've been there. You have died,* her doctor told her. She had, anyway, referred to herself impersonally for years as The Barnes.

Romaine Brooks began the decade's deaths for the expatriates in 1970 at the tremendous age of ninety-six. Thelma Wood, remember, died at the end of that same year. Natalie Barney died in 1972. Next came Emily, in 1974. She had been living for many years on the Catholic Worker Farm at Tivoli, New York. Strangely enough, in the final years it was Barnes who had made the greater effort to seeing to it that they stayed in touch. Emily had passionately wanted Djuna to follow her into Catholicism and was very disappointed that she didn't. Immediately after Emily Coleman's death a close friend visited Miss Barnes. She plied him with questions about Emily's final days and was, he reported to me, visibly moved to learn that her stormy and violent friend had died in a state of religious peace surrounded by friends whom she loved and who loved her. Janet Flanner had a serious stroke that left her in a haze with moments of sudden clarity before she died. The last to go was Peggy in 1980. Now virtually all her contemporaries who had been close to her, with the exception of her brother Saxon and Berenice Abbott, were dead. The last close friend left to her was Valerie Eliot, who would visit her whenever she came to New York. In the midst of all these deaths, Barnes herself experienced the greatest terror of her life when suddenly she was convinced that the moment of her own death had arrived. Nothing happened. She attended to her will. She still had several years to wait. Patchin Place was no longer the nook for artists that it had once been. The neighbourhood had deteriorated badly. Cockroaches ran wild in the chaotic little kitchen. Her home was now a hovel, her life, too, had come apart.

About her final literary work there were only clues from remarks made to close friends. It would be a long poetic work in cantos. In fact, the work consists of individual poems, most of them unfortunately never put in final form. They are dense in the fashion of *The Antiphon,* and like that play they contain some of the most powerful lines ever written by Barnes. Their theme, of course, is the old family story. They are quiet and intense. How would one describe them? Perhaps as poems by an Emily Dickinson in Hell. One title that she

242

mooted was *Poems In Passing.* Another title she had used was *The Book of Dan.* She spoke of it as being a calm retrospective vision of life by a tired and wise old man. In 1965 she told the Bouchés that she was on the thirteenth canto. She sent a copy of the poems she had completed to Faber & Faber before going into hospital in 1968, just in case. They then had the provisional title *Satires,* and she described them as a kind of "resurrection pie" of songs and observations on life by a certain Don Pasquin. This would be a reference to Pasquino, the name jocularly given to a mutilated statue that was dug up in Rome at the beginning of the sixteenth century and set up again near the Piazza Navona. It became the custom to address this statue with satirical verses on St. Mark's Day, and from this comes the word pasquinade to denote a certain kind of satirical verse or lampoon, usually quite caustic.

In her final months Barnes said that she wanted everything in her apartment destroyed, including all drafts of the long poem. Though this did not happen, it is uncertain when these last poems will be published.

What was to be the final Barnes work prepared during her lifetime was a little book of animal alphabet rhymes, *Creatures in an Alphabet.* She lived to correct the galleys, but the book appeared in October 1982; Miss Barnes died, at Patchin Place as she had wished, on Friday night, June 18, 1982, six days after her ninetieth birthday.

A month before her death, she had had to be taken to hospital suffering malnutrition. She had seemed to recover her health there on a diet of ginger ale and Häagen-Dazs coffee ice cream, a standard medical diet for those recovering from malnutrition because of the therapeutic effect of caffeine. It is not known whether she had simply forgotten to eat or had decided not to eat. She had been given a Senior Fellowship by the National Endowment for the Arts a few months before. The important thing is that it developed after her death that she was rather comfortable.

Her last published poem in her lifetime appeared as "Work-in-Progress" in the New York quarterly *Grand Street* in the Spring 1982 issue:

Rite of Spring

Man cannot purge his body of its theme
As can the silkworm on a running thread
Spin a shroud to re-consider in.

It was a fine gossamer wafting on which to depart. There was hope

243

for the promised book of poems in these quiet and minimalist "post-modern" lines.

Unfortunately, *Creatures in an Alphabet,* when it appeared, was not a new work but a series worked up from a "black alphabet" she had played with doing many years before. It is a slight work. The familiar Barnes themes are all there, but only a few of the rhymes draw upon the particular Barnes power. The cycle was a sad end, really, to a career in which she had disappeared for long periods but always returned like a distant comet. One stanza at least is a magnificent hard-lined engraving of how Djuna Barnes saw old age:

> —Somewhat sullen, many days,
> The Walrus is a cow that neighs.
> Tusked, ungainly, and windblown,
> It sits on ice, and alone.

In the first version of the quatrains she had an amusing refrain line asking a Mr. Physter and Miss Peugh what creation was coming to.

xiii

In her last years the "idiot children" with their PhDs had begun to come at her in earnest. Observing the growing passion for the Twenties and the Lost Generation, Barnes wondered just what these children would have done had they been there themselves. She felt that most of them did not really care at all; at best, that some of them probably "meant well."

Barnes frowned at the autobiographical and biographical efforts of Hemingway, Parker Tyler, Virgil Thomson, Kay Boyle, and other of her fellow expatriates. As writers died the media wanted comments. She always refused. Occasionally the early Man Ray photographs of her would flash by on her television screen.

Apart from the Raymont interview in connection with the publication of her poem in *The New Yorker,* the only real exception in regard to interviews, because of Hammarskjöld, was for Swedes. Several Swedish reporters were received by her. One interesting fact which had escaped record before it emerged from an otherwise uninteresting Swedish interview was that Barnes had been friendly with Scott Fitzgerald. The best of the Swedish interviews is the one by Folke Isaksson (*Dagens Nyheter,* February 25, 1963). It provides an excellent portrait of Miss Barnes relaxed in her old age:

244

—We search for a place. —*A bar for young men or for old ladies?* says Djuna Barnes. I suggest the latter. It is a shady place, and we are revived.

—*Young man,* she says over her glass of juice, —*what do you want of me?*

She focuses her gaze on the young man and for a moment lets him feel scrutinized. —*You must understand I live like a Trappist monk.*

... I say something like —*I have thought of you, imagined this conversation. As I would also very much like to have met Chekhov, Marilyn Monroe* ...

Then we talk about her with mutual concern, and Djuna Barnes comments: —*The poor girl ... Like a white dove ... One that hunters throw up in the air and shoot as a target.* Her empathy is not sentimental. It is a reality washed by the turbid water of life for Djuna Barnes. She is shy, on the defensive, angered, when we talk about atomic bombs and the inhumanity of humanity, but there is also something elfin in her, a teasing sparkle in the depths of her eyes. All her strength is in her gaze.

In her peculiar dark-blue ski-cap she reminds me of an old actress, a Naima Wifstrand, marked (as it is said about Miranda in *The Antiphon*) by a "dignified shrivel." She speaks of aging as a role. She knows it very well.

Miss Barnes spoke with feeling to Isaksson about Hammarskjöld and Monroe, people whom everyone knew and no one knew. (It was a fate that much appealed to Djuna Barnes, since that is how she saw herself.) She tells Isaksson that the public seems gradually to be growing up to *Nightwood* and laughs as she recounts how she has already rejected five offers to film the novel (Barnes protested her poverty but was indifferent to money), including one from an imaginative producer who wanted to cast Groucho Marx as Doctor O'Connor. She passes severe judgment on contemporaneity:

—*People have become half-hearted and goalless! Nobody wants to sacrifice anything. Even artists do not want to pay the price required.*

It is Miss Barnes' absolute conviction, says Isaksson, that one must pay with suffering in life. She tells him —*Well, I have come to sit tight here,* and she strikes him as being like an immigrant without a ship at a harbour dock full of people eager to be on their way to security, ties and common values. Dusk falls, and he escorts her back to Patchin Place.

Her next major exception to her self-imposed isolation occurred in

245

1970 when it was time for the first book about her. Professor James Scott of the University of Bridgeport had undertaken to write the volume about her for the endless Twayne series of books about modern writers. He wrote to Miss Barnes and received an appointment to see her. However, when he arrived and learned from some people coming into her building which buzzer it was (there was no nameplate), there was no response to his ring. He went for a walk. It started to rain. He returned to the buzzer, tried again, and this time an elderly woman with thin white hair poked her head through an open window above and to the right of him and asked in an irritated voice: — *Yes. What is it?*

She received him in her nightgown and flannel dressing gown at three in the afternoon. After the meeting he wrote down what had happened.

> —While I was standing, early in the meeting, she took the opportunity to look me over carefully, saying —*Let me see you. I haven't really seen you yet.* I stood the scrutiny of her intense gaze, her face about a foot from mine, and removed my glasses . . . I had half a fleeting thought, as I took off the glasses, that she might hit me. But she seemed satisfied.

She told Scott that she didn't see anyone anymore, and that the last time she had received someone like this in her room had been twenty-five years before. (A reference to the *Time* article in connection with the Art of This Century Gallery showing of her paintings.) She told him that, since she had once worked on newspapers, she knew what reporters are capable of doing:

> —*They'll stop at nothing to get what they want.* I told her I, too, had worked on a newspaper, for five years. —*Well, you know what I mean then! Lately I'm trying to write poetry. But there are so many interruptions! Lately everybody wants something of me! But I just won't give it!* (There seems to be an exclamation point at the end of each sentence she says.) —*I'm the most famous unknown in the world, you know that, don't you?*

Scott found that he was getting a headache as he talked with her. Without his saying anything about it, she divined it and offered him two coated aspirin and a glass of water:

> —*I have been told that I give everyone I talk to a headache,* she said.
> —*You're so intense!* I said.
> —*Yes. I know.*

She went on to depress Scott even further by insisting that, since he was writing the book, it would have to be a work that would do them both credit and put the critics to shame. She told him that the Caedmon people were currently after her to record *Nightwood*, but that she wouldn't do it:

>—*My voice is deteriorating. You can tell it's the voice of an asthmatic, can't you? Well, can't you?*
>—*Well*, I confessed, —*a little bit.*
>—*Of course! I know! I can hear myself.*

When she began to speak about her health, she suddenly stopped and declared:

>—*Old people should be killed! You know that? There should be a law. This business of keeping them alive—it's inhuman! I'm already dead. Do you know that? I've already died, and they brought me back. Now I have to go through the whole horrid business again! It's terrible!*

Scott was struck by the way in which her speech rushed forward, veered, and even contradicted itself just like Miranda's in *The Antiphon*. She was charming, petulant, angry, and sometimes she became lost in herself, and it was as if he weren't there, until suddenly she turned back to him with her wide smile.

When I myself met Miss Barnes in March 1977, I had been warned beforehand of the difficult time that was had by the last person known to have seen her more than six months before, an editor who was devoted to Barnes' work and was abused by her. My meeting confirmed both the timespan of silence and that difficulty, for Miss Barnes immediately began to recount that meeting as though it had just taken place. Before I came we had had a telephone conversation lasting an hour. Just when it seemed clear to me that there would be no meeting, she had said: —*Well, I suppose I'll have to see you.* She told me that I would have to describe myself over the telephone so that she could prepare herself mentally. I was then wearing a rather full beard. She told me I would have to have it shaved off before she would see me, as she didn't like beards—her father had worn a full beard. I demurred but said that I would certainly at least have it trimmed before coming. And as we came onto the landing that afternoon she was standing in the hallway in her dressing gown and demanding in an imperious voice: —*What is this!? I agree to meet one person, and I'm confronted by two!!* —though quickly it is clear that she is more pleased with Meg than with me—and at one point she turned to you as if I wasn't in the room at all and asked: — *How can you marry a man with a beard?! Dis - gusting!!* and paused before continuing: —*No, it's better that way. You can't see their faces!!* I had brought her photographs of some of her early drawings. She talked about them all as if she had drawn each of them yesterday

247

and not sixty years before, thereby demonstrating what I knew, that she had a fine memory when it suited her. She warmed particularly to the afternoon when she had sketched the old entomologist, but then caught herself. —*He was a nasty old man. Like your Nabokov!* By far her strongest statement was reserved for the exaggerated posturing of the contemporary feminist movement: —*These women!! Why don't they do something? Or knit socks for their husbands!*

I felt that she was waiting for me to ask questions about her life. She met almost everyone with anger and waited for them to try and cheat her. I couldn't explain that I didn't want to ask questions. To my astonishment we talked for almost four hours. At several points Miss Barnes had very serious fits of coughing. We would half-rise to leave, but the coughing would subside, she would ask a question (Did I have a contract for my book about her? Did I prefer *The Antiphon* or *Nightwood*?), and so we stayed a little longer.

At the end of the longest afternoon in my life I was surprised, since I have had extremely difficult literary conversations before in my life, to notice that I could feel considerable sweat on the back of my shirt. Miss Barnes put her hand out to me through the crack in the door as we left. It was a gentle hand, shrunken with age but warm and confident all the same. Then she spoke very softly:

—*Why do you have to stir up all that old history, family matters? There's no point.*

—*I think there is point,* I replied, —*because you are Djuna Barnes.*

She died in pain, but a kind doctor gave her opiates which eased it. Her last wish: that her ashes be scattered in a dogwood grove at Cornwall-on-Hudson.

BIBLIOGRAPHY
AND SOURCES

The primary source of archival material for this book were the papers of the Djuna Barnes Collection held in the Porter Room of McKeldin Library at the University of Maryland, College Park, Maryland 20742. I wish to thank particularly Mary Boccaccio and Dr. Robert Beare for their assistance while my wife Meg and I were using this collection in 1977. Materials of great importance are at the Beinecke Library at Yale (and for several services there I should like to thank the then-director, Dr. Donald Gallup) and the Humanities Research Center at the University of Texas at Austin. The New York Public Library is an essential source for early newspapers and journals. Materials relating to the Natalie Barney circle are at the Bibliothèque Litteraire Jacques Doucet at the University of Paris, where assistance was given to me by the Director, François Chapon. The William Andrews Clark Library in Los Angeles has letters from Zadel Gustafson to Lady Wilde. Jean Chalon, the French biographer of Natalie Barney, kindly showed me Barney's annotated copy of *Ladies Almanack*. The librarians of Griffith University in Australia facilitated writing such a book from such a distance. There were several hundred people who spoke and corresponded with me and scores of libraries which diligently attended to my queries, and I must hope that this book will thank them for their efforts and graciousness. Those witnesses mentioned in the book who were there themselves are warmly thanked. Thanks are also due to Raija Nugent of Griffith, who did translations from the Swedish for me (and to Folke Isaksson for permission to use his article); to Albert Parry, who helped in regard to Bruno, and to the poet Bill Zavatsky, who helped with the Baroness; and to Nancy Kleinpoppen of Columbia and The New School, who paused in the completion of her own doctorate, which deals with Djuna Barnes, to do some vital research work for me in birth certificate searches and on the papers of Maurice Sterne at Yale, and did it very well. Her own finished research will be worthy of attention. I wish to thank Mrs. Valerie Eliot for permission to quote a line from an unpublished letter by T. S. Eliot, and also for her warm interest in this project. Andreas Brown and Bradford Morrow rendered very great services in regard to material relating to the final years of Barnes.

249

Though Barnes has been neglected in the broad context of modern criticism and scholarship, she has often been rather lucky in some of the critics she has had. In 1975, Dr. Douglas Messerli of Temple University published *Djuna Barnes: A Bibliography* (David Lewis, Rhinebeck, New York), which is a good bibliography, and so I do not repeat the listing of Barnes' works or the secondary literature in the bibliography to this book. Since the Messerli bibliography, *Ryder* has been republished (St. Martin's Press, 1979) and a 1916 Barnes article from *Pearson's Magazine* has been republished as a small book entitled *Greenwich Village As It Is* (the Phoenix Bookshop, New York, 1978). An important item missing from Messerli is Barnes' review of Gertrude Stein's *Wars I Have Seen* in *Contemporary Jewish Record*, vol. VIII, #3, June 1945, New York, pp. 342–3. The new publications since Messerli are *Creatures in an Alphabet* (Dial, New York, 1982), the brief poem in *Grand Street* (Spring 1982, New York), and *Smoke and Other Early Stories* (Sun and Moon Press, College Park, Md., 1982).

Of critical books on Barnes, I wish to focus upon *Djuna Barnes* by James Scott (Twayne, Boston, 1976), a very sensitive critical study. I am grateful to Professor Scott for giving me permission to use his notes on his meeting with Barnes, and I would also like to acknowledge use of an unpublished portion of his book which points to the concealed series of poems addressed to Mary Pyne, a discovery which I had also made. John Glassco's note on Mahoney was a marvellous gift. Of doctoral dissertations, special mention should be made of Dr. Jack Hirschman, *The Orchestrated Novel* (Indiana, 1961); Dr. Isobel Davis, *The People in Djuna Barnes's Nightwood* (SUNY at Stony Brook, 1978); and, most of all, Dr. Lynda Curry, *The Second Metamorphosis: A Study of the Development of The Antiphon by Djuna Barnes* (Miami University, Oxford, Ohio, 1978). The latter dissertation is a fine piece of scholarship examining all of the many drafts of *The Antiphon*, on which I have relied considerably in my discussion of that play.

My thanks to you, Meg, should be specific and not the usual meaningless gesture-to-a-spouse: You warmed the atmosphere in conversations on three continents, and several times that meant the difference between finding out and not. And you have the credit for the discovery of several of this book's most important historical sources.

It would please me to think that the bibliography which follows will help bring into play new interest in the people and times that are the subject of this book.

It should be obvious, but needs to be said anyway: this book is in no way an authorized biography of any sort. The sole involvement of Miss Barnes was to enter into an agreement whereby she was paid in advance of publication for citations from her works and reproduction of her pictures. Exactly a month before Miss Barnes' death, her editor at Dial and her literary agent, Irene Skolnick, both informed my publisher that she was alternately pleased and furious about the biography, which is all, I think, I might have dared to hope for.

A.F.

Abel, Lionel. "Bad by North and South." *Partisan Review* XXV: 461–66, Summer 1958. Reprinted in his *Metatheatre: A New View of Dramatic Form.* New York: Hill & Wang, 1963.

Ahman, Sven. "Omstritt geni i Greenwich Village: Exklusiv USA-forfattarinna i varldspremiar pa Dramaten." *Dagens Nyheter,* 24 Maj, 1959, p. 29.

Allan, Tony. *Americans in Paris.* Chicago: Contemporary Books, 1977.

Alvarez, A. "Chariot of Light." *New Statesman* LXII: 653, November 3, 1961.

American Writers in Paris, edited by Karen Lane Rood. Detroit: Bruccoli Clark, 1980.

Anderson, Margaret. "Conversation." *Prose,* no. 2:5–21, Spring 1971.
———. *My Thirty Years' War.* New York: Covici Friede, 1930. Horizon Press, 1969.

Anderson, Sherwood, *Letters of Sherwood Anderson.* Edited by Howard Mumford Jones and Walter B. Rideout. Boston: Little, Brown, 1953.

———. *Memoirs.* New York: Harcourt, Brace, 1942.

Les années vingt. Les écrivains américains à Paris et leurs amis, 1920–1930. Exposition du 11 Mars au 25 Avril 1959. Paris: Centre Culturel Américain, 1959.

Antheil, George. *Bad Boy of Music.* Garden City, N.Y.: Doubleday, 1945. London: Hurst & Blackett, 1947.

Atherton, Gertrude. *Adventures of a Novelist.* New York: Liveright, 1932.

———. *Golden Gate Country.* New York: Duell, Sloan and Pearce, 1945.

Autour de Natalie Clifford Barney. Recueil établi sous la direction de Georges Blin, par François Chapon, Nicole Prévot et Richard Sieburth. Paris; Bibliothèque litteraire Jacques Doucet, 1976.

"Babylon Revisited." *The San Francisco Chronicle,* July 2, 1963.

Bair, Deirdre. *Samuel Beckett: A Biography.* New York: Harcourt Brace Jovanovich; London: Jonathan Cape, 1978.

Baker, Carlos. *Ernest Hemingway: A Life Story.* New York: Scribner's, 1969.

Bald, Wambly. "La Vie de Bohème (As Lived on the Left Bank)." *Chicago (Paris) Tribune,* September 2, 1931, p. 5.

Banner, Lois W. *Elizabeth Cady Stanton: A Radical for Women's Rights.* Boston: Little, Brown, 1980.

Barnes, Djuna:

The Papers of Djuna Barnes are held in the McKeldin Library, University of Maryland, College Park, Md.

A listing of uncollected articles, plays, poems and stories is given in Douglas Messerli's Bibliography. Five items not in Messerli's Bibliography are:

"Matron's Primer" (Review of *Wars I Have Seen* by Gertrude Stein), *Contemporary Jewish Record* VIII, no. 3, June 1945, pp. 342–3.

Work in Progress: Rite of Spring. Grand Street, v. I, no. 3, Spring 1982, p. 66.

Ryder (French translation). Paris: Christian Bourgeois, 1982.

Creatures in an Alphabet. New York: Dial Press, 1982.

Smoke and Other Early Stories. Baltimore: Sun and Moon Press, 1982.

The Book of Repulsive Women: 8 Rhythms and 5 Drawings. Published November 1915 as v. II, no. 6, *of Bruno's Chap Books.*

A Book. New York: Boni and Liveright, 1923.

Ladies Almanack. Printed for the Author and Sold by Edward W. Titus. Paris: 1928. Facsimile edition published New York; Harper & Row, 1972.

Ryder. New York: Horace Liveright, 1928. Published with additional materials: New York: St. Martin's Press, 1979.

A Night Among the Horses. New York: Horace Liveright, 1929.

Nightwood. London: Faber & Faber, 1936. New York: Harcourt, Brace and Company, 1937. New York: New Directions, The New Classics no. 11, 1946.

The Antiphon: A Play. London: Faber & Faber, 1958. New York: Farrar, Straus & Cudahy, 1958.

Selected Works of. New York: Farrar, Straus & Cudahy, 1962.

Spillway. London: Faber & Faber, 1962. Reprinted New York: Harper & Row, 1972.

Greenwich Village As It Is. New York: The Phoenix Bookshop, 1978.

"The Barnes Among Women." *Time* XLI:55, January 18, 1943.

252

Barney, Natalie Clifford, "Djuna Barnes." In *Aventures de l'esprit*. Paris: Émile-Paul Frères, 1929.

————. *Selected Writings*. Edited with an introduction by Miron Grindea. London: Adam Books, 1963.

————. *Souvenirs indiscrets*. Paris: Flammarion, 1960.

————. *Traits et portraits*. Paris: Mercure de France, 1963.

Barry, Joseph. *The People of Paris*. New York: Doubleday, 1966.

Beach, Sylvia. *Shakespeare and Company*. New York: Harcourt Brace, 1959.

Beaton, Cecil. *Photobiography*. New York: Doubleday, 1951.

————. *The Wandering Years: Diaries 1922–1939*. Boston: Little, Brown, 1961.

Beer, Thomas. *The Mauve Decade*. New York: Knopf, 1926.

Beskow, Bo. *Dag Hammarskjöld: Strictly Personal*. New York: Doubleday, 1969.

Bessière, Jean. "Djuna Barnes nouvelliste et romancière. Du lieu commun à l'imprévisible sens: *Spillway* et *Nightwood*." *Revue de Littérature Comparée* 50:455–77, October–December 1976.

Bianciotti, Hector. "Djuna au bois dormant. Mais ou donc se cache la Garbo de la littérature américaine?" *Le Nouvel Observateur*, 19 fevrier 1979.

Blackmur, R. P. "The American Literary Expatriate." In David F. Bowers, ed., *Foreign Influences in American Life*. Princeton University Press, 1944.

Blakeston, Oswell (review of *Nightwood*). In "Recent Novels," *New English Weekly* X:455, March 18, 1937.

Blues: A Magazine of New Rhythms. V. 1–2, no. 9, February 1929–Fall 1930. Edited by C. H. Ford.

Bodenheim, Maxwell (review of *A Book*). In "Books," *Chicago Literary Times* 1:3, January 15, 1924.

————. "Djuna Barnes and W. Carlos Williams." *Chicago Literary Times* 1:10, July 1923.

————. "Djuna Barnes' Play." *The Little Review* VI:73, December 1919.

————. *My Life and Loves in Greenwich Village*. New York: Bridgehead Books, 1954.

Bookman: A Review of Books and Life. New York: v.1–76, no. 3, February 1895–March 1933.

Booster Broadside. Paris: Booster Publications, 1938–39.

The Boulevardier. Paris: v.1–6, no. 1, March 1927–January 1932.

Bourdet, Edouard. *La prisonnière; pièce en trois actes.* Paris: Librairie théatrale, 1926.

Bowen, Stella. *Drawn from Life.* London: Collins, 1941.

Bowles, Paul. *Without Stopping: An Autobiography.* New York: Putnam's, 1972.

Brassai. *Picasso and Company.* Translated by Francis Price. New York: Doubleday, 1966.

————. *The Secret Paris of the 30's.* Translated from the French by Richard Miller. New York: Pantheon Books, 1976.

Bremont, Anna, Comtesse de. *Oscar Wilde and His Mother.* London: Everett and Co., 1911.

Brome, Vincent. *Frank Harris: The Life and Loves of a Scoundrel.* New York: T. Yoseloff, 1960.

Brooks, Charles S. *Hints to Pilgrims.* New Haven: Yale University Press, 1921.

Brooks, Van Wyck. *Days of the Phoenix: The Nineteen-Twenties I Remember.* New York: Dutton, 1957.

Broom. Rome, Berlin, New York: v.1–6, no. 1, November 1921–January 1924.

Broun, Heywood. "Short Plays at the Provincetown in Good Bill: *An Irish Triangle,* by Djuna Barnes, Is Best of the New One-Act Pieces Now Presented." *New York Tribune,* January 15, 1920, p. 12.

Bruno, Guido. "Discovering America with Frank Harris I." *Pearson's Magazine* XLIX: 26–27, November 1923.

————. "Fleurs du Mal à la mode de New York." *Pearson's Magazine* XLV: 655–56, December 1919.

————. "Folklore from Montenegro." *Bruno's* 1,1:11, January 8, 1917.

————. *Fragments from Greenwich Village.* New York: privately published by the author, 1921.

————. "Memories of Prague." *Bruno's Review of Two Worlds* 1,1:20–23, November 1920.

————. "President Thomas Carrigue Masaryk: A Portrait." *Bruno's Review of Two Worlds* 1,6:146–48, April 1921.

Bruno's Bohemia: Magazine of Life, Love and Letters. New York: v.1, no. 1–(7), March–September 1918.

Bruno's Chap Books. New York: v.1–3, no. 5, 1915–16. Edited by Guido Bruno.

Bruno's Garret. New York.

Bruno's. New York: v.1, no. 1–3, 1917. Edited by Guido Bruno.

Bruno's Review of Two Worlds. New York: v.1, 1920–21.

Bruno's Weekly. Edited by Guido Bruno in His Garret on Washington Square. New York: C. Edison.

Bruno's Weekly, Frank Harris Issue. V.20, no. 2, May 13, 1916. Edited by Guido Bruno. New York: Charles Edison, 1916.

Bryher [Annie Winifred Ellerman]. *The Heart to Artemis: A Writer's Memoirs.* New York: Harcourt, Brace, 1962.

Buddington, Thomas Cushman. *Dissolution or Physical Death, and How Spirit Chemists Produce Materialization, by M. Faraday.* 2nd ed., Springfield, Mass.: Star Publishing Co., c. 1887. Houdini pamphlets: mediumship and mediumistic writings, v.3, no. 8, given through the mediumship of Thomas C. Buddington.

————. *Historical Revelations of the Relation Existing Between Christianity and Paganism Since the Disintegration of the Roman Empire. By the Roman Emperor Julian (Called the Apostate).* Boston: Colby & Rich, 1886.

Budington, Henry Aaron. *The Leyden Branch of the Budington Family.* N.d. (c. 1910).

————. *Man Makes His Body, or The Ascent of the Ego Through Matter.* Springfield, Mass.: Star Publishing Co., 1899.

Burgess, Gelett. *Bayside Bohemia.* San Francisco: Book Club of California, 1954.

Burke, Kenneth. "Immersion." *The Dial* LXXVI: 460–61, May 1924.

————. "Version, Con- Per, and In- (Thoughts on Djuna Barnes' Novel *Nightwood*)." *Southern Review* II: 329–46, April 1966. Reprinted in his *Language as Symbolic Action.* Berkeley: University of California Press, 1968.

Burra, Peter. "Fiction." *The Spectator* CLVII: 962, November 27, 1936.

Butts, Mary. *The Crystal Cabinet.* London: Methuen, 1937.

Calhoun, L. "A Woman's Hero." *The Argonaut* CIV: 12, September 1, 1923.

Callaghan, Morley. *That Summer in Paris: Memories of Tangled Friendships with Hemingway, Fitzgerald and Others.* London: MacGibbon and Kee, 1963.

Calmer, Edgar. In *Blues,* v.2, no. 7, Fall 1929.

Carey, John. "Edwin Muir: One Foot in Eden" (review of *An Autobiography* by Edwin Muir). *The Sunday Times,* August 24, 1980.

Carr, Virginia Spencer. *The Lonely Hunter: A Biography of Carson McCullers.* Garden City, N.Y.: Doubleday, 1975.

Chalon, Jean. *Portrait d'une séductrice.* Paris: Stock, 1976.

Charters, James. *This Must Be the Place: Memoirs of Jimmie the Barman (James Charters) as Told to Morrill Cody; with an Introduction by Ernest*

Hemingway. New York: Lee Furman, Inc., 1937. English edition: *This Must Be the Place: Memoirs of Montparnasse*. Illus. by Ivan Opffer & Hilaire Hiler. London: H. Joseph, 1934.

Chicago Art Institute. *Surrealism and Its Affinities: the Mary Reynolds Collection. A Bibliography*. Compiled by Hugh Edwards, 1956.

Chisholm, Anne. *Nancy Cunard*. London: Sidgwick & Jackson, 1979.

Churchill, Allen. *The Improper Bohemians: A Re-Creation of Greenwich Village in Its Heyday*. New York: Dutton, 1959.

————. *The Literary Decade*. Englewood Cliffs, N.J.: Prentice Hall, 1971.

Clarke, Austin. "Family Reunion." *Irish Times,* April 19, 1958, p 8.

Cleaton, Irene and Allen. *Books and Battles: American Literature 1920–1930*. Boston: Houghton Mifflin, 1937.

Clurman, Harold. *All People Are Famous (Instead of an Autobiography)*. New York: Harcourt Brace Jovanovich, 1974.

Coates, Robert M. *The View from Here*. New York: Harcourt, Brace, 1960.

Cocteau, Jean. *My Contemporaries*. Edited by Margaret Crosland. Philadelphia: Chilton, 1968.

————. *Professional Secrets: An Autobiography of Jean Cocteau*. Edited by Robert Phelps. New York: Farrar, Strauss & Giroux, 1970.

Coleman, Emily Holmes. *The Shutter of Snow*. New York: Viking, 1930; London: Routledge, 1930. Republished London: Virago, 1981.

Colette. *Earthly Paradise: An Autobiography Drawn from Her Lifetime Writings*. Robert Phelps, ed. Herma Briffault, Derek Coltman et al. trans. New York: Farrar, Straus & Giroux, 1966.

————. *The Pure and the Impure*. London: Secker & Warburg, 1968.

Contact. New York: no. 1, December 1920–no. 5, 1921.

Contact *Collection of Contemporary Writers*. Paris: Contact Editions, 1925. Edited by Robert McAlmon.

Cowley, Malcolm. *After the Genteel Tradition: American Writers Since 1910*. New York: Norton, 1937.

————. *—And I Worked at the Writer's Trade: Chapters of Literary History, 1918–1978*. New York: Viking, 1978.

————. *Exile's Return*. New York: Viking, 1951.

————. *A Second Flowering*. New York: Viking, 1973.

————. "Those Paris Years" (review of *Being Geniuses Together, 1920–1930,* by Robert McAlmon, rev. ed. by Kay Boyle). *The New York Times Book Review* LXXIII, no. 23, June 9, 1968.

Craig, Hardin. *The Enchanted Glass*. Westport, Conn.: Greenwood Press, 1975. Reprint of 1952 edition.

Crane, Hart. *The Letters of.* Edited by Brom Weber. New York: Hermitage House, 1952.

The Criterion. London: v.1–18, no. 2, October 1922–January 1939.

Crosby, Caresse. *The Passionate Years.* New York: The Ecco Press, 1979. Reprint of the 1953 ed. published by the Dial Press.

Cummings, E. E. *Selected Letters of.* Edited by F. W. Dupee and George Stade. New York: Harcourt, Brace & World, 1969.

Curry, Linda Catherine. *The Second Metamorphosis: A Study of the Development of "The Antiphon" by Djuna Barnes.* PhD thesis, Miami University, Oxford, Ohio, 1978. Ann Arbor: University Microfilms International, 1981.

D'Alvarez, Marguerite. *Forsaken Altars.* London: Rupert Hart-Davis, 1954.

Damon, Gene, and Lee Stuart. *The Lesbian in Literature: A Bibliography.* San Francisco: The Daughters of Bilitis, 1967.

"A Daughter for Inquisitor" (review of *The Antiphon*). *Times Literary Supplement,* April 4, 1958, p. 182.

Davis, Isabel. *The People in Djuna Barnes's "Nightwood."* PhD thesis, State University of New York at Stony Brook, December 1978. Ann Arbor: University Microfilms International, 1981.

Day, Douglas. *Malcolm Lowry: A Biography.* New York: Oxford University Press, 1973.

De Casseres, Benjamin. *Mirrors of New York.* New York: J. Lawren, 1925.

Delaney, Edmund T., and Charles Lockwood. *Greenwich Village: a Photographic Guide, With Photos by George Roos.* New York: Dover, 1976.

Dell, Floyd. *Homecoming.* New York: Farrar & Rinehart, 1933.

———. "Irrelevant" (review of *A Book*). *The Nation* CXVIII:14–15, January 2, 1924.

———. *Love in Greenwich Village.* New York: Doran, 1926; London: Cassell, 1927; New York: Avon, 1949.

Demetillo, Ricaredo. *"Nightwood:* An Explication." *Diliman Review* III:175–90, April 1955.

Deutsch, Helen, and Stella Hanau. *The Provincetown: A Story of the Theatre.* New York: Farrar & Rinehart, 1931.

The Dial. Chicago, New York: v.1–86, no. 7, May 1880–July 1929.

"Djuna Barnes 75." In *Die Welt,* June 5, 1967, p. 5.

The Double-Dealer. New Orleans: v.1–8, no. 1–48, January 1921–May 1926.

Earnest, Ernest. *Expatriates and Patriots: American Artists, Scholars and Writers in Europe.* Durham: Duke University Press, 1968.

Eastman, Max. *Love and Revolution: My Journey Through an Epoch.* New York: Random House, 1964.

Eaton, Walter. *The Theatre Guild; The First Ten Years, with Articles by the Directors.* New York: Brentano's, 1929.

Eberhart, Richard. "Outer and Inner Verse Drama." *Virginia Quarterly Review* XXXIV:618–23, Autumn 1958.

Eddy, Frederick W. "News of the Art World . . ." *New York World,* November 7, 1915, Section two, p. 5.

Edwards, Hugh, comp. *Surrealism and Its Affinities: The Mary Reynolds Collection: A Bibliography.* Chicago Art Institute, 1956.

The Egoist. London: v.1–6, no. 5, 1914–19.

Eliot, T. S. Reprint of his Introduction to the first American edition of *Nightwood.* In *The Criterion* XVI:560–64, April 1937.

Ellman, Richard. *James Joyce.* New York: Oxford University Press, 1982.

The Exile. Dijon, then Chicago and New York: no. 1–4, Spring 1927–Autumn 1928. Edited by Ezra Pound.

Falkowski, Ed. "Guido Bruno: Romantic Ghost." *The Bookman,* April 1929, pp. 167–69.

Farrar, John, ed. *The Literary Spotlight.* New York: Doran, 1924.

Ferguson, Suzanne C. "Djuna Barnes's Short Stories: An Estrangement of the Heart." *Southern Review* 26:41, January 1969.

Finch, Pearl. *History of Burley-on-the-Hill, Rutland.* London: Bale and Danielsson, 1901.

Fitts, Dudley. "Discord and Old Age" (review of *The Antiphon*). *New York Times Book Review,* April 20, 1958, p. 22.

Fitzgibbon, Constantine. "Dylan Thomas" (letter to the editor). *Times Literary Supplement,* April 2, 1964, p. 273.

———. *The Life of Dylan Thomas.* Boston: Little, Brown, 1965.

———. *Paradise Lost and More.* London: Cassell, 1959.

Flanner, Janet. *An American in Paris.* New York: Simon & Schuster, 1940.

———. "Americans in Paris." *New York Times Book Review,* March 8, 1959.

———. "Letter from Paris." *New Yorker* XXXV:154–60, March 21, 1959.

———. "Letter from Paris." *New Yorker* XXXVI:83–88, August 27, 1960.

———. *Men and Monuments.* New York: Harper's, 1957.

———. "Oscar Wilde's Niece." *Prose Magazine,* Fall 1972.

———. *Paris Journal, 1944–65.* Edited by William Shawn. New York: Atheneum, 1965.

———. *Paris Journal, 1965–1971.* Edited by William Shawn. New York: Atheneum, 1971.

———. "Paris Letter." *New Yorker* III:35–37, December 24, 1927.

———. *Paris Was Yesterday.* Edited by Irving Drutman. New York: Viking, 1972.

Flanner, Janet, and Solita Solano. *Archive,* held at the Library of Congress, Washington, D.C.

Fletcher, Helen. "Fiction à-la-mode." *Time and Tide* XVII:1607–1608, November 1936.

Flory, Sheldon. *The Writings of Djuna Barnes.* MA thesis, Columbia University, New York, 1952.

Ford, Charles Henri. *ABC's.* Prairie City, Ill.: The Press of J. A. Decker, 1940.

———. "Diary of a Decade." Unpublished manuscript.

———. *Flag of Ecstasy: Selected Poems.* Edited by Edward B. Germain. Los Angeles: Black Sparrow Press, 1972.

———. *The Garden of Disorder and Other Poems with an Introduction by William Carlos Williams and a Frontispiece by Pavel Tchelitchew.* London: Europa Press, 1938; Norfolk, Conn.: New Directions, 1938.

———. *The Overturned Lake.* Cincinnati: The Littleman Press, 1941.

———. *A Pamphlet of Sonnets. With a Drawing by Pavel Tchelitchew.* Majorca: Caravel Press, 1938.

———. *Poems for Painters.* New York: View Editions, 1945.

———. *Sleep in a Nest of Flames.* With a Foreword by Edith Sitwell. Norfolk, Conn.: New Directions, 1949.

Ford, Charles Henri, and Parker Tyler. *The Young and Evil.* Paris: The Obelisk Press, 1933. Reprinted New York: The Arno Press, 1975.

Ford, Ford Madox. "A Haughty and Proud Generation." *Yale Review,* v.2, no. 2, pp. 703–17, July 1922.

———. *It Was the Nightingale.* New York: Lippincott, 1933.

———. *A Mirror to France.* London: Duckworth, 1926.

———. "Young America Abroad." *Saturday Review of Literature,* v.1, no. 8, pp. 121–22, September 30, 1924.

Ford, Hugh, ed. *The Left Bank Revisited: Selections from the* Paris Tribune, *1917–34.* Philadelphia: Pennsylvania State University Press, 1972.

———. *Published in Paris.* New York: Macmillan, 1975.

Fowlie, Wallace. "Woman; *Nightwood* of Djuna Barnes." In his *Clown's Grail: A Study of Love in Its Literary Expression.* London: Dobson, 1948. Reprinted in *Love in Literature: Studies in Symbolic Expression.* Bloomington: Indiana University Press, 1965.

Frank, Joseph. "Spatial Form in Modern Literature: An Essay in Three Parts." *Sewanee Review* LIII:221–40, April–June 1945; LIII:433–56,

July–September 1945; LIII:643–52, Autumn 1945. Reprinted in his *Widening Gyre: Crisis and Mastery in Modern Literature*. New Brunswick, N.J.: Rutgers University Press, 1963.

Frank, Waldo. *Time Exposures*. New York: Boni & Liveright, 1926.

Freedman, Ralph. *The Lyrical Novel: Studies in Herman Hesse, André Gide, and Virginia Woolf*. Princeton University Press, 1963.

Freeman, Joseph. *An American Testament: A Narrative of Rebels and Romantics*. New York: Farrar & Rinehart, 1936.

Freytag-Loringhoven, Elsa, Baroness von. "Selections from the Letters of Elsa, Baroness von Freytag-Loringhoven, with an Introduction by Djuna Barnes." *transition*, no. 11, pp. 19–30, February 1928.

Friede, Donald. *The Mechanical Angel: His Adventures and Enterprises in the Glittering 1920's*. New York: Knopf, 1948.

Friedman, Melvin. *Stream of Consciousness: A Study in Literary Method*. New Haven: Yale University Press, 1955.

Frisch, Michael. *Town Into City: Springfield, Massachusetts, and the Meaning of Community, 1840–1880*. Cambridge: Harvard University Press, 1972.

Gallup, Donald, *A Bibliography of Ezra Pound*. London: Hart-Davis, 1963.

————, ed. *The Flowers of Friendship: Letters Written to Gertrude Stein*. New York: Knopf, 1953.

Gargoyle. Paris: v.1–3, no. 2, August 1921–22.

Gascoyne, David. *Journal 1936–37*. London: The Enitharmon Press, 1980.

Gay Sunshine Interviews. V.1. Edited by Winston Leyland. San Francisco: Gay Sunshine Press, 1978.

Gelb, Arthur and Barbara. *O'Neill*. New York: Harper, 1962.

Gildzen, Alex, ed. *A Festschrift for Djuna Barnes on Her 80th Birthday*. Kent, Ohio: Kent State University Libraries, 1972. Includes among others: a photograph of Barnes, by Berenice Abbott; "Quarry," by Djuna Barnes; "For Djuna Barnes on Her 80th Birthday," by John Glassco; untitled tribute, by Lawrence Durrell; an introduction to, and, "On Meeting Miss Barnes," by James Laughlin; untitled tribute, by Richard Eberhart; "Six for Djuna Barnes," by David Ignatow; untitled tribute, by Ned Rorem.

Gilmer, Walker. *Horace Liveright: Publisher of the Twenties*. New York: David Lewis, 1970.

Glackens, Ira. *William Glackens and the Ashcan Group*. New York: Crown Publishers, 1957.

Glaspell, Susan. *The Road to the Temple*. New York: Stokes, 1941.

Glassco, John. *Memoirs of Montparnasse*. New York: Viking, 1973.

Glendinning, Victoria. *Edith Sitwell: A Unicorn Among Lions*. New York: Knopf, 1981.

Goodwin, K. L. *The Influence of Ezra Pound.* London: Oxford University Press, 1966.

Gorlier, Claudio. "Tre Esperienze Narrative." *Galleria,* v.4:349–59, 1954.

Gould, Jean. *The Poet and Her Book: A Biography of Edna St. Vincent Millay.* New York: Dodd, Mead, 1969.

Graham, Stephen. *New York Nights.* New York: Doran, 1927.

Grainger, B. "Patchin Place." *Plain Talk,* November 1927.

Green, Martin. *Children of the Sun: A Narrative of "Decadence" in England After 1918.* Rev. ed., London: Constable, 1977. New York: Basic Books, 1976.

———. "Lawrence Durrell: A Minority Report." *Yale Review* XLIX:496–503, Summer 1960. Reprinted in his *World of Lawrence Durrell.* Carbondale, Ill.: Southern Illinois University Press, 1962.

Greene, Graham. "Fiction Chronicle" (review of *Nightwood*) *The Tablet* CLVIII:678–79, November 14, 1936.

Greenwich Village. New York: no. 1–3, January–November 1915. Merged into *Bruno's Weekly.*

Greenwich Village Quill. New York: v.1–20, no. 7, June 3, 1917–May 1929. 1917–26 as *Quill: A Magazine of Greenwich Village.*

Greenwich Villager. New York: no. 1–44, July 9, 1921–May 6, 1922.

Greenwich Village Spectator. New York, v.1–2, no. 3, April 1917–June 1918.

Greiner, Donald J. "Djuna Barnes' *Nightwood* and the American Origins of Black Humor." *Critique* 17:41–54, no. 1, 1975.

Guggenheim, Peggy. *Out of This Century: The Informal Memoirs of Peggy Guggenheim.* New York: Dial, 1946. Republished as *Out of This Century: Confessions of an Art Addict.* New York: Doubleday, 1980.

Gunn, Edward. "Myth and Style in Djuna Barnes's *Nightwood.*" *Modern Fiction Studies* XIX:545–55, Winter 1973–74.

Gurko, Miriam. *Restless Spirit: The Life of Edna St. Vincent Millay.* New York: Crowell, 1962.

Gustafson, Axel and Zadel. *The Foundation of Death.* London: Hodder and Stoughton, 1888.

Gustafson, Zadel Barnes (works by Zadel Barnes were published under the names Gustafson, Budington, and Buddington). "Bernadotte Family," *Harper's New Monthly Magazine* 64:3.

———. *Can the Old Love? A Novel by Zadel Barnes Buddington.* Boston: J. R. Osgood, 1871.

———. "The Children's Night: A Poem." *Harper's New Monthly Magazine* 50:153, January 1875.

————. *Genevieve Ward. A Biographical Sketch from Original Material Derived From Her Family and Friends.* Boston: Osgood, 1882.

————. "Karin: A Romance of Swedish Life." *Harper's New Monthly Magazine* 60:588, March 1880.

————. "Laquelle? A Story." *Harper's New Monthly Magazine* 65:418.

————. "Lambeth Palace, or 'Ye Archbishop's Inne.' " *Harper's New Monthly Magazine* 67:3, June 1883.

————. "Maria del Occidente Brooks." *Harper's New Monthly Magazine* 58:249.

————. *Meg: A Pastoral, And Other Poems.* Boston: Lee & Shepard, 1879.

————. "Nicaise de Keyser." *Harper's New Monthly Magazine* 67:688, October 1883.

————. "The Prisoner, a Poem." *Harper's New Monthly Magazine* 43:511.

————. "Rune of the Vega's Rudder, a Poem." *Harper's New Monthly Magazine* 70:211.

————. *Sir Moses Montefiore: A Biographical Sketch.* Cincinnati: The Bloch Pub. & Print. Co., 1883. Reprinted from *Harper's Magazine.*

————. "Sir Walter Scott: The Bard of Abbotsford." *Harper's New Monthly Magazine* 43:511.

————. "Voice of Christmas Past." *Harper's New Monthly Magazine* 42:187.

————. "Where Is the Child?" *Harper's New Monthly Magazine* 46:229.

Hall, Radclyffe. *The Well of Loneliness.* New York: Covici Friede, 1928.

Hamnett, Nina. *Laughing Torso: Reminiscences.* London: Constable, 1932; New York: Long & Smith, 1932.

Hapgood, Hutchins. *A Victorian in the Modern World.* New York: Harcourt, Brace, 1939.

Harris, Frank. *My Life and Loves.* Edited and with an introduction by John F. Gallagher. New York: Grove, 1963.

Hartley, L. P. "The Literary Lounger." *The Sketch* CLXXVII:86, viii, January 13, 1937.

Hartley, Marsden. *Adventures in the Arts.* New York: Boni & Liveright, 1921.

————. *Selected Poems.* New York: Viking, 1945.

————. *Twenty-Five Poems.* Paris: Contact, 1923.

Hawkes, John. "Fiction Today: A Symposium." Reprinted in *Massachusetts Review,* Fall 1962.

————. "Notes on the Wild Goose Chase." *Massachusetts Review* III:784–88, Summer 1962.

Hawkins, A. Desmond. "Views and Reviews: Miss Djuna Barnes." *New English Weekly* XI:51–52, April 29, 1937.

Hemingway, Ernest, in "Chroniques." *Transatlantic Review* I:356, May 1924.

—————. *A Moveable Feast.* New York: Scribner's, 1950.

—————. "The Sea Change." In *The First Forty-Nine Stories,* new ed. London: Cape, 1962.

—————. *Selected Letters 1917–1961.* Edited by Carlos Baker. London: Granada, 1981.

—————. *The Sun Also Rises.* New York: Bantam Books, 1954.

Heppenstall, Rayner. *The Fourfold Tradition: Notes on the French and English Literatures, with Some Ethnological and Historical Asides.* New York: New Directions, 1961

Hirschman, Jack. *The Orchestrated Novel. A Study of Poetic Devices in Novels of Djuna Barnes and Hermann Broch, and the Influences of the Works of James Joyce Upon Them.* PhD thesis, Indiana University, 1961.

History of the County of Rutland. London: St. Catherine Press, 1935.

History of Woman Suffrage, v.1–3. Edited by Elizabeth Cady Stanton, Susan B. Anthony, and Matilda Jocelyn Gage. New York: Fowler & Wells, 1881–82; Rochester, N.Y.: Susan B. Anthony, 1886. V.4, edited by Susan B. Anthony and Ida Husted Harper. Rochester: Susan B. Anthony, 1886.

Hobhouse, Janet. *Everybody Who Was Anybody.* New York: Putnam's, 1975.

Hoffman, Frederick. *The Twenties: American Writing in the Postwar Decade.* New York: The Free Press, 1965.

Horton, Philip. *"Nightwood,* by Djuna Barnes." In "Fiction Parade," *New Republic* LXXXX:247, March 31, 1937.

Horwood, Harold. "Djuna Barnes and the Sense of the Cosmos." *Protocol* 5:17–20, Fall 1948.

Huddleston, Sisley. *Back to Montparnasse: Glimpses of Broadway in Bohemia.* Philadelphia and London: Lippincott, 1931.

—————. *Europe in Zigzags.* Philadelphia and London: Lippincott, 1929.

—————. *Paris Salons, Cafés, Studios.* Philadelphia and London: Lippincott, 1928. English edition: *Bohemian Literary and Social Life in Paris: Salons, Cafés, Studios.* London: Harrap, 1928.

Hunt, Violet. *I Have This to Say: The Story of My Flurried Years.* New York: Boni & Liveright, 1926.

Hyman, Stanley Edgar. "The Wash of the World." *New Leader* XVL:22–23, March 19, 1962.

Hymes, Dell. "Journey to the End of Night." *Folio* XVIII:43–62, February 1953.

Imbs, Bravig. *Confessions of Another Young Man.* New York: The Henkle-Yewdale House, 1936.

"In Our Village." *Bruno's Weekly* I:104, October 7, 1915; *Bruno's Weekly* II:642–43, April 1916.

"In Our Village: Djuna's Exhibit." *Bruno's Weekly* I:142–43, October 21, 1915.

Isaksson, Folke. "Folke Isaksson portratterar Djuna Barnes: Ensamhet i Megalopolis." *Dagens Nyheter,* February 25, 1963, Part A, p. 4.

Jacobson, Paul H. *American Marriage and Divorce.* New York: Rinehart, 1959.

Johnsen, William A. "Modern Women Novelists: *Nightwood* and the Novel of Sensibility." *Bucknell Review* XXI:29–42, Spring 1973.

Johns, Orrick. *Time of Our Lives.* New York: Stackpole, 1937.

Jolas, Eugene, in "Glossary." *transition* 16–17:326, June 1929.

Jolas, Maria, ed. *A James Joyce Yearbook.* Paris: Transition Press, 1949.

Joost, Nicholas. *Ernest Hemingway and the Little Magazines: The Paris Years.* Barre, Mass.: Barre Publishers, 1968.

—————. *Years of Transition: The Dial, 1912–1920.* Barre, Mass.: Barre Publishers, 1967.

Josephson, Matthew. *Life Among the Surrealists.* New York: Holt, 1962.

—————. *Portrait of the Artist as American.* New York: Harcourt, Brace, 1930.

Joyce, James. *Letters.* V.I, edited by Stuart Gilbert. New York: Viking; London: Faber & Faber, 1957. V.II and III, edited by Richard Ellmann. New York: Viking; London: Faber & Faber, 1966.

Kannenstine, Louis F. *The Art of Djuna Barnes: Duality and Damnation.* New York: New York University Press, 1977.

Kazin, Alfred. "An Experiment in the Novel: Djuna Barnes, in *Nightwood,* Makes a Strange Excursion in the Technique of Fiction." *New York Times Book Review,* March 7, 1937, p. 6.

Kellner, Bruce. *Carl Van Vechten and the Irreverent Decades.* Norman: University of Oklahoma Press, 1968.

Kemp, Harry. *More Miles: An Autobiographical Novel.* New York: Boni & Liveright, 1926.

—————. *Tramping on Life: An Autobiographical Narrative.* New York: Boni & Liveright, 1922.

Kenner, Hugh. *A Homemade World: The American Modernist Writers.* New York: Knopf, 1975.

————. *The Pound Era.* Berkeley: University of California Press, 1971.

Kiki [Prin, Alice]. *Kiki's Memoirs.* Translated from the French by Samuel Putnam. Introduction by Ernest Hemingway. Paris: E. W. Titus, 1930.

Knoll, Robert, ed. *McAlmon and the Lost Generation: A Self-Portrait.* Lincoln: University of Nebraska Press, 1962.

Kramer, Hilton. "Period Piece." *The Reporter* XXVII:38–40, July 5, 1962.

Kreymborg, Alfred. *Troubadour: An Autobiography.* New York: Liveright, 1925.

Kunitz, Stanley J., and Howard Haycraft, eds. *Twentieth Century Authors: A Biographical Dictionary of Modern Literature.* New York: H. W. Wilson, 1942.

Laney, Al. *The Paris Herald: The Incredible Newspaper.* New York: Greenwood, 1947.

Langner, Lawrence. *The Magic Curtain.* New York: Dutton, 1951; London: Harrap, 1952.

Lanier, Henry W. *Greenwich Village, Today and Yesterday.* Photographs by Berenice Abbott. New York: Harper, 1949.

Le Gallienne, Richard. *From a Paris Garret.* New York: Ives Washburn, 1938.

————. *From a Paris Scrapbook,* New York: Ives Washburn, 1939.

Lemon, Courtenay. *Free Speech in the U.S.* New York: Free Speech League, 1916. Republished from *Pearson's Magazine,* v. 36, no. 6, December 1916, pp. 531–39.

Levy, Julien. *Memoir of an Art Gallery.* New York: Putnam's, 1977.

Levy, William Turner, and Victor Scherle. *Affectionately, T. S. Eliot: The Story of a Friendship, 1947–1965.* Philadelphia: Lippincott, 1968.

The Little Review. Chicago, then New York: v.1, March 1914–v.12, no. 2, May 19, 1929.

Loeb, Harold. *The Way It Was.* New York: Criterion, 1959.

London Bulletin. London: April 1938–June 1940.

Longstreet, Stephen. *We All Went to Paris; Americans in the City of Light, 1776–1971.* New York: Macmillan, 1972.

Lost Generation Journal. Tulsa, Okla., May 1973 to date.

Lottman, Herbert R. "In Search of Miss Barney." *New York Times Book Review,* September 28, 1969, pp. 2, 46–47.

Loy, Mina. *Lunar Baedecker.* Paris: Contact Editions, 1923.

————. *The Last Lunar Baedecker.* Edited and Introduced by Roger L. Conover. East Haven, Ct.: The Jargon Society, 1982.

265

Lueders, Edward. *Carl Van Vechten and the Twenties*. Albuquerque: Univesity of New Mexico Press, 1955.

Luhan, Mabel Dodge. *Intimate Memories*. New York: Harcourt, Brace, 1933.

Lutz, Alma. *Created Equal: A Biography of Elizabeth Cady Stanton 1815–1902*. New York: John Day, 1940.

Macdougall, Allan Ross, comp. *The Gourmets' Almanac*. New York: Covici, Friede, 1930.

MacGowan, Kenneth. *Footlights Across America: Towards a National Theater*. New York: Harcourt, Brace, 1929.

MacShane, Frank. *The Life and Work of Ford Madox Ford*. London: Routledge and Kegan Paul, 1965.

Mahoney, Daniel A. "Perfumes." *The Ignatian*, v.6, no. 3, June 1916 (St. Ignatius High School publication, San Francisco).

Mariani, Paul. *William Carlos Williams, a New World Naked*. New York: McGraw-Hill, 1981.

McAlmon, Robert. *Being Geniuses Together: 1920–1930*. Revised, with supplementary chapters by Kay Boyle. Garden City, N.Y.: Doubleday, 1968.

———. *Distinguished Air (Grimms Fairy Tales)*. Paris: Contact Editions, 1925. Includes *Miss Knight*.

———. *The Portrait of a Generation*. Paris: Contact Editions, Three Mountains Press, 1926.

———. "Why Do Americans Live in Europe?" A Symposium. *transition* 14:98–100, Fall 1928.

McCormick, John. *The Middle Distance: A Comparative History of American Imaginative Literature: 1919–1932*. New York: Free Press, 1971.

McMillan, Dougald. *transition: The History of a Literary Era 1927–1938*. New York: Braziller, 1976.

Mellow, James. *Charmed Circle*. New York: Praeger, 1974.

Mencken, H. L. *The American Language*. 4th ed. New York: Knopf, 1936; reprinted 1973.

Messerli, Douglas. *Djuna Barnes: A Bibliography*. Rhinebeck, N.Y.: David Lewis, 1975.

———. [Review of] Djuna Barnes' *Ryder*, 1979. *American Book Review*, v.3:17, March 1981.

Millay, Edna St. Vincent. *Letters of*. Edited by Allan Ross Macdougall. New York: Harper, 1952.

Miller, Henry. *Letters to Anaïs Nin*. Edited and with an introduction by Gunther Stuhlmann. New York: Putnam's; London: Peter Owen, 1965.

Monnier, Adrienne. *Les Gazettes d'Adrienne Monnier 1925–1945*. Paris: René Juilliard, 1953.

———. *Rue de l'Odéon*. Paris: Albin Michel, 1960.

Monroe, Harriet. *A Poet's Life: Seventy Years in a Changing World*. New York: Macmillan, 1938.

Moore, Harry T. "Gothic Surprises That Are Her Own" (review of Barnes' *Selected Works*). *New York Times Book Review*, April 29, 1962, pp. 5, 40.

Morris, Lloyd. *A Threshold in the Sun*. London: Allen and Unwin, 1948.

Muir, Edwin. *An Autobiography*. London: The Hogarth Press, 1980. Reprint of 1939 Folcroft Press edition.

———. "New Novels." *The Listener* XVI:832, October 28, 1936.

———. *The Present Age from 1914*. London: The Cresset Press, 1939; New York: McBride, 1940.

Muir, Willa. *Belonging: A Memoir*. London: Hogarth Press, 1968.

Nadeau, Robert L. "*Nightwood* and the Freudian Unconscious." *International Fiction Review* 2:159–63, 1975.

Nadel, Norman. *A Pictorial History of the Theatre Guild*. New York: Crown.

Neagoe, Peter, ed. *Americans Abroad: An Anthology*. The Hague: Servire Press, 1932.

Nelson, Gerald B. "Dr. O'Connor." In his *Ten Versions of America*. New York: Knopf, 1972.

Nemerov, Howard. *Reflexions on Poetry and Poetics*. New Brunswick, N.J.: Rutgers University Press, 1972. Includes reprint of his "Response to The Antiphon." *Northwest Review* 1:88–91, Summer 1958.

The New Review. Paris: v.1, no. 1–5, January/February 1931–April 1932.

"Nightmare of the Soul" (review of *Nightwood*). *Times Literary Supplement,* October 17, 1936, p. 835.

Nin, Anaïs. *Journals*. Edited by Gunther Stuhlmann. London: P. Owen, 1967–78.

Norman, Charles. *E. E. Cummings: The Magic-Maker*. Indianapolis: Bobbs-Merrill, 1972.

———. *Ezra Pound*. Rev. ed. New York: Funk and Wagnalls, 1969.

———. *Poets and People*. Indianapolis: Bobbs-Merrill, 1972.

Oberle, Jean. *L'Américain at Home*. Paris: La Palatine, 1962.

———. *La vie d'artiste*. Paris: Denoël, 1956.

Parry, Albert. *Garrets and Pretenders*. New York: Covici, Friede, 1933.

"Patchin and Mulligan Tenants Unite to Preserve Quiet Corner." *New York Times,* September 30, 1963, p. 31.

Paul, Elliot. *The Last Time I Saw Paris*. New York: 1942; London: The Cresset Press, 1951.

Pearson, John. *Façades: Edith, Osbert and Sacheverell Sitwell*. London: Macmillan, 1978.

Philippe, Charles Louis. *Bubu de Montparnasse, roman*. Paris: Editions de la revue blanche, 1901. Translated as *Bubu of Montparnasse* by Laurence Vail. Preface by T. S. Eliot. Paris: Crosby Continental Editions, 1932.

Playboy. New York: v.1–2, no. 2, January 1919–June 1924.

Pochoda, Elizabeth. "Style's Hoax: A Reading of Djuna Barnes's *Nightwood*." *Twentieth Century Literature*, v. 22, no. 2, May 1976.

Poli, Bernard J. *Ford Madox Ford and the Transatlantic Review*. Syracuse, N.Y.: Syracuse University Press, 1967.

Ponsot, Marie. "Careful Sorrow and Observed Compline." *Poetry* XCV:47–50, October 1959.

Pougy, Liane de. *Mes cahiers bleus*. Paris: Plon, 1977.

Pound, Ezra. *Letters of, 1907–1941*. Edited by D. D. Paige. New York: Harcourt Brace, 1950; London: Faber & Faber, 1951.

Pritchard, William H. *Seeing Through Everything: English Writers 1918–1940*. London: Faber & Faber, 1977.

Putnam, Samuel. *Paris Was Our Mistress: Memoirs of a Lost and Found Generation*. Carbondale: Southern Illinois University Press, 1947.

Quennell, Peter. *Genius in the Drawing Room: The Literary Salon in the Nineteenth and Twentieth Centuries*. London: Weidenfeld and Nicolson, 1980.

———. "New Novels." *New Statesman and Nation* XII:592, October 17, 1936.

Rahv, Philip. "The Taste of Nothing." *New Masses* XXIII:32–33, May 4, 1937.

Raine, Kathleen. "Lutes and Lobsters." *New Statesman* LV:174–75, February 8, 1958.

Ransome, Arthur. *Bohemia in London*. New York: Dodd, Mead, 1907.

Rascoe, Burton. *A Bookman's Daybook*. Edited by C. Hartle Grattan. New York: Liveright, 1929.

———. "The Land of Promise." *New York Tribune Magazine and Books*, October 14, 1923, p. 25.

———. *We Were Interrupted*. Garden City, N.Y.: Doubleday, 1947.

Rauh, Ida. *And Our Little Life*. New York: Bookman Associates, 1959.

Ray, Man. *Self-Portrait*. Boston: Little, Brown, 1963.

Raymont, Henry. "From the Avant-Garde of the Thirties: Djuna Barnes." *New York Times,* May 24, 1971, p. 24.

Reed, John. *The Day in Bohemia.* New York: privately printed, 1913.

"Reports and Reporters: Contributors and Others." *View* I:4, September 1940.

Rexroth, Kenneth. "Djuna Barnes." *Contemporary Novelists,* 2nd ed. London: St. James Press; New York: St. Martin's Press, 1976.

―――. Letter in *Blues,* v.2, no. 2, Fall 1929.

Roditi, Edouard. Interview with Edouard Roditi by Daniel Halpern. *Antaeus* 2:99, Spring 1971.

Rogers, W. G. *Ladies Bountiful.* New York: Harcourt, Brace, 1968; London: Gollancz, 1968.

―――. *When This You See Remember Me.* New York: Rinehart, 1948.

Russell, John. *Paris.* New York: Viking, 1960.

Sarason, Bertram D. *Hemingway and the Sun Set.* Washington, D.C.: NCR Microcard Editions, 1972.

Sargent, W. *Oakham Through the Centuries.* Oakham: 1950.

Schwarz, Arturo. *Man Ray: The Rigour of Imagination.* London: Thames and Hudson, 1977.

Scott, James B. *Djuna Barnes.* Boston: Twayne, 1976.

Secession. New York: no.1–8, Spring 1922–April 1924.

Secrest, Meryle. *Between Me and Life: A Biography of Romaine Brooks.* New York: Doubleday, 1974.

Seven. London: v.1–7, 1938–47.

Seven Arts. New York: v.1–2, 1916–17.

Shattuck, Roger. "*Nightwood* Resurrected." *Village Voice,* May 24, 1962, p. 10.

Sheaffer, Louis. *O'Neill, Son and Playwright.* Boston: Little, Brown, 1968.

Sherman, Frederic Fairchild. *Albert Pinkham Ryder.* New York: privately printed, 1920.

Shi, David E. *Matthew Josephson, Bourgeois Bohemian.* New Haven: Yale University Press, 1981.

Simon, Linda. *The Biography of Alice B. Toklas.* New York: Doubleday, 1977.

Simonson, Lee. *Minor Prophecies.* New York: Harcourt, Brace, 1927.

Sitwell, Edith. *Taken Care Of.* New York: Atheneum, 1965; London: Hutchinson, 1965.

Smoller, Sanford J. *Adrift Among Geniuses: Robert McAlmon, Writer and Publisher of the Twenties.* University Park, Pa.: Pennsylvania State University Press, 1974.

The Soil: A Magazine of Art. New York: The Soil Publishing Company, 1916–. V.1, 1916.

Soupault, Philippe. *Last Nights of Paris.* Translated by William Carlos Williams. New York: Full Court Press, 1982. (First published 1928.)

Stanton, Elizabeth Cady. *Eighty Years and More (1815–1897), Reminiscences.* London: T. Fisher Unwin, 1898. Republished, New York: Source Book Press, 1970.

Stearns, Harold E. *Civilization in the United States.* New York: Harcourt, Brace, 1922.

———. *The Street I Know.* New York: Lee Furman, 1935.

Stein, Gertrude. *The Autobiography of Alice B. Toklas.* New York: Harcourt, Brace, 1933.

———. *Paris France.* London: Batsford, 1940.

Sterne, Maurice. *Shadow and Light.* New York: Harcourt, Brace, 1965.

Stonier, G. W. *Gog Magog.* New York: Books for Libraries, 1966. Reprint of 1933 edition.

Susman, W. I. *"A Second Country." Texas Studies in Literature and Language.* V.3, no. 2:171–83, Summer 1961.

Sutton, Walter. "The Literary Image and the Reader: A Consideration of the Theory of Spatial Form." *Journal of Aesthetics* XVI:112–23, September 1957.

Sylvia Beach (1887–1962). Paris: Mercure de France, 1963.

Symons, Julian. *The Thirties: A Dream Revolved.* Rev. ed. London: Faber & Faber, 1975.

Tambour. Paris, 1929–30.

Tarbell, Ida M. *All in the Day's Work.* New York: Macmillan, 1939.

This Quarter. Paris and Milan: v.1, no. 1, Spring 1925; v.5, no. 2, October/December, 1932.

Thomas, Dylan. "Nightwood." In *Light and Dark,* March 1937, pp. 27, 29.

Thomson, Virgil. *Virgil Thomson.* New York: Knopf, 1966.

Toklas, Alice. "They Who Came to Paris to Write." *New York Times Book Review,* August 6, 1950, pp. 1, 25.

———. *What Is Remembered.* New York: Holt, Rinehart and Winston, 1963.

Tomkins, Calvin. *Living Well Is the Best Revenge.* New York: Viking, 1971.

Toynbee, Philip. "The Power and the Glory" (review of the 1963 Faber & Faber edition of *Nightwood*). *The Observer,* December 15, 1963, p. 25.

The Transatlantic Review. Paris: v.1, no. 1, January 1924–v.2, no. 6, December 1924.

transition. Paris: no. 1, April 1927–no. 27, April/May 1938.

Traylen, A. R., comp. *Oakham in Rutland.* Oakham: Rutland Local History Society, 1977.

Troubridge, Una Elena, Lady. *The Life and Death of Radclyffe Hall.* London: Hammond, Hammond, 1961.

Tyler, Parker. *The Divine Comedy of Pavel Tchelitchew: A Biography.* London: Weidenfeld and Nicolson, 1969.

———. "Pained Sex: Elizabethan Style" (review of 1946 New Directions edition of *Nightwood*). *Kenyon Review* VIII:323–25, Spring 1946.

Unterecker, John. *Voyager: A Life of Hart Crane.* New York: Farrar, Straus & Giroux, 1969.

Urquhart, Brian. *Hammarskjöld.* New York: Knopf, 1972.

Van Doren, Mark. In "Fiction of This Quarter" (review of *Nightwood*) *Southern Review* III:159–82, Summer 1937.

Van Vechten, Carl. *Fragments from an Unwritten Autobiography.* 2 vols. New Haven: Yale University Library, 1955.

———. *Sacred and Profane Memories.* New York: Knopf, 1932.

———. "Some Literary Ladies I Have Known." The Yale University Library *Gazette,* v. 26, no. 3, January 1952.

Vella, Michael. "Djuna Barnes Gains Despite Critics' Pall." *Lost Generation Journal* 4:6–8, Winter 1976.

Venable, John D. *Out of the Shadow: The Story of Charles Edison.* East Orange, N.J.: Charles Edison Fund, 1978.

View. New York: View, Inc. v.1, September 1940. Editor, 1940–, C. H. Ford.

Villard, Oswald Garrison. *Fighting Years: Memoirs of a Liberal Editor.* New York: Harcourt Brace and Company, 1939.

Vorse, Mary Heaton. *Footnote to Folly.* New York: Farrar and Rinehart, 1935.

Wain, John. "Second Curtain" (review of *The Antiphon*). *The Observer,* February 2, 1958, p. 14.

Waldau, Roy S. *Vintage Years of the Theatre Guild, 1928–1939.* Cleveland: Press of Case Western Reserve University, 1972.

Ware, Caroline. *Greenwich Village 1920–1930.* Boston: Houghton Mifflin, 1935. Reprinted Octagon, 1977.

Weintraub, Stanley. *London Yankees: Portraits of American Writers and Artists in England, 1894–1914*. New York: Harcourt Brace Jovanovich, 1979.

Weisstein, Ulrich. "Beast, Doll and Woman: Djuna Barnes' Human Bestiary." *Renascence* XV:3–11, Fall 1962.

Wescott, Glenway. *Fear and Trembling*. New York and London: Harper, 1932.

Wesleyan University, Middletown, Conn. *Alumni Record*. 5th ed. 1921; Centennial (6th) ed. 1931.

Whittemore, Reed. *William Carlos Williams: Poet from Jersey*, Boston: Houghton Mifflin, 1975.

Wickes, George. *The Amazon of Letters: The Life and Loves of Natalie Barney*. New York: Putnam's, 1976.

———. *Americans in Paris*. Garden City, N.Y.: Doubleday, 1969.

Wickham, Harvey. *The Impuritans*. New York: Dial, 1929.

Wilde, Oscar. *Letters of.* Edited by Rupert Hart-Davis. New York: Harcourt, Brace, 1962.

Williams, William Carlos. *Autobiography*. New York: Random House, 1948.

———. *Selected Letters of.* Edited by John C. Thirlwall. New York: McDowell, Obolensky, 1957.

Williamson, Alan. "The Divided Image: The Quest for Identity in the Works of Djuna Barnes." *Critique: Studies in Modern Fiction* VII:58–74, Spring 1964.

Wilson, Edmund. *The Twenties*. New York: Farrar, Straus & Giroux, 1975.

Wilson, Robert Forrest. *Paris on Parade*. Indianapolis: Bobbs-Merrill, 1924.

Wolff, Geoffrey. *Black Sun: The Brief Transit and Violent Eclipse of Harry Crosby*. London: Hamish Hamilton; New York: Random House, 1977.

Wood, Clement. "The Fleshly School of American Fiction." *New York Herald Magazine and Books,* January 13, 1924, pp. 15, 19.

———. *Greenwich Village Blues*. New York: H. Harrison, 1926.

Wood, Thelma (review of her work, "Un Elogio a La Señora de Las Girafas"). In *Amauta,* Ano. IV, Lima, Junio–Julio 1930.

———. (review of her silverpoint exhibition at The Milch Gallery). In *The Arts* 16:493, March 1930.

———. "Silverpoint." *The Arts* 16, February 1930.

———. "Study." *Gargoyle,* no. 3, p. 27, September 21, 1921.

Woollcott, Alexander. "Second Thoughts on First Nights: The Provincetown Plays." *New York Times,* November 9, 1919, Section 8, p. 2.

———. "Second Thoughts on First Nights." *New York Times,* April 4, 1920, Section 6, p. 6.

Young, Art. *On My Way.* New York: Horace Liveright, 1928.

Young, Katherine. *My Old New York Neighborhoods.* New York: Profile Press, 1979.

Zolla, Elemire. "Djuna Barnes." *Studi Americani,* v. V:301–13, 1959.

INDEX

276

College Inn, The, 147
Colum, Padraic, 231
Compton-Burnett, Ivy, 225
Confessions of Another Young Man (Imbs), 120
Conjunctions, 60
Contact Collection of Contemporary Writers, 125, 134
Contemporary Jewish Record, 104
Cook, George Cram ("Jig"), 58, 86
Cornwall-on-Hudson, 13, 248
Cosmopolitan, 198
Coupole, La, 131
Cowley, Malcolm, 42, 59, 63–64, 70–72, 119–120, 131
Crane, Hart, 70, 79, 81, 133
Creatures in an Alphabet (Barnes), 202, 243–244
Crepuscolari, 96
Criterion, The, 213
Crosby, Harry, 137
Crowninshield, Frank, 55, 162
Cummings, E. E., 20, 41, 231
Cunard, Nancy, 120, 137

Dada, 83
Dagens Nyheter, 244–245
Dali, Salvador, 235
Darantière Press, Dijon, 125
Darley, George, 225
Davies, Mary, 84
Day, Dorothy, 59
Deirdre of the Sorrows (Synge), 28
Delarue-Mardrus, Lucie, 122
Dell, Floyd, 59, 63, 89
Dempsey, Jack, 45, 53, 55
Deslandes, Ilse, Baroness, 124
Deux Magots, Les, 131
Dial, The, 92
Dilly (cat), 152
Dingo, The, 132, 136
Distinguished Air (McAlmon), 138

Divine Comedy of Pavel Tchelitchew, The (Tyler), 164–165
Djuna Books, 86
Dodge, Mabel, 13, 48, 50, 120
Dome, The, 131
Doolittle, Hilda, *See* H. D.
"Doris the Dope," 55–56
Dostoevsky, Fyodor, 94, 99
Double Dealer, The, 102, 172
Douglas, Lord Alfred, 55
Douglas, Norman, 125
Dove, The (Barnes), 92, 95
Dowd, Harrison, 16, 65, 117, 234, 235
Dreiser, Theodore, 14, 69, 231
Dubliners (Joyce), 94, 110
Duchamp, Marcel, 19, 60, 116, 235
Dumond, Frank Vincent, 44
Duncan, Isadora, 117
Durrell, Lawrence, 20, 41

Eastman, Max, 59, 87
Eberhart, Richard, 21, 224
Eddy, Mary Baker, 220
Edison, Charles, 72
Edna (Kreymburg), 72
Education of Henry Adams, The (Adams), 38
Eliot, T. S., 18, 20, 21, 32, 43, 63, 70, 104, 107–108, 118, 120, 130, 145, 158, 172, 201–212, 213, 214, 215, 218, 219, 220, 221, 222, 223, 225, 229, 235, 238, 241
Eliot, Valerie (Mrs. T. S. Eliot), 235, 242
Ell, Christine, 86
Ellis, Charles, 59
Encratites, 169
Ernst, Max, 205
Exile's Return (Cowley), 119–120
Expatriation, 17–19, 39–40, 113, 116–118, 120, 125
Expressen (Stockholm), 228

H. D., 120
Hall, Radclyffe, 69, 124
Hallinan, Vincent and Vivian, 142
Hamlet's Custard Pie (Barnes), 192
Hammarskjöld, Dag, 20, 21, 227, 228, 229, 244
Hammarskjöld Foundation, 229
Hamnett, Nina, 42, 132, 136–137
Hanfstaengl, Putzi, 15, 61–62, 117, 165
Hapgood, Hutchins, 95
Harcourt, Brace, 214, 220
Hari, Mata, 121
Harland, Henry, 147
Harper & Row, 130
Harper's (New Monthly) Magazine, 26, 45, 92
Harrie, Ivar, 228
Harris, Frank, 14, 55, 74–76
Hartley, Marsden, 15, 27, 61, 116–117, 136
Hartmann, Sadikichi, 98
Harvard University, 21, 215, 223
Havel, Hippolyte, 59, 74, 98, 200
Hawkins, Desmond, 213
Hayford Hall, 18, 195, 198, 205, 207
Hayward, John, 213, 215
Heap, Jane, 16, 41, 63, 79, 80, 98, 102, 120, 134, 165
Heart to Artemis, The (Bryher), 106
Hellman, Lillian, 36
Hemingway, Ernest, 16, 40, 42, 106, 113, 125, 130, 131–132, 135–136, 172, 197, 244
Hemingway and The Sun Set (Sarason), 135
Hiler, Hilaire, 131, 133, 157
Hints to Pilgrims (Brooks), 79
Hirschman, Jack, 109–110
Hitler, Adolf, 117

Hoare, Peter, 19, 192, 199, 201, 205, 210, 216, 227, 235, 240
Hoare, Sir Samuel, *See* Hoare, Peter
Holladay, Polly, 59
Holmes, Oliver Wendell, 173
Holms, Dorothy, 200, 205
Holms, John, 18, 195, 200, 201, 202–205
Hotel d'Angleterre, 113, 116, 136
Houdini, Harry, 177
Huddleston, Sisley, 130
Hush Before Love (Barnes), 103

Ibsen, Henrik, 155
Imbs, Bravig, 120
In Our Time (Hemingway), 130
Intruder in the Dust (Faulkner), 20
An Irish Triangle (Barnes), 90
Isaksson, Folke, 244–245
Ivanov (Chekhov), 95

Jack, Peter, 218
James, Edward, 211
James, Henry, 39, 172, 208
"James Joyce: a Portrait of . . ." (Barnes), 109
Javsicas, Erma and Gabriel, 142
Jenkins, Susan, 42, 57, 63
Jockey, The, 131
Jones, Jefferson, 130
Josephson, Matthew, 39, 40, 41, 59, 81, 113, 116
Joyce, James, 16, 18, 20, 24, 32, 33, 60, 79, 94, 99, 100, 104, 107–111, 120, 125–126, 137, 145, 155, 190, 219
Joyce, Nora, 108, 155
Jurgen (Cabell), 129

Kafka, Franz, 35
Kazin, Alfred, 20
Kemp, Harry, 14, 103
Kenton, Edna, 84
Kiki, 129

283

Oakham, Rutland, 187–188, 192
Oates, Titus, 187–188
Oberle, Jean, 167, 168
O'Connor, Robert, 141, 144
On Returning from Abroad (Barnes), 129
O'Neal, Hank, 24
O'Neill, Eugene, 14, 59, 87–89, 90, 103, 197
Orage, A. R., 60
Oscar (Barnes), 93, 94, 173
Others, 91
Out of This Century (Guggenheim), 19, 157, 202, 203–204

Pankhurst, Emmeline, 33
Paradise (Barnes), 103
Paris Tribune, The, 200
Paris Was Yesterday (Flanner), 125
Parisienne, The, 91
Parry, Albert, 66
Partisan Review, 225
Pascal, Blaise, 140, 208
A Passion Play (Barnes), 91, 146
Patchin Place, 19, 22, 218, 230–248
Pearson's Magazine, 74, 96
Perlmutter, Tylia, 165
Petite Chaumière, La, 148
Philippe, Charles-Louis, 157–158
Pickering, Ruth, 84
Playboy, 90
Playboy of the Western World, The (Synge), 28
Poe, Edgar Allan, 30, 96, 184
Poetry, 41, 103
Poetry Centre, The, 219
Poets and People (Norman), 103
Poets' Theatre, The, 223
Polly's, 59, 102
Ponsot, Marie, 224
Porter, Katherine Anne, 120

Portrait of the Artist as American (Josephson), 39
Postman Always Rings Twice, The (Cain), 197
Pound, Ezra, 16, 42, 104, 106–108, 125, 225
Power of Darkness, The (Tolstoy), 129
Pratt Institute, 44
Present Age from 1914, The (Muir), 99
Princeton University, 21, 239
Proust, Marcel, 35, 145, 150
Provincetown Players, 16, 48, 58, 84, 86–89
Pyne, Mary, 14, 84, 103–104, 231

Quarry (Barnes), 241
Quennell, Peter, 213
Quill, The, 67

Rabbit, The (Barnes), 96
Rabelais, François, 35, 123, 152
Rachilde, 122
Rahv, Philip, 215
Raine, Kathleen, 224
Rascoe, Burton, 108
Rauh, Ida, 59, 89
Ray, Man, 16, 40, 60, 116, 244
Raymont, Henry, 21, 36
Read, Sir Herbert, 227
Reed, John, 56, 87, 231
Religio Medici (Browne), 208
Reptilia (C. H. Ford), 167
Rexroth, Kenneth, 60
Reynolds, Mary, 235
Richards, I. A., 223
Ridge, Lola, 116
Rihani, 83
Rite of Spring (Barnes), 243
Roditi, Edouard, 137, 141, 142
Rodman, Henrietta, 83
Rohrer, Alice, 207
Rotonde, La, 116, 131
Royal Dramaten Theatre, 228
Ruskin, John, 33

285

Thomas, Dylan, 20, 199, 212, 213
Thomson, Virgil, 123, 244
Three from the Earth (Barnes), 89, 94, 111
Three Sisters (Chekhov), 95
Tice, Clara, 76–77
Tidings Brought to Mary, The (Claudel), 129
Time, 23, 25, 206, 246
Time and Tide, 219
Times Literary Supplement, The, 23, 214, 225
Tiny Alice (Albee), 90
Titus, Edward, 40
To the Dogs (Barnes), 92
Toklas, Alice, 104
Tolstoy, Leo, 129
Tomkins, Calvin, 172
Town, The, 20
Transatlantic Review, 40, 106
transition, 82, 110, 200
Trotsky, Leon, 131
Trowbridge, Lady Una, 124
Tsvetaeva, Marina, 120
Twain, Mark, 38
Twentieth Century Authors (Kunitz), 19
Tygon, The (Coleman), 201
Tyler, Parker, 163–164, 196, 244
Tzara, Tristan, 64

Ulysses (Joyce), 60, 108–109, 110, 111, 120, 126, 145
University of Maryland, 23
Unterecker, John, 81
Urquhart, Sir Thomas, 152

Vagabonde, La (Colette), 122
Vagaries Malicieux (Barnes), 109, 112
Vail, Laurence, 15, 61, 131, 157–158, 205
Valéry, Paul, 121

Van Vechten, Carl, 48, 64, 197, 229
Van Vechten, Fania, *See* Marinoff, Fania
Vanity Fair, 16, 17, 55, 91, 109, 128
A Victorian in the Modern World (Hapgood), 95
Virginia Quarterly Review, 224
Vivien, Renée, 121
Vogue, 26
Vorse, Mary Heaton, 59, 86

W.P.A., 198
Walking-mort, The (Barnes), 241–242
Wandering Jew, The (Sue), 13, 25
Ward, Genevieve, 173
Ward Number Seven (Chekhov), 201
Wars I Have Seen (Stein), 104
Washington Square Players, 86
Wasteland, The (Eliot), 225
Weaver, Harriet, 107, 120
Well of Loneliness, The (Hall), 69, 124
Wellesley College, 199
Wells, "Harper," 130
Wescott, Glenway, 36, 42
West, Nathanael, 125, 238
Westley, Helen, 45
Wharton, Edith, 63
Whistler, James, 147, 172
White, Antonia, 18, 195, 198, 203, 206, 209
Whitney, Gertrude Vanderbilt, 59
Who's Afraid of Virginia Woolf? (Albee), 90
Wickham, Anna, 122
Widening Gyre, The (Frank), 145
Wiedersweiler, Mrs., 230–231
Wilde, Dorothy ("Dolly"), 124, 210, 237

286

287